MW00534286

BOOK 23

For more O Canada Crosswords, go to
nightwoodeditions.com/collections/o-canada-crosswords

O CANADA CROSSWORDS

BOOK 23

75 All New Crosswords

GWEN SJOGREN

NIGHTWOOD EDITIONS

1 2 3 4 5 — 26 25 24 23 22

Nightwood Editions
P.O. Box 1779
Gibsons, BC
VON 1VO
www.nightwoodeditions.com

Edited by Murray Lewis
Proofread by Patricia Wolfe

Printed in Canada

ISBN 978-0-88971-434-2

The folk art on the cover is by Mitchell Fancy (moose) and Pat Ryerson (lobster),
from the gallery Hubert and Belle's, hubertandbelle.com.

Contents

1 The Sporting Life

Go teams!

ACROSS

1. 1996 Margaret Atwood Giller Prize winner: *Alias* _____
6. Told a fib
10. Cummerbund
14. Symbol of Canada: _____ leaf
19. Of the kidney
20. British pop singer Murs
21. Lenovo competitor
22. Combined metal
23. All by oneself
24. Flood prevention barrier
25. Barrels that weigh a lot?
26. Vancouver Island municipality
27. US hardware retailer in Canada: True _____
28. Esso product
29. Famed WWII battle island: Iwo _____
30. 1997 Shania Twain hit: "Don't Be _____ (You Know I Love You)"
31. Suncor VP, say
32. Canadian hockey star Crosby, for short
33. Chic chapeau
34. Really small
35. *Blazing Saddles* actress Madeline
37. Sheep known for its high-quality fleece
38. Like a dodgy Dodger?
42. Free from one kind of eye trouble
46. Canadian Screen Awards science or nature show prize: _____ Stewart Award
48. Fork point
49. Crazy
50. See 49-A
51. It's 5 per cent in some provinces
52. Seed shell
53. Land around a lagoon
55. Basement
58. Victoria's Murchie's, for example
60. California city
63. Hayes who appeared in a famous photo taken on 29-A
64. Cob of corn
65. Toboggan
66. **Winnipeg's CFL team**
70. Hollywood luminary?
74. Livestock grazing area
75. Former *Coach's Corner* commentator Cherry
76. Seemingly
78. Famed British ballerina Margot
82. Egyptian president Gamal (1956–70)
85. Cavern, to Shakespeare
86. Keep clear of
87. Canadian attorneys' org.
89. Security guard's duty
92. South China _____
93. Zingy flavour
94. Stage light sheet
95. Former pharmacists?
98. Description of slippery streets
100. Half a set of dentures
102. Chi-chi fundraising event
103. "Losing My Religion" US band
104. Fill with joy
105. Bob the bait
106. Ancient Briton
110. Pieces of pizza
113. Protrudes
114. Take a quick note
115. RONA or Roots
116. Cigar type for Castro?
117. Rani's dress
118. Confined (with "up")
119. Halifax's Lord Nelson, for one
120. Apartments and condos
121. Myanmar money
122. Sicilian spewer, on 2/17/21
123. Give an address
124. Untidy
125. _____ of Wight
126. "A nod _____ good…"
127. Town in southwestern Ontario

DOWN

1. Sombre
2. Enjoy some R&R
3. Arboreal lizard
4. **Vancouver NHLers**
5. USS *Robert* _____
6. Airbnbs and inns
7. Tale about Troy (with "The")
8. **Edmonton's CFL squad**
9. Get rid of your grey
10. Like Jonathan Swift works
11. Shrewdness
12. **Ottawa NHLers**
13. Shoppers Drug Mart window info
14. MBA word
15. **Montreal's CFL team**
16. Old Alka-Seltzer jingle word
17. Mischievous Norse god
18. Ogled an optometrist?
29. *Star Trek: Voyager* actress Ryan
30. Collect DNA orally
32. Front part of the leg
33. Areca nut
36. Leaning
37. Horse's hair
39. Tilapia or tuna
40. Bible preposition
41. Spring
42. Gather at a church service?
43. Region of South Africa
44. Venerate
45. It's across from Hong Kong
47. Mammals with webbed feet
51. Latch onto
52. La Brea pits substance
54. Canadian '50s pop quartet member
56. **BC CFLers**
57. Fogo Island community: Joe Batt's _____

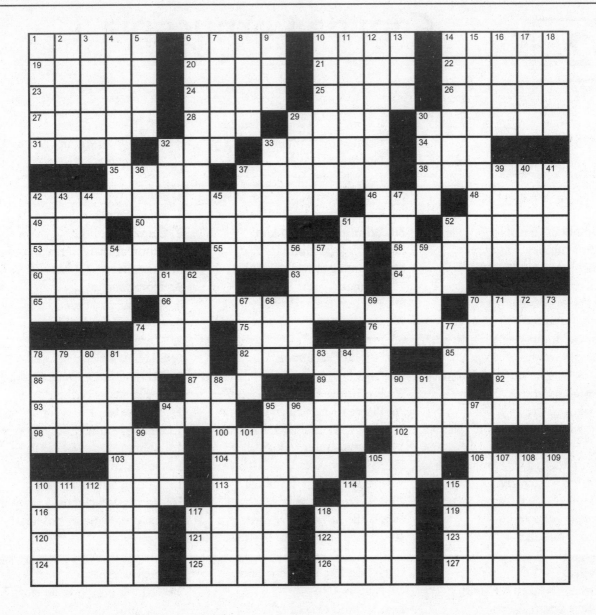

59. 15-D and 81-D are in this CFL Division
61. Comply with orders
62. Quick peek
67. Pulitzer-winning writer Ferber
68. Feathery neck wrapper
69. 1999 David Suzuki book: *You Are the _____*
70. Actor Kiefer, to Donald Sutherland
71. Rwandan ethnic group
72. Be of the same opinion
73. Flightless birds
74. Conducted the Hamilton Philharmonic Orchestra
77. Acceptable for Islamic diets
78. Suet and lard

79. Richmond Olympic _____
80. Zero
81. **Hamilton's CFL squad**
83. Plant reproductive cell
84. Dines
88. **Toronto MLBers**
90. Competitions for boats
91. Ontario Coalition Against Poverty (abbr.)
94. Workout facilities
95. Mineral found by a hungry geologist?
96. Pats a poodle?
97. **Toronto's NBA team**
99. See 34-A
101. Not singular, in grammar

105. Canadian Strickland who won a Nobel Prize in Physics in 2018
107. Little bits, on 108-D?
108. Largest Greek island
109. Fax predecessor
110. Pond surface algae
111. Debussy suite movement: "Clair de _____"
112. Wading bird
114. **Winnipeg's NHL squad**
115. Toronto tourists' attraction: Bata _____ Museum
117. Enjoy a winter's day at Blue Mountain
118. Canada's smallest prov.

SOLUTION ON PAGE 158

Canada Cornucopia 1

2

ACROSS

1. Canadian short story scribe Gallant
6. Canadian product: Peameal _____
11. Tresses
15. Small metric measurement
19. Acid type found in proteins
20. "Give a dog _____ …"
21. Problem with pimples
22. _____-mutton
23. Salient points
24. Ranee's wrap
25. Rock type found in Nahanni National Park
26. Buckeye State
27. 1986 Howard Jones hit: "No One _____ Blame"
28. Mythological sea nymph
29. Wound with a dagger
30. Paddles
31. Area around an altar
33. Minor mistake
35. Canadian Brass, for one
37. Gutters
39. Toronto NHLer, for short
41. Haul a wreck
42. 1972 April Wine hit: "_____ Side of the Moon"
45. Canadian education savings plans (abbr.)
47. Adjudge, like a judge
49. Fill a cannon again
54. UFO crew member
56. Collections for Canada's Bianca Andreescu?
58. Southern Alberta city
60. Canadian nickel critter
62. Uses a fake ID to extort online
64. Houseplant type
65. Bantu spear
67. _____ culpa
68. That guy
69. Arizona landforms
70. Isolated from others
74. Not quite round
78. Former musical pair: _____ & Tina Turner Revue
79. Chardonnay, in Chibougamau
80. Advice columnist Ann
85. Pastry type (var.)
86. Encouraged by the cardiac surgeon?
89. Western University city
90. Dessert developed on Canada's prairies
92. "Pronto!" acronym
94. CBC _____-Canada
95. Electronic eye, e.g.
96. Places to stay overnight
98. Groove caused by a glacier
100. Tirana country (abbr.)
101. Saskatchewan U18 AAA team: Regina _____ Canadians
103. Baby's early syllables
105. Cliffside home for birds
107. Three-season reality show: *The _____ Canada*
112. Canadian children's book author Ohi
114. Summon via cellphone?
118. Entice
119. Bryan Adams song: "(Everything I Do) I _____ For You"
121. Sauerkraut-filled sandwich
123. Be overly fond of
124. Ovule coat
125. Facts
126. Missed the mark
127. BC Lower Mainland city
128. Arrived
129. World's longest river
130. Noise heard in the night
131. Willow tree type
132. Eager
133. Disco-era band: The Bee _____
134. Hammer's partner
135. Paul Brandt's first album: *Calm Before the _____*

DOWN

1. 1968 Steppenwolf song: "_____ Carpet Ride"
2. Mennonites' Ontario brethren
3. "Hasta la _____, baby"
4. Repeat a mantra
5. Scouring pad brand name
6. Without foundation?
7. "Three men walk into _____ …"
8. CANDU reactor centres
9. *Married…with Children* star Ed
10. More impoverished
11. Toques, et al.
12. Severely urgent
13. Baby
14. Soaks up for a second time
15. Doom's mate
16. Recovery facility
17. 1958 show tune: "I Enjoy Being _____"
18. Mammal found in every province and territory
28. Guelph-born *Scream* star Campbell
32. NYC concert venue since 1891: _____ Hall
34. Russian emperor (1796–1801)
36. Jug with a handle and a spout
38. Architect's plan detail, for short
40. Extra pounds, say
42. *Ali _____ and the Forty Thieves*
43. Some Molson libations
44. Guadalajara greeting: Buenos _____
46. Speaking hesitantly
48. Moral principle
50. Louise Penny's first Gamache mystery: *Still _____*
51. Bards' output
52. Taj Mahal locale
53. Bears' lairs

55. Genesis mother
57. Wind-up watch part
59. Blood related
61. Sought a seat as an MP
63. French dog breed: Basset _____ de Bretagne
66. More slippery, on winter streets
69. Bombardier produces this type of transportation system
71. Congo animal
72. Bulgarian–Canadian actress Dobrev
73. NFL Cowboys city (abbr.)
74. Braggarts: Show-_____
75. Disgusting
76. Order of Canada musical honouree Doyle

77. Toys that spin
81. Paternity suit substance
82. Old Scandinavian literary opus
83. Stir up
84. Pretentious person
86. Foreshadowing with fanfare?
87. Barbershop quartet voice
88. See 125-A
91. Jorge Mario Bergoglio's Catholic title, since 2013
93. Comes before
97. Most tart
99. Tehran nation
102. Two-tone Canadian coin
104. Chafing dish fuel
106. Most senior, among siblings

107. November sales event: _____ Friday
108. Migraine symptoms (var.)
109. The RCMP fights this
110. _____ of Troy
111. Search through a gun vault?
113. One of Canada's Great Lakes
115. Compilation of Shakespearean plays
116. Canadian-made plane: Twin _____
117. Provide with more weapons
120. Foot parts
122. Baffin Bay ice mass
127. Initial scale notes

3

A Dozen Theme Clues...

From a classic fantasy film

ACROSS

1. Athabasca oil _____
6. Con's game
10. 1978 Village People chart-topper
14. Three-time world figure skating champ Patrick from Canada
18. GPS helps you do this
20. Hoopla
21. Pair's pronoun
22. For sure, colloquially to a Brit
23. **Colour of a brick road**
24. Unauthorized military absence
25. Chew like a dog with a bone
26. **The Gales lived on this**
27. Convince
28. Zebra's tresses
29. Jamaican cuisine fruit
31. Irish actor Stephen
32. Room for work or play
33. The _____ Rovers
35. Like CFL or NHL players
37. Canadian Forces _____ Suffield
40. Is inclined to
42. Query
44. *Superman* antagonist Luthor
45. _____ de Triomphe
46. Last exam at McMaster?
47. Cape Breton's Men of the Deeps, for one
49. Synagogue leader
53. Became shallow at the shore
55. Flin Flon airport code
57. Bikes with one wheel
59. **Dorothy's home state**
60. Goblet or tumbler
62. Place to get pampered
63. Primate in Peru
64. Kettles release this
65. Loud merrymakers do this
67. Famed Fabergé creation
69. Furry family member
70. August birthstone

72. Darlington and Pickering produce this type of power in Ontario
75. _____ de plume
78. Weep
79. Lad who delivers the paper
81. Fundamental
85. Vancouver General Hospital ward
87. It comes before Vegas
89. Squirrels nest in these
90. **The Good Witch**
91. Old English coin
94. Former provincial premiers Schreyer and Stelmach
95. It might be ingrown
96. Take hold of the wheel
97. Hollywood star Matt
99. Claims against properties
101. TO museum since 1912
102. Restaurant server's gratuity
104. Stags' amorous season
105. Longed for
106. Wagers at Edmonton's Century Mile Racetrack
107. Carpentry work support
111. Campers' canvas covers
113. Ontario Waterpower Association (abbr.)
115. Alberta Band Association (abbr.)
116. Gag
118. Daddy, in Durango
119. Type of test
123. **Dorothy's dog**
125. Scarlett O'Hara's place
126. Cheddar description
127. **Miss Gulch**
128. Pupil part
129. Horse's moderate pace
130. CIBC Run for the _____
131. Like informal phrases

132. Extra benefit
133. Ornamental evergreens
134. Dick Tracy's Trueheart
135. South American range

DOWN

1. Source of tofu (var.)
2. Mars' Greek counterpart
3. Zeroes, at an FC Edmonton game
4. Bamboozle
5. Disturb your spouse at night
6. Endurance
7. **Companion of Dorothy**
8. Aphrodite's gorgeous guy
9. Spicy chocolate sauces
10. Tranquil exercise regime
11. **Little people**
12. Rail family bird
13. Additionally
14. Canadian Dermatology Foundation (abbr.)
15. **The Tin Man's missing part**
16. 1974 Joni Mitchell lyric: "I was _____ man in Paris"
17. Desert wanderer
19. "Roaring" decade
30. Board for manicuring nails
34. Comedian's triumphant interjection?
36. Extremely precise
37. Enjoys the limelight
38. Buddhist who attains nirvana
39. Biscuit served with jam and cream
41. Finish
43. Trifle, in Témiscaming?
46. Calgary's NHL team
47. Price of shopping at Leon's?
48. In a fully matured manner
50. Radar screen dot
51. _____ noire
52. "_____ something I said?"

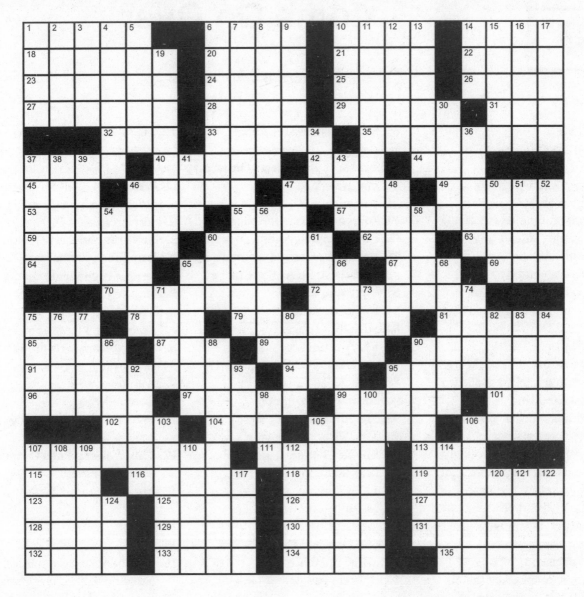

54. PDQ synonym
56. Abstained from eating
58. Pen
60. Margaret Laurence novel: *A Jest of* _____
61. Had a hunch
65. *Titanic* never won this: Blue _____
66. **Dorothy's flashy footwear**
68. *Anne of Green* _____
71. Neo, for Canada's Keanu Reeves
73. Romaine lettuce
74. Frequent BC coast precipitation
75. Montreal-based religious group: Grey _____
76. "You can bank _____"

77. Shania song: "Any Man of _____"
80. Small brown bird
82. Trapper's drum?
83. Ninny
84. Lulls before the storm?
86. Molars and incisors
88. **See 7-D**
90. Venetian canal transports
92. Earlier (with "to")
93. World's second-largest bird
95. Start of a par 3 at Crowsnest Pass Golf Club
98. PEI-born former NHLer Steve
100. Guts
103. Comely
105. Czechoslovakian city

106. A Caped Crusader
107. Rose from reclining
108. Overhead
109. **Dorothy melted the Wicked Witch of the West with this**
110. Gaze rudely at
112. Make _____ with the devil
114. American frontier life writer Cather
117. '80s Canadian band: Men Without _____
120. Glen Campbell classic: "Gentle on My _____"
121. Prod
122. Speaks like Simon?
124. Nova Scotia island of note

SOLUTION ON PAGE 158

13

4 Come On Over

International bridges

ACROSS

1. Hitchhiker's query: "Can I _____ ride?"
5. Provide many provisions?
10. Kaplan of *Welcome Back, Kotter*
14. Front bumper cover
17. Olympic golden Canadian wrestler Wiebe, at al.
20. Two-door car
21. Queen of scat Fitzgerald
22. Like uncooked ground beef
23. Small eatery
24. Photocopier cartridge filler
25. Hit the road, like Nickelback
26. Cotswold kitchen appliance
27. Most simplistic
29. Buddhism belief
31. Adjective for Enya music
33. Jewish mourning ritual
34. Dreadlocks sporter, for short
36. Important toupée wearer?
38. Sara, to Tegan, in Cdn. music
39. Concept, in Chibougamau
40. Actor DeLuise
41. Shoelace ends
45. They're often asked (abbr.)
47. Wash out, in the washer
48. Something, in Britspeak
50. Beasts that pull plows
51. Contiguous boundaries
53. Yellow pigment
54. Clean a whiteboard
55. Canada's Keanu Reeves played this role four times
56. Michael Bublé holiday track: "_____ Beginning to Look a Lot Like Christmas"
57. Coke, for one
58. Dog's greeting or warning
60. _____ Aviv
61. Skimps
63. Nebraska's eastern neighbour
64. Ready, _____, fire
65. Stand for Canada's Robert Bateman
67. **Bridge that connects Ontario and New York**
71. Papier _____
74. Sun, in Spain
75. Creamy cheese with a crust
76. Appalled
80. Ontario Brain Institute (abbr.)
81. Weeny amount
83. Innocent person
84. Stick for snooker
85. Kiwi's extinct cousin
86. Canada joined this org. in '49
88. Wild Asiatic asses
90. Nicaraguan banknotes
92. Pre-eminent pilots, say
93. Mrs. Shrek, in the movies
94. The Keg entrees listing
95. Informant, in a gaol
96. 1970s dance clubs
98. Manulife offering (abbr.)
99. Whale's offspring
100. Diddley and Derek
101. Brief reference
103. "There you have it," in Quebec City
104. Take back one's words
107. Dispossess (with "of")
110. _____ the beans
112. Hag
114. "Evil Woman" supergroup
115. Earns income from trawling?
117. Some lilies
119. CBC skating show: *Battle of the _____*
120. Chignon
121. Oscar-winning director Kazan
122. Alter electoral districts, say
123. Olden days description
124. Devious
125. Scouse or cawl
126. Boxer Liston or singer Bono
127. U of R program: Master of Fine _____

DOWN

1. Little children, in Chambly
2. Heep created by Dickens
3. **Span that connects Quebec to Vermont**
4. Exercise proponent?
5. Emulate Canada's Ryan Gosling
6. Quick peek
7. Resembling a new moon
8. BC performing arts group: Vancouver _____
9. Semester at UBC
10. Comprehend
11. 1966 The Association hit: "_____ Comes Mary"
12. **This crossing links Ontario with Michigan**
13. Insect you may have heard about?
14. Crow
15. Fury
16. Newfoundland-set musical based on 9/11: *Come from _____*
18. Locations
19. Ship's emergency call
28. Ontario Court of Justice proceedings
30. Weapon of mass destruction
32. Shining
35. Calculates the total
37. Unable to move
40. Where Russian politicians legislate
42. Highway 400 off-ramps
43. Plains abode (var.)
44. Fish-hook line
45. Leaf lovers, in Toronto?
46. Help a felon
47. 40-A starred in this "hefty" film

48. Restaurants' self-serve counters
49. Terrestrial lizard
52. Paid a tenth to the church
53. Graduation ceremony robe
57. Canadian mining resource
59. Towed with an anchor
62. Utmost, in math
63. Weather map lines description
64. "Like, no way!"
66. Volcanos spew this
68. Taking illicit drugs, say
69. Symbol of Quebec: Blue flag _____
70. Island in Micronesia
71. Single-cell organism
72. Primitive calculators (var.)

73. Quotes a reputable source
77. **Bridge that connects Windsor and Detroit**
78. Fly like an eagle?
79. To-do list entry
82. **Span that links Maine and New Brunswick (with "Franklin Delano")**
83. Notable Scottish loch
84. Chinwag
87. Canadian jazz great Peterson
89. 1996 game: Trivial Pursuit _____ IV
90. Phone for a prisoner?
91. Some Six Nations people
94. Canada Post employee

97. Offers an opinion
99. Op-ed piece in the *Calgary Herald*
100. Pick on from the pulpit?
102. Adjust your shoelaces
103. Petite grey bird
105. Catkin
106. Positive votes
107. They're the belles of a southern ball
108. Jewish month
109. Wee horsey
111. Average scores, at Cabot Cliffs
113. Diminish
116. Carpenter's adage?
118. Espionage operative

5 Drive Time

Tunes for your trip

ACROSS

1. Oliva Dionne was this to the famed Canadian quintuplets
5. Looey's underling, in the army
10. Philosophy suffix
13. Stream of revenue or water
19. Mine entry point
20. Make butter, in olden days
21. Tuber type
22. Team spirit, say
23. **1972 America chart-topper**
26. Summary
27. Captivate your fiancée?
28. Enjoy a favourite book again
29. 2017 horror film: *It _____ Night*
30. At the house of, in Hochelaga
32. Number one Nickelback song: "_____ Away"
33. Vacillate, at the park?
35. Mosquito bite irritation
38. Lucien or Lise, in Lachine
40. *Mal de _____*
42. With scalloped edges
46. Fondue sauce
49. Polos and pullovers
51. Jellystone Park cartoon bear
52. Suffix with musket
53. Old-style prayer
55. Arduous burden
56. Land feature at Elora, Ontario
57. Scottish terrier breed
59. Pessimist's potential scenario?
61. Most prevalent
62. Too
63. Former moniker of the Maritimes
64. Ultimate objective
67. Entreaty
68. **1978 Gerry Rafferty hit**
70. Casino chances
74. Less sharp, like a knife
76. Roof of a gourmand's mouth?
77. _____ Parmigiana
78. Finally

81. Music convention's significant speech?
83. Mystery or romance, say
84. Divvy up
85. Drained a rad
87. Diamond retailer with stores in three provinces
89. Canadian *Weekend at Bernie's* director Kotcheff
90. Atomic particle
91. Pathos inducing
93. Respectfully regarding
95. Honest Ed's in Toronto was one
97. Famed Canadian artist Thomson
99. Guy Lafleur's Canadiens jersey number
100. Poker pot payment
101. Classified section notice
103. It's tapped from trees in Quebec
105. Auctioneer's final word
107. Bulldozer or baler
110. First Flames game of the year: Home _____
113. These slot into mortises
117. Genetic variant
118. **1983 Eddy Grant hit**
120. Rude onlooker
121. "Okay"
122. Tear to shreds
123. 2021 movie remake: *West _____ Story*
124. They're a hit at Rogers Centre?
125. Quebec compass point
126. It precedes beth
127. Staircase riser

DOWN

1. Upgrade from gravel to asphalt
2. Red Sea port city
3. _____-Pong
4. Canadian embassy employee's case?
5. YVR security employee

6. "Eureka!"
7. Industrial region in Germany
8. Charlie Brown catchphrase: "Good _____!"
9. Memory trace
10. Corn Belt state
11. Lots of jackfish?
12. Victoria Day month
13. Forces one's will on others
14. _____ Wells NWT
15. **1985 Aretha Franklin song**
16. Memphrémagog and Mistassini, in Quebec
17. Garnier hair colouring brand
18. AB-based think tank: Canada _____ Foundation
24. "That's gross!"
25. 2013 Avril Lavigne song: "_____ to Never Growing Up"
29. Popular breath mints brand
31. Astrological signs adjective
34. Hosiery shade
35. Polar headgear?
36. 1985 Gene Autry TV movie: _____ *American Cowboy*
37. Cherry, in Chibougamau
39. Error
41. Some Greek letters
43. Harshly criticized: _____ into
44. Sunny side up plateful
45. Weight watcher's regime
47. Farley Mowat's WWII reminiscence: *My Father's _____*
48. Explosive situation at the armoury?
50. Encroach on others' rights
54. Black, in Beaupré
56. Sudbury-born C&W singer Grand
58. **1992 Ozzy Osbourne chart-topper**
60. Hoarse
61. Critique
63. Adroitly done, say

65. Most tidy
66. Diplomatic thaws
69. Summer skin tones
71. Molar material (var.)
72. Doesn't have the guts
73. "When a Man Loves a Woman" singer Percy
75. To the utmost, in brief
78. Hobbled by pain
79. UVic reunion attendee
80. Spill the pigs' feed?
82. Revise wording
83. "Holy cow!"

85. Thug
86. Tibetan priest
88. Ottawa's National War Memorial, for example
91. Some metalworkers
92. Trig function
94. Insanity
96. He might complain about CN service?
98. Repetitive phrase in meditation
102. Hands out pineapple?
104. Dangerous situation
106. Bulgarian currency unit

107. 1962 novelty song: "Monster _____"
108. Palo _____
109. Sea mollusc
111. Person who's a nuisance
112. Like a juicy plum
114. Reacting right away
115. Naked
116. Trickle out
118. Beauty is in this of the beholder
119. Top NHL prize: Stanley _____

SOLUTION ON PAGE 159

6 Across the Aisle

Former leaders of the federal opposition

ACROSS

1. Puffball part
6. **Liberal John**
12. Lip of a cup
16. Competition TV show: _____ *Chef Canada*
19. City on the Nile
20. Circle around a pupil
21. Sitar music style
22. Indigenous New Mexico people
23. Suggestions or opinions
24. Tune in to CBC Radio, say
25. Clearasil might clear this up
26. Classic Canadian film: _____ *oncle Antoine*
27. Tree near the seashore?
28. From B to B, in music
29. Cup of Earl Grey
30. In the near future
31. Roil
33. Hussar's horse
35. Sights and sounds, say
37. _____ Club of Edmonton
39. Atlas page feature
41. Season to
42. Jewish month
43. Buddies, in Barcelona
47. Groundhog or gopher
49. Cares for your Ps and Qs?
51. Kitchen cooker
52. Terse attorney's document?
53. Conceited
57. Four-legged family member
58. Bathroom fixture: _____ rack
60. Court officer
62. Mo. that can bring spring showers
63. Circular object
64. Canadian Armed _____
65. Northern Canada snow house
67. **NDPer Thomas**
71. **Conservative Joe**
72. **Reformer Preston**
74. Eastern Christian church member (var.)
75. Cling to
77. Tear wrapping paper
78. Envy or gluttony
79. Gave a guarantee
81. Work with Canada's Tatiana Maslany?
84. Letter in some US sorority names
87. Dele opposite, to an editor
89. Type of saxophone
90. It precedes processing
91. Public acclaim
93. Headpiece made of flowers
95. Tithing amounts
97. Nickname of a Calgary Stampede event: Half-mile of _____
98. Compare
100. Draped Indian garments
102. Jerusalem country
104. Absconded with
106. Assuages a hunger
108. Winnipeg-based philanthropist: The _____ Foundation
109. Shipboard okays
110. House of York monarch: Richard _____
112. Knight's knave?
114. Air Supply song: "Making Love Out of Nothing _____"
117. Grp. that fundraises for a school
118. Bics and Montblancs
119. Sense
120. Egyptian peninsula
121. Man who looked ahead, not back, in the Bible
122. K-6 school
123. African country: _____ Leone
124. Holy city in Saudi Arabia
125. Compass pt.
126. Tallies up
127. **Conservative Stephen**
128. Express disdain

DOWN

1. Smooth-talking
2. Moon, in Montreal
3. Like parents-to-be?
4. **Bloc Québécois leader Lucien**
5. Canada's ninth prime minister Meighen
6. Bird of prey's claw
7. _____ acid
8. Respites for musicians?
9. Margin jotting
10. High rolls, in craps
11. Rajahs' mates
12. *Enfant terrible*
13. Hightails it to the Honda Indy Toronto?
14. **Liberal Michael**
15. Canadian singer-songwriter Moore
16. Abnormal cell growth
17. **Conservative Erin**
18. Pre-euro Finnish currency unit
30. Former South African statesman Jan
32. Scandinavian rug
34. Western Canada oil field structure
36. Rustic lodgings
37. Slope for a wheelchair
38. *Garfield* dog
40. Patterned fabric
44. Cut the lawn
45. "_____ had it!"
46. It holds a hairstyle in place
48. Thomas Paine advocated for this in *The Age of Reason*
50. Layers, to a geologist
52. Practice rail for National Ballet of Canada dancers

54. West African nation
55. "Once" follower, in a fairy tale
56. Pirate ship potable
59. Kimono accoutrement
60. You play Trivial Pursuit on this
61. Limited by a time span
63. Ontario Camps Association (abbr.)
64. Express contempt, old style
66. Gross National Product (abbr.)
67. No fuss, no this
68. Pint of blood, say
69. Part of a poem
70. Demolished a building, in Berkshire
71. Measurements of colour purity

73. Car anagram
76. Sandy mounds
80. Conservative Robert
81. Trash bin
82. Canada's capital city (abbr.)
83. A doctor tells you to say this
84. Type of sale at Leon's
85. In good health
86. "_____ just take a minute"
88. Movie set scenes
90. AWOL military member
92. Liberal Jean
94. Prefix that means "new"
95. Queen of the fairies, in folklore
96. Lisa, to Maggie, for short

98. NDPer Jack
99. Conceive of
101. Captivate
103. Series of twitches
104. Southern BC city: _____ Ridge
105. Amerced
107. Sound made by a noisy soup eater
108. Perfume sourced from petals
111. Basic beliefs, for short
113. Historic name for Ireland
115. Handkerchief or wedding dress trimming
116. He's guilty of perjury
118. Round veggie

SOLUTION ON PAGE 159

7 Famous Fauna?

You'll know their names

ACROSS

1. Fashion forward
5. _____ au rhum
9. Top a pot?
14. "Wherefore art _____ Romeo?"
18. Paul Henderson in a '72 game
19. **Golf great Woods**
20. "_____ With Me"
21. **CNN personality Blitzer**
22. Russian mountain chain
23. 1987 Paul Carrack hit: "Don't Shed _____"
24. String quartet's favourite liqueur?
26. Repair
27. Germ-free state
29. Some CBC shows
30. Pool hall signals?
32. Bad habit
33. Mouse spotter's shriek
34. Produces a copy of *Canadian Geographic*?
37. The shakes, say
40. Score of a Flames–Jets game
44. **Country Music Hall of Fame inductee Wells**
45. It precedes chi
46. Covered in morning moisture, old style
48. American Department of Health org.
49. Jersey numbers for Plante and Parent
50. Open pies filled with fruit
52. Picked a plot for a house
53. Southwest Newfoundland town: _____ aux Morts
54. Parliament Hill caucus group: _____ Democratic Party
55. Old Pontiac model for nana?
57. **"Peace Train" singer Stevens**
58. In all honesty
59. Splashing about
61. Netherlands river

63. Where ocean creatures sleep?
64. Sirloin tip, for one
65. Niagara-on-the-Lake museum: _____ Secord Homestead
66. Strong blasts of wind
67. As of now
69. Titter (var.)
70. Vancouver pro soccer player
73. Speaks hoarsely
74. **Reality TV bounty hunter**
75. State of being stuffed
77. Famous Quebec City street: _____ du Petit Champlain
78. Grey complected
79. Nobel-winning scientist Marie
81. Canadian metric weight measurement
82. Phoenician queen
83. 52, to Nero
84. Some non-biological children?
86. Go mouldy
87. ***Good Morning, Vietnam* star Williams**
88. Father-and-son Canadian TV magnates Izzy and Leonard
90. Passes on an illness
92. Trade advocacy group: _____ Association of Canada
93. Stuck in a _____
94. NASA flight cancellation
95. Penny, say
96. Pump gas at Esso, say
99. Plant preferred by baseballer Hank?
102. Labyrinth
106. Extremely angry
108. Car you can plug in
109. _____ formaldehyde
110. **US political commentator Gingrich**
111. British county
112. ***The Cosby Show* cast member: _____-Symoné**
113. Parasitic ova

114. Singer Shannon, et al.
115. Tourism slogan: _____, Natural British Columbia
116. European peaks
117. When Canadian troops stormed Juno Beach

DOWN

1. Pal at a TO radio station?
2. Bryan Adams song: "_____ I Am"
3. With 91-D, Reagan-era scandal name
4. Loblaws deli purchases
5. Mooring posts
6. Pulitzer-winning author James
7. ***Man vs. Wild* host Grylls**
8. Land at YWG
9. Feline owners' fabrics?
10. Roman judge's incidental remarks?
11. Canadian soldiers succeeded here in WWI: _____ Ridge
12. Doe anagram
13. Delivered a verdict
14. Adjusts a bit
15. Ian who starred in Atom Egoyan's *The Sweet Hereafter*
16. _____ podrida
17. Roswell sightings
19. Shoots with a stun gun
25. Religious group's principles
28. Leg or arm
31. One-eighty turn
34. Eastern church art pieces (var.)
35. Tendon
36. WestJet crew's attentiveness?
37. 2011 Rihanna R&B song: "Do Ya _____"
38. Citrus fruit peel
39. Wiry hairs
41. Opt out of Internet notifications
42. City in northern France
43. Contraction for "Those people would"

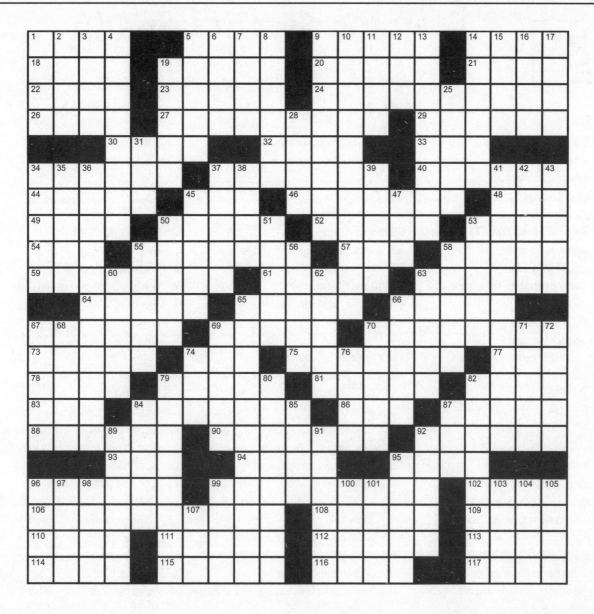

45. Sow seeds
47. Frequent Ucluelet weather forecast word
50. Curly-haired dog: Bichon _____
51. HGTV Canada shows star Richardson
53. See 106-A
55. Stairways to the Ganges
56. Pouts
58. Moody, at a U of M mid-term?
60. In a lather?
62. Tim Hortons Timbit, for example
63. Château Laurier room type
65. French Armed Forces member
66. Belgian city
67. Start of a musical refrain
68. Saharan spring
69. Bodily trunks (var.)
70. Sots
71. Attend a non-credit U of C course
72. Showy garden flower
74. Unexploded ordinance
76. Wrongful act, in law
79. Be cheaper
80. Ex-Leaf Williams was one
82. City in Germany
84. Thin porridge
85. Utah state flower
87. 2010 Barenaked Ladies single: "You _____ Away"
89. Explodes, like Mount Etna
91. See 3-D
92. Roomy car
95. Canadian bookstore chain
96. South African currency
97. Weapon for a duel
98. Poultry
99. "Take _____ from me"
100. **Mononymous soul singer**
101. Respond to an invite
103. Dry
104. Epsilon follower
105. 2021 Adele hit: "_____ on Me"
107. Celebrated Calgary-born pianist Wesley

SOLUTION ON PAGE 159

8

Home Sweet Canada

Popular treats

ACROSS

1. Cajole
5. It follows gab or slug
9. Large flightless birds
13. Dancer's sliding step
19. Diamond Head island
20. Tibetan holy man
21. Insubstantial (var.)
22. More lively, at Honda Indy Toronto?
23. Make a garment with yarn
24. "Urgent" acronym
25. HGTV star Jonathan Scott, to brother Drew
26. 1990 Neil Young and Crazy Horse song: "Days That _____ Be"
27. Self-interest
30. Johnnycake
32. Crone
33. Scouts Canada group
35. Bluish-green ocean fish
36. Former US telco
37. Append your two cents?
40. *I Love Lucy* star Arnaz
42. Long-time Canadian children's entertainers: Sharon, Lois and _____
44. Axle adjunct
46. Jumps
48. Scotiabank Arena ice fixture
50. 1971 Poppy Family song: "Where _____ Grows"
52. Take over territory in wartime
55. Wile E. Coyote's retailer
56. Atelier tripod
58. Gladden
60. Let _____ a secret
61. Like some bath mats
63. Matchsticks game
65. Former CBC host-turned-filmmaker Lewis
66. Pelvic bones
67. Got anagram
68. Snake charmer's snake
70. Most mentally ill
72. Public luminary, for short
75. **Treat in a yellow box**
78. Publishing submission encl.
79. Worshipping false gods
81. Cockneys drop this letter
82. Original *Antiques Roadshow* network (abbr.)
84. West Coast shrub
85. _____ and tonic
87. Receive
88. Green with envy
92. 2003 Margaret Atwood novel: _____ *and Crake*
93. Lost soul, say
95. Happen once more
97. Southern US cooking pod
98. Use Royal LePage again
100. Snag
102. *Good Bones* demolition pro Starsiak
103. Artificial, at the theatre?
104. Groups of three
106. Mayberry's town sot
108. 1985 novel by Canada's Brian Moore: *Black _____*
110. Positive answer
111. Be offensively inquisitive
113. "Hardly!"
115. Ancient Grecians gathered here
117. Lummox or lout
119. These help you listen
122. Some dabs
127. One type of discriminator
128. Via, informally
130. Rank and _____
131. Cad
132. Curdled milk
133. Coconut fibre
134. Chimney component
135. _____ *qua non*
136. Fly that transmits sleeping sickness
137. It goes with an eye
138. Bees' enclosure
139. William Shatner series: *Star _____*

DOWN

1. See 1-A
2. Pushed a doorbell
3. Akron state
4. These potato chips are made in Canada: Old _____
5. Water pipe part
6. _____ Coast
7. **Sugar-coated chocolate spheroids**
8. South American forest ungulate
9. **Chewy peanut/ toffee/chocolate confection**
10. Kitten's sound
11. Type of acid
12. Gathering of church officials
13. **Honeycomb toffee treat**
14. No-longer-popular celebrity
15. Maple genus
16. Fleeting looks from the corner of your eyes
17. Relieve: _____ ease
18. Wear away, like a shoreline
28. *CSI: Crime Scene Investigation* star George
29. Have a bawl?
31. Uncooked
34. Repair a road
37. Glass Tiger singer Frew
38. Art Nouveau period successor: Art _____
39. Rhett's expletive
41. Open pea pods
43. Mrs. Mulroney
45. Perrier rival
47. Ant or aphid
49. Male vocal range
51. Extravagant
53. Backs, anatomically

54. Related through mom
56. Number of Olympic bronze medals won by Canada in Beijing in 2008
57. Tripoli country
59. Campbell's soup containers
62. Near to your home
64. **Large bar**
66. Sassy ballroom dance
68. 1987 Roy Orbison and k.d. lang duet
69. Make a modification
71. Opposite of intoxicated
72. Motorcycle helmet part
73. Throw down the gauntlet: "_____ you!"
74. Styrofoam material

76. *Cogito, _____ sum*
77. Square dance group, e.g.
80. Less strict
83. Set
86. Notable Roman emperor
88. Canada has won seven medals in this at the Olympics
89. Give the green light
90. See 1-A
91. Utters
93. **Chocolate-dipped raisin bit**
94. _____-tat-tat
96. **Bar with a famous advertising question**
99. Serves as an intermediary
101. **"Delightful" nougat bar**

103. Scorch steak
105. Set the dog on
107. …Fah-_____-lah…
109. Little gal who lost her sheep
111. Long-time Rush drummer Neil
112. Fits of anger
114. Get the ball, like Fido
116. Ornate collar fringes
118. Assembly of _____ Nations
120. Glass of ale
121. Easy victor: _____-in
123. Canadian band: _____ Rodeo
124. Black, in La Belle Province
125. Whistler's whistle
126. Hide-and-go-_____
129. Brazilian seaside city, for short

SOLUTION ON PAGE 159

23

Toys in the Attic

9

But they sometimes come out to play!

ACROSS

1. Alone, to a stage actor
6. CBC milieu
11. Former Ontario premier Rae, et al.
15. Party invitation acronym
19. Medium for Alex Colville
20. Cutting foresters from the workforce?
21. Assist
22. Foil's kin
23. **Mechanical drawing toy**
25. HGTV Canada show: *Save My* _____
26. Prefix meaning "Chinese"
27. Cyclist's stunt
28. Seedy
30. Regular Tim Hortons customer, say
32. Greek alphabet starter
34. Pronounce like Daffy Duck?
36. Condemns to a woeful fate
37. Idly veg
40. Spicy Caribbean drink
44. In the midst of
46. 1977–79 government initiative: Task Force on Canadian _____
48. 1970 Joni Mitchell hit: "Big _____ Taxi"
49. Blue Jays and Argos
50. Annual fundraising event: Terry Fox _____
53. Allergy symptoms
55. Pain free, in the dental chair
56. Deep male voice
57. Mob bigwig
58. Monaco and Singapore, e.g.
60. Churchy choral composition
61. Picks one
62. Open for business time (abbr.)
63. Toronto tourist's aid
64. Slowly trickle out
65. Salmon type (var.)
66. **Game that hooks kids in**

72. Assembly of witches
75. Amphibian type
76. Sun Life product (abbr.)
77. Netherlands river
80. Related to?
81. Missouri tributary
83. Atlantic side African country
87. Produced puppies, say
88. Palindromic man's name
89. Prince's platform
90. _____-squat
91. Caught a glimpse
92. Clarified butter, in Indian cuisine
93. Root vegetable
95. Withered old woman
96. _____ Jaw SK
98. Between the earth and the moon
100. Decor jug
101. *The Maltese Falcon* PI Sam
103. Friends
105. Painful sound?
107. It loves company
109. Native of northeast India
113. South American game bird
117. Kids' song: "The _____ Go Marching"
118. Ontario-born Thicke who starred in *Growing Pains*
120. **See 68-D**
122. Teapot dregs
123. Weird, to a hip-hopper
124. Extremely successful, on Broadway
125. White House workers
126. Vega is in this constellation
127. Cramped, to Gumby?
128. TSX word
129. Facial grimace

DOWN

1. Erupt like Etna
2. Governor General's avowal
3. Scalp pests

4. Ill
5. Antiques market booth
6. Profit, like a farmer?
7. Microsoft Windows filename ender
8. Morse code signals
9. Imperial ruler measurement
10. Old-style Turkish title (var.)
11. **She debuted in 1959**
12. Follows instructions
13. Famed Canadian horse: Big _____
14. Cease or desist
15. _____ one's laurels
16. **Geometric drawing kit**
17. Scorpion's poison
18. Menial labourers
24. Takes a tiny taste
29. Extinguished the cake candles
31. Foofaraws
33. Old-style "with regard to"
35. Break down syntax
37. *The Addams Family* butler
38. Broadcasting live, at a CTV studio
39. Leans, like a liner
41. Stick together?
42. Donations, old style
43. Hold up a TD branch
45. Nearly all
47. He always agrees?
49. Eucharist bread plate
51. _____ the minute
52. Pinocchio's "tell"
54. Newspaper name in Windsor and Sudbury
56. **Punchable clown toy**
57. Sweet whisperings
59. It precedes May (abbr.)
60. Canadian coach Ellen Burka, to skater Petra
64. Frequently, for short
65. Charitable organization: _____ Fibrosis Canada

66. Ontario community: Grand _____
67. Anagram for eaten
68. **Classic building toy**
69. Be in arrears
70. White wine drink
71. Canadian medical field pioneer: _____ Johnson MacLeod
72. These pick up passengers at YYC
73. Creole cooks' ingredient
74. **Picturesque discs toy**
77. Give to Lakehead University
78. Author who created Piglet and Pooh
79. "You Make Me Feel Like Dancing" singer Leo

81. Homophone for 64-A
82. Brew some oolong
83. Dolomite deposit
84. Ethnic group in Siberia
85. Unfairly exploiting
86. Hormone released during stress
89. Name a sir, say
92. Busy body?
93. Heinie
94. Had some, say
97. Place name shared by Saskatchewan, Ontario and Ukraine
98. **Stairclimbing toy**
99. Muddy the waters, maybe?

101. Second Cup order size
102. Like some air freshener scents
104. Surprised: Taken _____
106. Actress Faris, et al.
108. Cry of complaint
110. Priests' vestments
111. Crowd's melee
112. The 411, say
114. Pie à la _____
115. Moulding shape
116. Historical hockey rival of CDA
119. Southeast Asian people
121. Canadian Film Centre (abbr.)

Canada Cornucopia 2 Challenger

No three-letter answers

ACROSS

1. Cloud formation in Alberta: Chinook _____
5. CPS personnel
9. Horseshoe Falls spray
13. Mountain range segment
19. Road Runner's foe: _____ E. Coyote
20. Tortoise's foe in a fable
21. Early Peruvian
22. Enter the picture
23. In thermodynamics, occurring without gain or loss of heat
25. Sudden decrease on the Dow Jones, say
26. Canadian country pop superstar Twain
27. Loads a Web page again
28. Lavish with adoration (with "on")
29. Fire truck alarms
30. Flaky behaviour
31. Venetian blind board
32. Give up control
33. Wedding party fellow
34. Did some DIY
36. Like Goethe's literary pact?
40. Picturesque, at BC's Panorama Resort?
42. Unit of barometric pressure
43. Do nothing
44. Equal, to a Quebecer
49. Wedding invitation acronym
50. 14-D, for example
51. Like some fast-food meal purchases
52. Rot
54. They're known as "Canadian" birds
55. Draw new boundaries
56. CFL trophy
57. Barely detectable amount
60. Affirmative answers (var.)
61. Organic compound used in gasoline and gin
62. Anne Murray #1 hit: "I Just Fall _____ Again"
67. Small eatery in France
69. Baking product in a box
70. Michael Ondaatje's 2000 Giller Prize winner: _____ *Ghost*
74. Standing tall
75. Australian Indigenous person
77. Toronto-born Austin Powers franchise actor (with 87-A)
78. Unpleasant smell
79. HGTV Canada airs this: *Flip or _____*
80. Jotted down pertinent info
81. Check your sleeping infant: Look _____
82. Breathe labouriously
83. Program a Crock-Pot timer
85. Just hanging around?
87. See 77-A
88. Capricious ideas
93. 1985 Canadian Football Hall of Fame inductee Gabriel
94. Shelter for sheep or pigeons
95. Aggravate an extraterrestrial?
98. Manly men, in Madrid?
101. "What _____ God wrought?"
102. Nonsensical remarks
103. Act I, Scene III *Macbeth* line: "_____ thee, witch!"
104. Armoury contents, for short
105. Mechanic's apparel
106. Lassie's breed
107. Author Trotsky
108. Second-to-last fairy tale word
109. That, in Montreal
110. Influencer
111. Subdivision tracts
112. Papas
113. Seatback drop-down on a jet

DOWN

1. Juno, for example
2. Governor General's Ottawa home (with 101-D)
3. They're white, in Dover
4. Fireplace floor
5. Tag players, say
6. Courtroom avowals
7. Tarot deck card: The High _____
8. Jiffies
9. One of 88 on a piano
10. Encroachment
11. HGTV Canada reno guru McGillivray
12. Ruler made of cloth
13. These spa employees rub you the right way
14. Plant-eating insects
15. Extra hours?
16. Samoan currency
17. Nova Scotia premier elected in 2021 (with 55-D)
18. Benedictine bros
24. *Nota* _____
31. Freud's stumble?
32. OPEC is one
35. GIC or RRSP
36. Discovery in Alberta's Badlands
37. The same, to an old Roman
38. Piece of plankton
39. One type of tide
41. Potatoes are the leading this in New Brunswick
42. One who abstains from alcohol, in Arkansas
44. Like the jittery fashion designer?
45. *American Gigolo* actor Richard
46. High or low cards
47. 1930s Hollywood star Myrna, et al.
48. Roast hosts
50. Tubular pasta with diagonally cut ends

53. Kitty or cat
54. Old CBC kids' show: *The Friendly* _____
55. See 17-D
58. Barnyard baby bird
59. False witness
61. Sailboat rope
63. Toy you might ogle?
64. Fail to say
65. Climbing plant
66. Crossed out
68. Some seizures may indicate this illness

69. Manage reasonably well
70. In the centre of things
71. This ship sailed in 1492
72. Russian church relic (var.)
73. In a long-winded manner
76. Lively Brazilian dance
78. Never married woman, old style
79. At no charge
83. Big snakes
84. They work with rope
86. Quintessentially Canadian coin
87. Kingfisher's kin
89. Legatee

90. Canadian insurance company
91. Canada Post delivery?
92. Pilsner popular in Canada: _____ Artois
94. Star's brief screen role
96. Washed oneself
97. English course assignment
98. They're big at McDonald's?
99. Get one's ducks in _____
100. Fizzy beverage
101. See 2-D
102. Decorated a cake

11 Give Me a C...

For these Canadian cities

ACROSS

1. Service at Toronto's St. Patrick's Church
5. Domestic servant in Asia
9. Some playing marbles
13. Shove
17. "Wanna make _____?"
18. Vane anagram
19. Not at all suitable
21. Post-coup military ruling group
22. **BC's sixth-largest city**
24. Farm bull
25. Night sky hunter
26. Disentangle string
27. **City on Newfoundland's west coast**
29. George Strait #1: "_____ in the Hole"
31. Breakaway religion group
32. Rock Hudson comedy: *Has Anybody Seen My _____?*
33. Back part of a bunny?
34. Cambria or Calibri
36. Enrol at York University
39. Pigeon-_____
40. Make up for a financial loss
42. In 2019, TELUS bought this home security co.
43. Sends in a bill payment
45. Snapshot, for short
48. Cineplex _____
49. 1985 Canadian charity song: "Tears _____ Not Enough"
50. Actress Blanchett and her namesakes
51. Cache
53. Uncouth
55. Licorice-flavoured seeds
57. Partner of Zeus
58. **This Alberta city includes a Canadian Forces Base**
62. The "U" in UHF
63. Cold weather cap part
65. Inuit-invented jackets
66. Fireplace nook, in Felixstowe
67. Person released from Stony Mountain Institution
68. Withdraw
69. CBC Radio show: *Ontario _____*
70. **Ontario's easternmost city**
71. Movie awarded a Genie in 2008: _____ *from Her*
72. Corporate plunderer
74. _____ profundo
75. Inlet in the heart of Vancouver: _____ Creek
77. Tall and tapered, like a turret
78. Cdns. give thanks in this mo.
79. Filled a ship's hold
84. Bud on a spud
85. Style of skiing
87. Scrooge's interjection of contempt
88. Stupidity
89. Canada won three Olympic silver medals in this state
90. Reaching the best-before date
93. 2020 Neil Young track: "We Don't Smoke It No _____"
94. Cólon sunhats?
97. 20-year NHLer from Sarnia Verbeek
98. Toddler's transgression
100. Water-soaked soil
101. **New Brunswick city on the Restigouche River**
103. Influential avenues?
105. Use to one's advantage
106. Raise a glass at Oktoberfest
107. **Ontario city at the confluence of the Grand and Speed rivers**
110. River with a famed left bank
111. More tender to the touch
112. Bibliographical abbr. for additional authors
113. Put on pounds
114. Seabirds (var.)
115. Ring-around-the-rosy bloom
116. Refuse to admit
117. Popular 1990s band: 'N _____

DOWN

1. Hamilton's university, for short
2. Blood-typing classification letters
3. Order of occurrence
4. Flabbergast
5. Belgian port city
6. Spitefulness
7. Like innovative artists
8. Component of blood pigment
9. Oman's capital
10. With a narrow-minded attitude
11. *Beverly Hillbillies* star Max
12. Exhausted by a shopping excursion?
13. The happy cat did this
14. Front Street landmark in Toronto: _____ Station
15. Oscar Peterson recorded this classic: "My Heart _____ Still"
16. Country music star from Nova Scotia Snow
20. Dissertation
21. Unemployed
23. Gender-neutral pronoun
28. Public disturbance
29. Hairstyle for Hendrix
30. Like some sports teams
32. Cdn. tax since 1991
35. Further
37. Brainstorm, in Baie-Comeau
38. Call it a day at work, for good
41. Denuded
44. It's east of Phoenix
45. Rice dish flavoured with saffron
46. Haifa country
47. Wedding venue
49. North Sea birds
50. **Alberta's most populous city**

52. Toss an afghan?
54. Fall leaf gatherer
56. US retailer that closed in Canada in 2018
58. Coffee serving vessel
59. Like some downtown streets in 50-D
60. Neck of the woods, say
61. Squirrels' nests
62. Provides insufficient light
64. Ex-governor of California Schwarzenegger
66. Orange antiseptic liquid
67. Canadian newspaper: *National* _____
69. Shelter on the Great Plains (var.)
70. Laugh loudly, old style
73. Covers a street with tar
74. Humdrum hog?
76. Safe for consumption
80. Intention
81. After Armageddon
82. Lighter shade of beige
83. Changed from brunette to redhead
86. In need of a cane
87. Minuscule amount
88. In a mean-spirited manner
89. Takes the tails off the donkeys?
91. Food storage cupboard
92. Famed Canadian physician Bethune
94. Patio slab
95. Full speed, to Admiral Nelson
96. Boat with one mast
99. Paddle
101. Labatt Blue two-four
102. Source of poi
103. Tim Hortons menu option: _____ coffee
104. Archaeologists' milieux
108. Nova Scotia's Still Fired Distilleries makes this: Fundy _____
109. SASE, for one

Take Off, Eh!

Come fly with us

ACROSS

1. Adjective for a Hamelin piper
5. Fish catch in many provinces
9. **Australia's national airline**
15. Upper body garment
19. Long-time retailer: Canadian _____
20. Trifling sum
21. Disquietude
22. Vehicle shaft
23. **WestJet rival**
25. Muscle coordination disorder
26. Garishly bright
27. Alberta Motor Association (abbr.)
28. Antiquity, in antiquity
30. Expresses one's opinions again
32. 1972 Temptations #1: "Papa Was a _____ Stone"
35. Secluded mountain tracts
38. A lot of this falls in Canada
39. Hot beverage, in Beauceville
40. Don Ho instrument, for short
41. Traditional Welsh soup
43. Feathered friends, say
45. Lose your temper
47. **UK flyer**
51. It's as good as a mile?
54. Effortless
55. Prefix meaning "within"
56. Wreck a car, colloquially
58. Wood strip
60. _____ Patricia's Canadian Light Infantry
64. Remembrance Day mo.
65. Nigerian monetary unit
66. Frightened away the cobbler?
69. Devour lunch, say
71. **Largest Russian airline**
73. Tennis player's soft shot
74. US fitness chain in Canada: Gold's _____
76. Stonecrop
78. Toronto mayor Ford (2010–14)
79. Series starring Canada's Sandra Oh: *Killing* _____
80. **Rome-based airline (1947–2021)**
83. Swift
85. Pitch type at Rogers Centre
87. Flower leaf
88. Sunscreen tube info
90. Number of Saskatchewan Roughriders appearances in the Grey Cup (as of 2021)
92. Civil court litigant
93. Unadorned
95. Eyelid hair
96. _____ von Bismarck
100. You might see one at Cineplex Odeon
102. **Airline based in Amman**
106. Diplomatic skill
108. "Born This Way" singer: Lady _____
109. Rainy weather systems
110. Acronym of Canada's major trading floor until 2002
111. US retailer in Canada: _____ Navy
114. It can be oily or dry
116. Southern Ontario conservation area: _____ Cotta
118. Sees James Bond?
120. Sycophant
123. Nonetheless
124. Indochinese language
125. TTC charge
126. Calgary Stampede interjections
129. **Flag carrier of Ireland**
134. Visa alternative
135. Dress a king for his coronation
136. 1963 part for Liz
137. Workstation surface
138. 1972 Edward Bear hit: "_____ Song"
139. **Airline based in Jeddah**
140. Song of praise
141. Dispatch a dragon

DOWN

1. "Harper Valley _____"
2. Nine minus six, to Caesar
3. Goof or muff
4. Windshield sticker
5. Yellow fruit
6. American attorneys' assn.
7. Oblique peek
8. Play for time
9. *Sine* _____ *non*
10. Pantry pest
11. Close
12. PST and GST
13. North and South Koreans
14. Like Whistler sports
15. Blade on a windmill
16. Use your influence
17. Otiose mammal
18. Uptight
24. Buddies, in Bologna
29. Car feature used in winter
31. Did laps in the pool
32. Pulitzer Prize-winning cartoonist Goldberg
33. Edible plant pod
34. Polynesian floral garlands
36. Joni Mitchell song covered by Sinatra: "Both Sides ____"
37. Law enforcement tactical grp.
42. Mulroney and Reagan sang this at an '85 summit: "_____ Irish Eyes are Smiling"
44. Former prime minister: William _____ Mackenzie King
46. Dish of seasoned rice
48. Keyboarding error
49. Inventors' brainstorms
50. Passageway for Plato
52. Set out on a ship
53. Tried hard (to)
57. Strongly state
59. Bigot

61. Scotch brand: Chivas _____
62. Pastoral poem (var.)
63. Khartoum country
65. Like a lofty lord?
66. Open-handed blows
67. Hide on the fairway?
68. _____ dictum
70. Relating to an eye part
72. Alberta's official flower: Wild _____
75. Niagara Falls sightseers' craft: Maid of the _____
77. "Queen of Rap" Nicki
81. The Magician deck
82. On _____ with
84. In a forlorn manner

86. Get _____ the ground floor
89. Leaping amphibian
91. Via variant
93. BC salmon type (var.)
94. Myanmar spending money
97. South American primate
98. Temporarily stun with a gun
99. In 1989, Canada discontinued these bills
101. Rigging support
103. For some, it's just a number
104. Obsess over, at home?
105. Very, musically
107. Albania's largest city
111. Abattoir viscera
112. Andean animal

113. Challenges
115. India's first prime minister
117. A young Stephen Harper appeared once on this show: _____ for the Top
119. Ducks' water holes
121. Send a message via cellphone
122. Crucifix
127. Kimono sash
128. Long-time Newfoundland band: Great Big _____
130. Stage of sleep
131. Type of toothpaste
132. Many CFLers come from here
133. Canadian singer Amy

SOLUTION ON PAGE 160

Ooh, a Trip to BC

Places that double your pleasure

ACROSS

1. CBC ex-news anchor Knowlton
5. Golden or chocolate dogs
9. Timbuktu nation
13. Saskatchewan capital
19. 1991 Sarah McLachlan single: "_____ the Fire"
20. Locale
21. *Doctor Zhivago* star Sharif
22. Oozed confidence, say
23. Shaped like an egg
24. **East Kootenay city**
26. Sent out an invoice
27. 200th anniversary celebrations
29. Steals
30. Canadian Rockies mammal
31. Optical Imaging Technology (abbr.)
32. Connecticut university
33. Unadulterated
34. TD investment option (abbr.)
35. Attaché for an attorney?
36. Ancient coffin
37. Limitless time span
41. Cavalry weapon (var.)
44. Petro-Canada station purchase
45. Canadian Mikita who won the Art Ross Trophy four times
47. Animal welfare agency: Calgary _____ Society
49. Colbie Caillat track: "Before _____ You Go"
50. It goes with gin
52. "It hit me like _____ of bricks"
54. Beverage for Stanley Cup-winning Leafs coach Imlach?
55. **City on the Fraser River**
57. Drawing lesson session
60. Fawn's mom
61. Nutrient-rich soils
62. Something you detest
63. Prepare for interment, in olden days
64. State that touches BC
66. **Okanagan Valley town**
67. Hardy's schtick partner
69. Statistics Canada stat, say
70. Liquid medicine dosage
72. Confidence in divinity?
73. Freud psyche construct
74. Parachute Club singer Segato
75. **Thompson Rivers University city**
78. Old Athens plaza
80. Scrapbooking paste
81. Indian loincloth
83. Snapshot, in Sicily
84. Andre De Grasse anchored Canada to two Olympic medals in these
86. Town north of Calgary
88. Luau instrument, in HI
89. Attach
90. Reality show: *Canada's _____ Race*
91. USMCA, for example
93. Chauffeur-driven ride
95. Bro's sibling
96. Colour of rosy cheeks
97. 1941 James Stewart movie: _____ *Gold*
98. _____ es Salaam
99. Ontario Public Service (abbr.)
102. Hollywood icon Judy
106. Courtroom wrangle over parentage
109. Beach Boys classic: "I Get _____"
110. **Coquitlam neighbour**
111. Brother of Michael and Marlon
112. More boring
113. Famed US general Robert
114. Yuri Andropov governed here (abbr.)
115. Not fully closed
116. Olfactorily offensive
117. Target of school bullies
118. Tennis players' collections?
119. Enjoy éclat

DOWN

1. She was turned to stone in mythology
2. Blacksmith's block
3. Make a pile
4. Golfer's target, on the green
5. Obtained from milk
6. Sherbrooke stop sign word
7. Green or yellow legume
8. Hindu fakir
9. *La Bamba* star Esai
10. Arcade amusement: Whac-_____
11. Vientiane is its capital
12. Annoy
13. Spiritual renaissance
14. Cast out of a country
15. _____ of St. Lawrence
16. Doing nothing
17. Old literary adverb
18. Tacks on
25. Predisposition
28. Movie genre: Film _____
29. Abscess liquid
33. Ground corn meals
34. "Scram!"
35. "I _____ Stop Loving You"
36. Get the picture
37. Former Australian flyer: _____ Airways
38. **District municipality near the centre of the province**
39. Regional airline: WestJet _____
40. Repair a pair of pumps
41. RSVP word
42. Frazier's bout foe
43. **BC Coast Mountains community**
44. Leaves
46. Applied permanent body markings
48. Opposite of downs

50. Shade of red in the garden?
51. Amazon rain forest description
53. '60s war country, for short
56. It abuts Victoria: _____ Bay
58. Synthetic fabric
59. Spicy pizza topping
62. _____ and battery
63. Shortened shorts?
64. Scared, in old days
65. He trails behind
66. This holds a paddle in place
68. Garlic, in Gatineau
71. Unit of work
72. Your destiny
74. Put down the law?
75. Famed gorilla who learned sign language

76. ESPN talk show since 2001, for short
77. Boston Red _____
79. Cleaner's cloth
82. Funny
85. Use a laundry appliance
87. You can't eat soup with this kind of spoon
89. Ethereal
92. *SCTV* duo: Bob _____ Doug McKenzie
94. List entry
95. Greek mythology creatures
96. "At Issue" discussion group on *The National*
97. Potato peeler

98. Shakespeare sonnet: "Why _____ thou promise such a beauteous day"
99. Seance board
100. Small round pockets for sandwiches
101. Long-legged bird
102. Roams
103. Jack-in-the-pulpit, e.g.
104. Part for Canada's Jim Carrey
105. Break in the action
106. Stanley Park art piece: Totem _____
107. Front end of a jet
108. Wild guess, colloquially
110. Animals' cage

SOLUTION ON PAGE 161

Spice Up Your Life...

By relishing these puns

ACROSS

1. Enjoy an activity at Banff Sunshine Village
4. Band founded by Canada's Bachman brothers, for short
7. Mistassini, in Quebec
10. It's more than a tsp.
14. American Allen who writes for *Maclean's*
18. More breezy
20. *The Barefoot Contessa* actress Gardner
21. Hebrew month
22. **Herb for a guru?**
23. Heart trouble description
24. Hit from 4-A: "_____ You"
25. Drawn-out tale
26. This Yukon place notched Canada's coldest ever temperature
27. **Herb served on a WWII Royal Navy corvette?**
29. Race, like an engine
31. Country bumpkins?
33. Broadcast, on Global
34. Root vegetable
37. Big mythological birds
38. "_____ written"
41. Inventive counterfeiter?
42. Ankara country (var.)
43. Ontario Racquet Club (abbr.)
46. Following one after the other
48. Impassioned
51. Long-running CBC documentary series: *The Passionate _____*
52. Doddering
53. State, with conviction
54. Fruity dessert: Peach _____
55. Wall board
57. Selfies and snaps
58. Intelligence, colloquially
60. Bros, e.g.
61. Canadian kidlit author Mélanie
63. Ontario town that shares its name with a French city
64. **Feline owner's herb?**
66. Get an eye for an eye
69. **Additive for a sailor?**
71. Princess Fiona, in *Shrek*
72. **Spice for dancer Rogers?**
73. Naysayers?
74. Hamburg lady of the house
75. Aborted mission, at NASA
76. Reddish-brown horse
78. Early '80s Police hit: "King of _____"
80. Me or I
84. Pseudonym
86. Indian restaurant bread
87. Canadian Safer who appeared on *60 Minutes* for 46 seasons
89. Pasture low
90. Producing shoots on sedge or grass
92. Improving
94. Jump off the deep _____
95. Principle of Chinese philosophy
96. Evaded
98. Like Hamilton, on a particularly polluted day
99. Paint or draw
100. Wanted
102. Canadian Agricultural Safety Association's awareness mo.
103. Summer thirst quencher
107. And so forth, in brief
108. **Herb for singer Clooney?**
112. On
113. Cabbage Patch Kid, for one
115. Have the flu
117. Aggressive South American fish
118. **Spice for Parliament Hill's sergeant-at-arms?**
119. Army munitions, for short
120. Health care pro
121. Calgary Spruce Meadows equestrian competitor
122. National non-profit group: _____ of Canada
123. Birds' domicile
124. Morning lawn moisture
125. Actor Alan Thicke, to singer Robin
126. Dispirited

DOWN

1. Clean a ship's deck
2. Cattle, in olden days
3. Fundamental, at the wheat farm?
4. Some stars
5. Canadiens or Canucks
6. Ship's lowest deck
7. It follows "soh"
8. Antipathetic
9. **Peppery additive for a Porsche driver?**
10. Yours, in Sherbrooke
11. Meh
12. Sweet 1966 Nancy Sinatra single?
13. Unfold, at the Shaw Festival?
14. Jennies and jacks
15. *Bête noire*
16. "Yikes!" old style
17. Journey segments
19. Numbers
28. Plan of attack
30. Compete
32. Stage curtain
35. Stirs up river sediment
36. Overcome adversity
38. Won a point off a serve, at the Rogers Cup
39. High protein bean (var.)
40. Ceremonial staffs, in the States
43. Many Canadians do this type of banking
44. Synagogue leaders

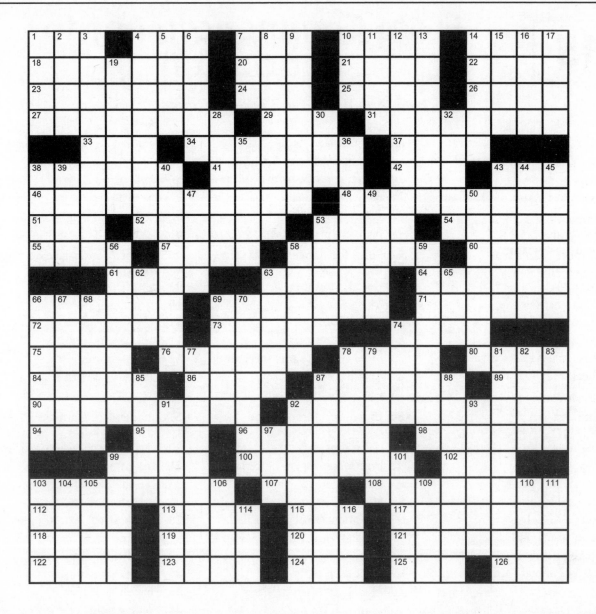

45. Holds onto
47. Condominium or apartment
49. Damp
50. When animals are in heat, in Hampshire
53. The Canadian National Vimy Memorial is near this French city
56. An FC Edmonton player never wants to score this
58. **Herb for actor Rathbone?**
59. They sneer
62. Mature
63. Plate used during mass
65. Ottoman Empire chief
66. Male line ancestor
67. Stradivarius instrument

68. Adorn with gold leaf
69. Wrap that clings
70. Really mad
74. Type of pastry (var.)
77. Russian Orthodox Church architectural feature
78. Gondolier, for example
79. More sere
81. New Canadians, say
82. Ontario provincial park: _____ Point
83. Fuddy-duddy (var.)
85. Indented
87. Alberta city: _____ Hat
88. Complained about the sweet potatoes?
91. Muslim month of fasting

92. **Spicy condiment for a Clue colonel?**
93. Without exception, for a guy?
97. Dennis who earned the Order of Canada for poetry
99. Ambles
101. Took PEDs, say
103. Metallic knit fabric
104. Latin abbr. found in footnotes
105. Ridicule
106. Stately deciduous trees
109. Hindu god (var.)
110. Perlman who played Carla on *Cheers*
111. Short gain for a CFLer
114. Subdivision space
116. The _____ Society of Nunavut

From Commencement to Conclusion

Find the letter pattern in these Canadian answers

ACROSS

1. Employees' supervisor
5. Vipers
9. Canadian Payroll Association (abbr.)
12. Strong lagers
17. Ready for picking
18. Sit still, like a Newfoundland
19. Annoy
21. Señora or señorita
22. Pennsylvania city
24. Veil anagram
25. Musical based on a Dickens novel
26. OPEC meeting dignitary (var.)
27. American author Truman
29. Felt sorry for someone
30. Bristle
32. Raised cattle, say
34. Tennis court call
35. Medical facilities
37. Took a TTC bus
39. Some gastropods live in these
41. Vocal pitches
42. **2012 Leonard Cohen track: "_____ Home"**
44. "He that cannot _____ cannot command"
45. Bitty branches
47. The National Gallery of Canada display
50. Lower Saxony city
52. Valérie Plante was first elected Montreal's this in 2017
53. Roast host
55. Welcome sight in the Sahara
56. Made amends
58. Lighten a burden
59. Gathers
62. Beds, in La Belle Province
63. Set
65. Outhouses
66. Harness racing horse
68. Large Atlantic sport fish
69. A doorway offers this
70. Starch sourced from palm trees
71. Baby rides in this
72. 16th Hebrew letter
73. Fly from Vancouver to Montreal, say
75. Ragout dish
76. Bracelet fastener
78. It precedes clock
79. State of purity
84. Shorten trousers
85. Light intensity measurements
87. Retailed on eBay, say
88. **Canada's largest bird of prey: Bald _____**
89. Alberta QEII divisions
90. Get a sense of?
92. Prep water for making rice
93. Bringing forth
95. 30-D, for example
96. Atlantic coastal waters fish
98. International Monetary Fund (abbr.)
99. Attack, verbally
100. Relatives by marriage
103. Musical triplet
105. Ask to a wedding
106. Peruse the *Ottawa Citizen*
107. They're just hanging around
111. Wrecked
112. Lollygag
113. Absent without leave military acronym
114. Potato salad sauce
115. Soups or salads, in restaurants
116. _____ de deux
117. Hamiltonian Lees who wrote lyrics recorded by Sinatra
118. Whole bunch

DOWN

1. You might buy one at la Vie en Rose
2. Canadian company: Imperial _____
3. Excellent
4. Appear to be
5. Fall flowers
6. Goods depositories
7. Dog's foot
8. Tune instruments, say
9. Suzette's servings?
10. Turn sharply
11. Deplaned
12. Indonesian language
13. Ear inflammation
14. **Statutory day in some provinces: _____ Holiday**
15. They're sometimes knobby
16. Type of quartz
20. Negatively charged particles
21. Ambling
23. National natural resources regulator (abbr.)
28. Nation friendly to Canada, for example
30. Roughrider rival
31. Angora or cashmere
33. Flotsam
36. French valley or river
38. Compass point (abbr.)
40. 1984 ZZ Top hit
43. Esoteric knowledge
45. Classical composer Erik
46. _____ Ilyich Tchaikovsky
47. **Nova Scotia educational institution: _____ University**
48. Feel indignant
49. High school enrollees
51. Most uncouth, at Rogers Centre?
52. **1961 posthumous Governor General's Award writing winner: _____ Lowry**
54. Cosmetics retailer in Canada: _____ Norman
57. 1990s sitcom: _____ *& Greg*

59. Diamond-patterned tartan

60. Governor General's Award for Fiction winner Toews

61. Garden perennial: Chilean _____

64. Poisonous gas

65. Fruit grown in Ontario and BC

66. Court dance of centuries past (var.)

67. Retirees: Golden _____

68. Act of invoking a curse

70. Young female retail clerk

71. Thickened skin

74. Noodle soup type

75. Glaswegian

77. Mollifies

80. Collar a criminal

81. Perfect state, in psychology

82. Opposite of portly

83. "To thine own _____ be true"

86. UCP in Alberta: _____ Conservative Party

87. Winter white stuff

89. Tall, spiky perennial

90. Sultan's decrees

91. Yellow-bellied Slider, for one

93. Lethargic state

94. Canadian environmentalist: _____ Suzuki

95. International hotel chain in Canada: Crowne _____

97. Dessert made with Saskatoon berries

99. Banting and Borden, formally

101. _____ tide

102. Smelting by-product

104. Canada's this turned 100 in 2021: Coat of _____

108. Have a mortgage with RBC

109. Canadian Club product

110. Mama pig

See solution page for letter pattern.

Rock On...

With singers who stepped in

ACROSS

1. Chit-chats
5. They're mined in BC
10. My, in Montreal
13. Scotiabank Saddledome home player, for short
18. Newfoundland landmark: Strait of Belle _____
19. *The Godfather* crime group
20. Chris Hadfield photography book: *You _____ Here*
21. Some Indian princes
22. It's "Arrêt" in Quebec
23. Rhetorical literary technique
24. **Mick Hucknall filled in for him in Faces**
26. Circles-and-exes game
28. Comes to the surface
29. Sailboat spar
30. Record keeping or data entry, for short
32. Hausa is this type of language
37. Gardening aid: Miracle-_____
40. Ben Mulroney, to Mila
41. Common person, informally
42. Poisonous salt
44. Mocking or teasing
46. Like a base baron?
48. 1985 Corey Hart hit: "_____ Surrender"
49. Woodworking tools
50. Glossy finish
52. American military flying org.
54. Marcel Marceau excelled at this
55. Spirograph and Slinky
56. Baking eggs in the oven
58. Iowa place: Cedar _____
60. ☺ and ☹
62. Ho-hum
64. Mare's baby
65. _____ Moines
66. Toronto's Rick Moranis voiced this *Brother Bear* character
67. Make ten from six plus four
68. Chianti, for one
70. Merino mom
73. Dump water from a leaky boat
75. Sushi bar beverage
77. Related to brain membranes
79. Rumple a coif
81. Traveller who goes on foot
83. Like the Kalahari
84. Kin of The Twist
85. Father of 64-A
87. Mammals seen on BC boat tours
88. Cite
89. Golden Italian liqueur
91. Saviour
93. Wooer
95. Chides
97. Back _____ a corner
98. Jasper, in EDM
99. Sign on a Leon's store, for short
100. African fly
101. Barbecuing utensils
103. Fit of twitching
105. Knight's tunic
107. Canadian Institute of _____ Accountants
111. **Arnel Pineda carried on his Journey journey**
115. A verified this clears you as a suspect
116. Margaret Atwood offering: *The Handmaid's _____*
117. Raring to go
118. Opus _____
119. Northern France city
120. Lebanon resident
121. Slow runs in the paddock
122. Northern European air carrier
123. Gdańsk residents
124. Canadian thespian Cariou, et al.

DOWN

1. Central point
2. Sparkling wine variety
3. La Belle Province-based party: _____ Québécois
4. Clans that gather on Labour Day?
5. 15th Greek letter
6. Sniper's final word?
7. 1970s Canadian band: _____ in Coldwater
8. Big Triumph hit: "Lay It on the _____"
9. 2010 Justin Bieber song: "Never _____ Never"
10. One official language of New Zealand
11. Sequential numbers
12. Famous loch or lawman
13. Rejuvenate
14. The _____ Society of New Brunswick
15. Steely Dan "Deacon Blues" album
16. Despoil
17. Brockville clock setting (abbr.)
24. Recurring Sylvester Stallone role
25. Gumshoes, for short
27. Most distant orbital point
30. 19th-C. US author Horatio
31. **Canada's Gowan stepped in for this Styx singer**
33. Red blood cell deficiency
34. **Sammy Hagar absorbed his Van Halen slot**
35. Twosomes or things
36. Prepare for burial, old style
37. Shredded cheese
38. Antenna enclosure
39. **Ronnie James Dio took over for this Black Sabbath singer**
41. Wharves
43. Bring up the _____
45. Vigour
47. Annoys an exterminator?
51. Not-so-veiled suggestions
53. Sigurd slayed this dragon
56. Oars

57. Okay from Don?
59. Indian hardwood tree
61. Colourful part of the eye
63. Turn _____ new leaf
67. Pseudonym letters
69. Like an inevitable jail sentence?
71. Milestones employee
72. First Nations leaders
74. Civic Holiday month in some provinces
76. Dazzles
77. Prefix meaning "large"
78. Asian ox
79. Actually plumbs?
80. Erie anagram

82. Worries excessively
84. Accurate piece of info
86. Stopping spot along Alberta's QEII Highway
88. Annual race in the North: Yukon _____
90. Gathers on command?
92. _____ Klassen, first Canadian to win five medals at one Olympics
94. Female reproductive organs
96. Gather crops
102. Perfume rootstock
103. Con artist's companion
104. Musical genre for 34-D and 39-D

106. The Brick sells these
107. History Muse
108. How some like their steak
109. See 45-D
110. First Reform Party MP Grey, et al.
111. Wimbledon unit
112. Paving crew's product
113. I, to Octavia
114. Retired Canadian Armed Forces member, for short
115. Matterhorn, for one

SOLUTION ON PAGE 161

Rock On 2...

17

In these Canadian places

ACROSS

1. Bunches of banknotes
5. Wintry woe in Canada: Cold _____
9. Former Canadian cable channel: Showcase _____
13. Not kosher
18. 2005–14 sitcom: *How _____ Your Mother*
19. Long-running CBC show: *This _____ Has 22 Minutes*
20. North African goat
21. Evil spirit (var.)
22. Mad, in Mexico
23. Common preposition
24. Petite car for a Brit?
25. Suitable for sowing
26. Main means of egress
29. **Parkland County AB town**
31. Tire patterns
32. Original Kiss guitarist Frehley
34. Savoury flavour, in Japan
35. Decompose
36. Canadian author and journalist Claire
37. Less fresh
39. Partner for life
41. European river
44. **Renfrew County ON village**
46. Food thickener
50. Official bird of Ontario: Common _____
51. Turtledove's murmur
52. RPM word
53. Canada had one in 2021
55. As sick as _____
56. Eddie Albert sitcom: *Green _____*
58. Follow commands
60. Kidney related
61. **Name of two New Brunswick communities**
63. Incoming flights, at YVR
64. Somewhat
65. Livestock field
66. _____–Japanese War
68. Biggest BC city (abbr.)
69. Motion detection device
73. Cookie containers
74. **BC city named for a beach boulder**
80. Glorify
81. Wolfish stare
82. Sleeper's night noise
83. *The Andy Griffith Show* sheriff's son
84. Terrier type
86. Ontario Veal Association (abbr.)
88. Battle between countries
89. Showed up
90. Eyelid inflammation
91. **It's north of Port Hood on Cape Breton Island**
94. Mongolian ruler: Genghis _____
95. Military-style hat
97. Communion tables
98. British aerial attack grp.
100. Stomach muscles, for short
103. Michael Bublé's milieu
105. Boston Bruins great Bobby
106. Asian temple
109. **Quadra Island community**
112. Containing gold
115. Immaturity, in legalese
116. Turn sharply (var.)
118. Annoying person or insect
119. Canadian Levant who wrote *Ethical Oil*
120. Complete
121. Make money
122. Noggin, in Rouyn-Noranda
123. Caulk
124. Cause alarm
125. Symbol on a staff
126. Winter ride for kids
127. Magnolia or maple

DOWN

1. Father of Canadian country music Carter
2. Apathetic, in olden days
3. Style matter on many HGTV Canada shows
4. **Saskatchewan municipality that shares its name with a Wiltshire wonder**
5. Cheaply built
6. Off-limits activities
7. Old agreement: Canada–US _____ Pact
8. Comparable, to a BC Lion?
9. Poorly lit
10. Everglades avian
11. Carburetor tube type
12. Adage
13. Bitumen deposit
14. _____ Canadian Superstore
15. Incarcerate, old style
16. Shakespearean volume, e.g.
17. About, old style
21. Hallucination, in the afternoon?
27. Chinese philosophy principle
28. Illegally peddles concert tickets
30. To wit
33. *A Shot in the Dark* star Sommer
37. Like a fleeced sheep
38. Blue Jays' fielding mistakes
40. Chemical compound
41. Israeli air carrier
42. 1969 Creedence Clearwater Revival song
43. Thunderous sound
44. Chocolatey beverage
45. Peace signs
47. 2005 Shania Twain song: "I _____ No Quitter"
48. Objective for an Oiler?
49. Mere
51. Supply meals for a banquet
54. JAL livery bird

40

O CANADA CROSSWORDS ▪ BOOK 23

57. Like Stephen King books
59. Father of Confederation George
62. A deadly sin
63. Buffoon
64. Father, informally
67. Open a sleeping bag
68. Like fast-spreading Internet memes
69. Attaches patches
70. Leave the Trans-Canada?
71. Hardly any, in the Hebrides
72. Aerodynamic
73. NU or YK
75. Coyotes' cries
76. **Partial Sherbrooke borough name**

77. Fish in some zoo aquariums
78. Canadian Independent Music Association (abbr.)
79. Avid
81. Act as an intermediary
82. World's largest desert
85. Person who's lost a limb
87. US president's bill rejection
92. Newfoundland fish dish (var.)
93. Enters forcefully
96. A Canadian in Paris, perhaps?
98. Went on a whitewater adventure
99. Bronze _____
100. Canada's first female MP MacPhail

101. Calgary Stampede Rodeo event: Saddle _____
102. He fills stockings
104. *Peer Gynt* playwright Henrik
106. Run at Tremblant
107. Construction site machine, for short
108. Halos (var.)
110. Depilatory brand
111. Circular tent
113. Virginia's favourite dance?
114. The Bay bargain day
117. Brandon-to-Portage la Prairie direction (abbr.)

Canada Cornucopia 3 Superchallenger

No Fill-in-the-blanks (FIBs) clues

ACROSS

1. Continually bother
7. Second Cup pot
13. Keyboard key
16. Dip bread in gravy
19. About to faint, old style
20. California's northern neighbour
21. Big Australian bird
22. Mobile state (abbr.)
23. Father of Confederation (with 63-A and 69-A)
24. Middle Ages men's coats
26. Seasonal malady
27. Overstimulated
29. Soft hit by a Blue Jay
30. City of 95-D
32. Souvenir shop buy (var.)
34. Taper
35. Orthodox Jew
38. Simplistic
39. Canadian Pointer, for one
40. Interfere
44. Nuclear particle
45. Stroke on a Glen Abbey green
46. Creation of Canada's Jean Paré
48. Wellington County ON town
49. Old West outlaw
51. Beirut country
52. Riverbed sediment
53. Wet dirt
54. Art Gallery of Ontario (abbr.)
55. Splinter group
56. Opposed to, in voting
58. Musical aptitude, say
59. Coins, but not bills
61. Calf's milk source
62. *The Fifth Estate* network
63. See 23-A
65. Disadvantaged, in society
69. See 23-A
72. Allow, at the Rogers Cup?
73. Kismet
74. Pungent red root
78. First-person pronoun
79. Prepares a planting bed
81. TTC's Bloor-Danforth, for one
82. Soupçon
83. Negative vote
84. Subj. for mathematicians
86. Diapers, in Derby
88. Canadian Supernault who won best actress at the 2013 American Indian Film Festival
90. Slope for tobogganing
91. Blue Mountain runs
92. Like a passé point
93. Business end of a hammer
94. US-born singer Bey honoured with the Order of Canada
96. James Bond's job
97. Edmonton and Regina, for short
98. Earth, to Minerva
99. Like this clue?
101. Enterprising commuter at Toronto's Union Station?
103. CIBC might give you one
106. Jerome who composed *Show Boat*
107. New Mexico city
111. Fertility clinic supply
112. Like the unlucky astronomer?
115. More base
116. Catch some rays
117. Utter a whopper
118. Millhaven Institution prisoner
119. Canadian opera star Stratas who won two Grammys
120. Large Alberta mammal
121. "Deck the Halls" syllables
122. Sri Lanka's previous name
123. Aromas

DOWN

1. It precedes "no fury" in a famous phrase
2. Like a pasty-faced chimney sweep?
3. Barter like a Brit
4. At an undetermined moment in the future
5. Inserted ammo into a firearm
6. Happen afterwards
7. Small component of a big machine
8. Scholar who studies the Middle East
9. Inter elsewhere
10. Commissioned salesperson, say
11. Halifax Citadel, for example
12. Stop
13. It goes in a mortise
14. Modification to the Constitution of Canada
15. Petticoated skirt support
16. Rogers Centre ump's shout
17. Pueblo pot
18. Ontario-born Coffey who played for nine NHL teams
25. Within the realm of possibility
28. False
31. Advises, in olden days
33. Really dislike
34. It comes before -Cola
35. Injures
36. Devoured dinner?
37. Weather balloon probe
39. Arrears
41. Not as moist
42. Fragrant spring bloomer
43. Ballot for a draw
45. Leafed through a book at Chapters?
46. Sets the record straight
47. Early Spanish explorer de León
50. Put on pounds
51. Literary father of Goneril, Regan and Cordelia
55. Seven, in Shawinigan
57. Form a mental picture
60. Feed an actor his lines
61. Commits a sin while committing a crime?

62. Quote
64. Alberta Doctors' Digest (abbr.)
66. British composer Edward
67. Moving company vehicles
68. Something for the mill?
69. Nocturnal flyers
70. Vatican governing body
71. Barbecue
75. It precedes Harbour in Victoria
76. More compos mentis
77. Dog-like African mammal
80. Among other things, to Octavius
81. Canada's Yvonne De Carlo played this Munster

82. Gives a car a jump-start
85. Brag
87. Gladys Knight's co-performers
88. Cord
89. Camera setting
92. Electrical generator
95. Large campus in La Belle Province
97. Horses' shelter
98. Madagascar mammal
100. Leers
101. Covered in microbes
102. Sensitive approaches

103. Speck of dust
104. Shape of a Calgary Olympic Games facility track
105. Colonel or major, in the Canadian military
106. 19th-C. Irish–Canadian painter Paul
108. Middle East port city
109. Ending for Oktober in Kitchener
110. Significant historical periods
113. Twitch
114. Cozy spot at home

Foods from across the pond

ACROSS

1. Stitch together, loosely
6. Costs for flying Air Canada
11. Former Royal Canadian Navy rank: _____ Seaman
15. It can be stuffed with hummus
19. Nighttime disorder: Sleep _____
20. Came out of a coma
21. Kill with kindness, say
22. Type of lily
23. **Traditional German roast**
25. Sea to Sky Highway provincial park: Porteau _____
26. *Cogito–sum* separator
27. As written, to Tiberius
28. Broadcast, like CBC
29. They sailed in steerage on White Star ships
31. Place to dip a quill pen
34. Edible roots
35. Lake southwest of Moose Jaw: _____ Wives
36. **Communal pot dish in Switzerland**
39. As tough as _____
42. Saturated with
45. NL's St. Patrick's Day falls in this mo.
46. Shooting marbles
48. Satisfied sigh
49. 1998 Bryan Adams *Unplugged* hit: "I'm _____"
50. Where to send Word documents
54. Niagara-on-the-Lake venue: Shaw Festival _____
56. Half-Canadian comedic pair: Cheech _____ Chong
57. Removes a rind
58. Old Alex Trebek show: *Reach for the _____*
60. Nicaraguan president Daniel since 2007
61. CTV newsmagazine since 1967: _____ *Period*
64. Some mites
66. Automobile sunshade
67. **Austrian veal meal**
71. Famed British racecourse
74. 1971 Stampeders hit: "_____ City Woman"
75. Symphony conductors
79. Polish composer Frédéric
81. _____ Quentin
82. Fen
84. Circus audience member's interjection
85. Old-style body armour (var.)
87. In a lively manner
89. Fad for fanatics?
91. Hit a Dodge truck?
92. Nutrient-rich dirt
94. New Brunswick-based business: Irving _____
95. Shared a Dalhousie dorm, say
96. Molokai welcome
98. **UK fare served in newspaper**
103. Landfill critter
104. Embezzlement, e.g.
105. Guiding light in the sky
109. Specialty of 54-A
112. Shorthand taker, briefly
114. Female gametes
115. Ping-_____
116. Highway 400 segment
117. **Staple in Belgium and France**
120. Naysayer
121. Helps
122. *The Canterbury Tales* character
123. Take the place of, forcibly
124. Imbroglio
125. Surveying document
126. Titleholder
127. In need of a fill-up at Esso

DOWN

1. Some male voices (var.)
2. "What _____ in the neck!"
3. Moved stealthily
4. A round of golf begins here
5. Play by _____
6. Flour, in Fabreville
7. Annual Canadian music industry event: Juno _____
8. Some learn by this method
9. Got every last drop, say
10. Red Chamber member (abbr.)
11. Meech Lake _____
12. Extinguish birthday cake candles
13. Couple's furniture piece?
14. Old-style ogler
15. **Valencian cuisine specialty**
16. Treats food with UV waves
17. Some Halifax Harbour boats
18. One of 12 minor biblical prophets
24. Bleated
29. Local Area Network (abbr.)
30. Saves energy, say
32. Soviet ballistic missile
33. Third-person pronoun
34. Law clerk's favourite cake?
37. Jannings who won the first acting Oscar
38. Rider Nation people, say
40. Slow, on a musical score
41. Give a ram a buzz
42. Basra country
43. Swiss Chalet handout
44. Issued a command
47. W.O. Mitchell novel: _____ *Has Seen the Wind?*
50. Low-level workers
51. Orders more *Chatelaine*
52. Inscribe with a stylus
53. Horse colouring
55. Not on the level?
57. 2011 Will Ferguson book: *Canadian _____*
59. 1996 Richard Gere film: _____ *Fear*
62. Exchanges (var.)
63. Arouse interest

64. Canadian legislation passed in 2014: Fair Elections _____
65. Boot-shaped country
68. Pare anagram
69. Samoan money
70. Alphabet ender in Colorado, but not Canada
71. Ghanaian city on the Gulf of Guinea
72. Sandbar
73. Large seabirds
76. Explore the Eternal City?
77. Slowly leak
78. Lose fur
80. _____-Georgian

82. Dermis is one layer of this
83. 1989 track from Canada's Luba: "_____ Heart"
86. Stern surround, on a ship
88. 1990s CBC show: _____ to Avonlea
89. Get by okay
90. 1998 golden Olympian from Canada Rebagliati
93. "The Brazilian Bombshell": Carmen _____
95. Finally freed from
97. **National dish of Scotland**
99. Most secure
100. US fast-food franchise in Canada: Pizza _____

101. Split
102. Nose, colloquially
106. Add, in England
107. Avoid a disaster
108. Gravelly, like a voice
109. Canned meat brand
110. Colour quality
111. Applaud
112. Braise
113. Pre-adult
117. Sold-out show sign (abbr.)
118. Street, in Sherbrooke
119. Institute for Supply Management (abbr.)

SOLUTION ON PAGE 162

Here's to the Habs

Celebrating the Canadiens 2021 Stanley Cup run

ACROSS

1. Calgarian McRae who charted big with "You Broke Me First" in 2020
5. Some Greek letters
10. Stew
16. 1974 Margaret Laurence novel: _____ *Diviners*
19. Acid type
20. Nebraska city
21. 1969 Margaret Atwood novel: *The* _____ *Woman*
22. Spat between scullers?
23. **In the 2021 first-round Stanley Cup playoffs, the Canadiens beat them in seven**
26. **Number of games the Canadiens won in the 2021 Cup final**
27. Humpty's breakfast offering
28. Make a comparison
29. Honour bestowed by our government: _____ of Canada
31. Rootlet
32. Baked beans container
33. Past its prime
36. Irritability, during an exam?
40. Lower-level nobleman, in Spain
44. Masonry block
48. Esso gas option, for short
49. Briefly visit
51. One of Henry VIII's six
52. Diaphanous
53. Canadian film director Kotcheff, et al.
54. Wallop
56. Northern Canada's Beaufort
57. _____-in-the-hole
58. Influence
59. Glass tube in a lab
60. German city
62. Tack on
63. Scientific study of nutrition
65. Talking about Tibetan oxen?
67. Scaleless fish
69. Summer season in Quebec
70. Like a solvent ship's captain?
71. 1984 Phil Collins soundtrack song: "_____ All Odds"
73. Denounce a writer's work?
75. Canada's southern neighbour (abbr.)
78. Saskatchewan provincial park: Athabasca Sand _____
79. Have a longing for
81. Sofia currency units
82. Middle Eastern gulf
83. Beldame
84. Completely wipe away
86. Savoury spread for crackers
87. Authorized absence at Eton
88. Pizza Pizza appliance
90. Italian screen queen Sophia
91. "The best things in life _____ free"
92. Tops of waves
93. Alberta mountain range where deer roam?
95. This blocks enzyme synthesis
98. Form of quartz
100. This partners with long.
101. New Zealand lizard
106. Gaspé goodbye word
109. Cantilevered window
112. Joe, as opposed to Joseph
113. **Number of years since a Canadian team had reached the Cup final**
114. **Team that defeated the Canadiens for the 2021 Cup**
118. History channel series: *The Curse of* _____ *Island*
119. Rabbitlike rodent of South America
120. Everly Brothers hit: "Wake Up Little _____"
121. Protection (var.)
122. 1942 movie: _____ *Miniver*
123. Snoozed
124. Lightened a load, say
125. The Canadian _____ Do Drugs Society

DOWN

1. Student's aide
2. Pleasant scent
3. Tuckered out
4. Harmful food bacteria
5. Soda factory employee
6. Overdramatizes
7. Docile
8. "Gotcha!" cry
9. Baby birches, say
10. Look for
11. Otiose
12. Countenances
13. Queen's University Smith School of Business deg.
14. Impish North Pole helper
15. Used Royal LePage again?
16. Trampled (on)
17. Sharpen
18. Decorative jug
24. Flower fluid
25. Blue Jay's hit: _____ drive
30. Gather the harvest
32. 1960s colouring technique
34. **Number of times the Canadiens have reached the final round (as of 2021)**
35. Indigenous group of Japan
37. International agreement
38. Joins film ends together
39. Zest and Ivory
41. Torpors
42. L.M. Montgomery classic: *Anne of* _____ *Gables*
43. Sumatran ape, for short
44. Nick and Nora's silver screen dog
45. Wearing clogs or oxfords
46. Heavy metal musician, say

47. Semi-conductor light source, for short
50. _____-Raphaelite
53. **Total number of Cups won by the Canadiens (as of 2021)**
55. Orange tea type
58. Canadians' gov. ID nos.
59. Spike for rock climbing
61. Reggae precursor
63. Thick
64. Earthly, as opposed to heavenly
66. *Fantastic Four* star Jessica
68. Falsehood, on a Glen Abbey fairway?
70. Ridges in the Rockies
71. Temporary, to Titus
72. Fruit used to make jelly

73. Woodbine trotter
74. Red wine from Bordeaux
76. MP's place in parliament
77. Aardvarks' grub
80. Potato Head piece
82. Tool for chopping wood
85. Ice mass off Newfoundland
86. Immobilize, in Ipswich
87. Like a stray shot
89. French Riviera resort city
92. Required Robitussin
94. Country between China and India
96. "Not guilty," for example
97. Groucho's cheap smoke
99. Get gas at Petro-Canada

102. Like a buff gym rat
103. Mate, in Málaga
104. Kidney enzyme
105. Sense of anxiety
106. Canadian film director Egoyan
107. 2012 Alice Munro collection: _____ *Life*
108. Pen fillers
110. Assess
111. In the same book (abbr.)
112. Canadian International Student Services (abbr.)
115. Ottoman Empire potentate
116. Floor cleaner
117. Embedded programming language

SOLUTION ON PAGE 162

47

Songs from the deeps?

ACROSS

1. Bone in the arm
5. Canadian actress/comedienne Caroline
9. Find
15. You can purchase puzzles on this Canadian website: _____ and Pieces
19. Rona buy
20. Long-eared mammal
21. Primeval god of darkness
22. Fencing sword
23. Part of modern-day Turkey
25. Kick out of Canada, say
26. A bit of heredity?
27. **1998 Eliza Carthy English folk tune**
29. Depressed
30. Physician who substitutes
31. _____ Pérignon
32. Popular potato chips brand in Canada
34. Think like a cow?
36. Settles down?
40. Garments for ladies in New Delhi
42. **1957 Patti Page gold record**
44. Some residents of Canada's north
46. Eminent
48. Ornamental pond fish
49. Relating to Texas or Tennessee
51. Oscar _____ Renta
52. Suffix with lemon
54. Was overly sweet on
59. WestJet jets fly here?
61. Violinist's bow coating
63. Fabric for blue shoes?
64. Trippin' drug
65. Instagram upload, for short
66. Sobs
67. Pack for a trip to Vermont?
68. **1987 Prince track**
75. Russian legislative body
77. Hen's offspring
78. Viral disease
79. Some pages in *Chatelaine*
82. Exhaust a supply
84. Beaverlike South American critter
85. Region surrounding the South Pole
88. Indigenous African people
89. *Wheel of Fortune* letter purchase
90. HGTV Canada show activity
92. Jacket for composer Maurice?
93. Bend in a pipe
95. Closest
98. Film critic, say
99. **1980 Raffi album and song title**
104. Beatles lyric: "He's _____ nowhere man"
106. Mother of a girl in Magog
107. Perfect, hypothetical substance
108. Ta ta _____ ta
110. _____ few rounds
112. Language spoken by 88-A
113. This can freshen your breath
115. **B-52's signature song**
121. The Three Stooges, for example
122. Old lithograph, for short
124. Beastly behaviour?
125. Take another stab at
126. Occur
127. Not any
128. Canadian mysteries novelist Emery
129. Lyrical poems
130. Atlas page inclusions
131. Had a CIBC mortgage
132. These share a pod

DOWN

1. Canadian men and women won Olympic hockey gold in this state
2. Take off some pounds
3. Black, in Sherbrooke
4. Defunct orchard spray
5. Some African animals, for short
6. You need perfect execution to win this game?
7. Another name for Cupid
8. These fall from space to earth
9. Marinas Trench description
10. Miners' discovery
11. Mushrooms with big tops
12. On the train
13. Three-birds-in-one serving
14. Quebec clock setting (abbr.)
15. "Scram!" in Shakespearespeak
16. Syrup of _____
17. Musical note stress symbol
18. Appeared to be
24. Partway
28. Like a twangy voice
30. Fatty acids
33. Sun, in Sagunto
35. Former Chinese chairman
36. Broadloom type
37. Those opposed
38. Beefeaters, for example
39. Takes a load off
41. Took Calgary Transit
43. Rented
45. Indian semi-classical vocal music
47. **Heart hit from 1977**
50. Lions' den
53. Device for storing data
55. Yorkshire river
56. Private conversation in Quebec?
57. Tokyo, before it was renamed in 1868
58. Citric soda: Mountain _____
60. NDP predecessor
62. Hog sound
66. Poker player's disc
69. Stretched tight
70. Stompin' Tom Connors, to many Canadians
71. Startling, like a horse
72. Many a time, in poetry

73. More than a bit of baby fat
74. Hullabaloo
75. Add sound effects to a film, say
76. Mexico's northern neighbour (abbr.)
80. More severe
81. Crowds cheer for Crosby when he does this
83. Colorado city
84. Toronto-born author Morley of *More Joy in Heaven*
85. Tim Hortons espresso offering
86. Rhinoplasty site

87. _____ chowder
91. Thalia's sister, in mythology
94. Long body part
96. Have breakfast
97. Movie trailer catchphrase
99. Café
100. Loved
101. *Persuasion* line: "Woe _____ him, and her too…"
102. Boorish Internet users?
103. Illegally seizes power
105. Hovered over the weaver?
109. Presses actor Jeremy's pants?

111. Grp. for US attorneys
114. Brood
116. 1995 Alanis Morissette smash: "You Oughta _____"
117. _____-happy
118. Trident part
119. It sometimes erupts in Sicily
120. Some bakery loaves
122. Greek letter
123. 2009 Michael Bublé hit: "Haven't _____ You Yet"

SOLUTION ON PAGE 163

22 Land O'Lakes

Saskatchewan bodies of water

ACROSS

1. Cold War participant (abbr.)
5. Morse _____
9. Vats
13. Distinctive feature
19. Back of the neck
20. Mrs. David Copperfield
21. Sole
22. 20-year MP Copps
23. **Lake that shares its name with an early explorer of Canada**
25. Toothy smile
26. Pelvis bone
27. Space under the eaves
28. Performing a ballroom dance
30. Regular maintenance chores, say
31. Used a mangle
33. National Social Work Month in Canada (abbr.)
34. Yukon-born author Berton
36. Split apart
37. Races alongside a Calgary Stampede chuckwagon during a heat
40. Deodorant type
45. Some condiments, in Quebec
47. Netflix show: *Cobra* _____
48. GOC program: _____ Age Security
49. Redo the driveway
50. Fertility clinics store these
53. *Superman* star Christopher
55. Related via mom's side
58. Mirren who won an Oscar for *The Queen*
59. Bamboo swords martial art
61. Little guy
62. _____ Frances ON
63. Passenger ships
64. **Rudolph might visit this lake**
66. Per _____
67. You might find one in a blanket?
68. Attacks
69. Sweet spread for bread
70. Places a picture again
75. OC Transpo transport
76. Clerical vestments
77. **It shares its name with a Quebec city**
78. Slavery or servitude
82. Plaintive request
83. Protrude
84. Insect development stage
85. _____ of Commons
86. Calgary Market Mall booth
87. Make modifications
89. Spunk
90. The Alouettes are in this CFL division
91. Workplace for Canada's Sandra Oh
92. Psychic ability in Seville?
94. Search for
96. Piece in *Maclean's*
98. Gym sessions
101. Research rodents
105. Canadian Armed Forces reserve member
107. Airbnb alternative
108. Knitted fabric
110. Sweet, in tone
114. Canada Post employee, for example
117. Port of ancient Rome
118. Disinclined toward
119. On the peak of Mount Assiniboine
120. **Lake with the same name as a British prime minister**
122. Canadian Ford model from 1949–76
123. Golden principle?
124. Kuril Islands Indigenous group
125. Seasonal La Belle Province visitor: Père _____
126. National Gallery of Canada stands
127. Drove too fast on Highway 417
128. Lovers' quarrel
129. Common conjunctions

DOWN

1. Inequitable, at the PNE?
2. 20th-C. French existentialist author
3. Exactly right, to a Dalmatian owner?
4. Repairs a book's spine
5. Canadian Depository for Securities (abbr.)
6. Gasps of amazement
7. Saw visions in your sleep
8. Put aside for the otolaryngologist?
9. Frat party garb
10. Not ready for picking
11. Buckwheat pancakes
12. *The Playboy of the Western World* playwright
13. Guaranteed
14. Woodworking tool
15. *Spellbound* **star Gregory shares this lake's name**
16. Old name for Ireland
17. Crime-solving tipoff
18. Press down on
24. Tim Hortons Brier surface
29. Juno-winning jazz musician Skonberg
32. Fruits-and-veggies company founded in 1851
35. Raspy breath
38. Not at all utile
39. **Lake named for a Canadian prime minister**
41. Unwrap a gift
42. Bargain event, at The Brick
43. Done
44. Part of a pair of glasses
46. Like beaches or levees
48. The Sens home game city
50. Gumbo recipe ingredient

51. Flying formations for Canada geese
52. Some black birds
54. Alt. spelling indicator in a crossword clue
56. Fifth canonical hour
57. Like a pretentious painter?
58. Swell time in the Bay of Fundy?
60. Gene component, for short
63. Legal claim
65. It comes before Tishrei
66. Canadian bookstore since 1940
67. Complain
69. Angel's ring of light
71. Upper body limb
72. Anagram for 19-A
73. Hamilton ON park

74. Spill
77. Flower for your mother?
78. "Take _____ Train"
79. Wintertime rime
80. Brownish-red shade
81. Piedmont vintners' region
82. Abyss
83. Popular plants in Tokyo?
86. Enthusiastic
88. Get ready for a newborn?
91. Some roofers
93. Scrape your knee, say
95. Religious group since 1966: Hare _____
97. Poisonous phenol
98. Rode to the top of the CN Tower
99. Baltimore major leaguer

100. Remove cargo
102. Director's cry
103. Worked hard
104. Conks out, like a car
106. Food thickening gums
109. Mythological bird
110. In 2018, Canada's Moya Greene was granted this title by Queen Elizabeth
111. Eye layer
112. Allows
113. **An Indigenous Canadian group shares this lake's name**
115. *National Post* commentary
116. Feline food flavour
121. Bumpy road groove

Catch(phrase) Me If You Can

Memorable TV slogans

ACROSS

1. Dazzle a drunkard?
6. Oscar-winning singer-songwriter: Lady _____
10. Look at a British lord?
14. Neighbour of Niger
19. Scent
20. Absolutely authentic
21. Shaft beneath a vehicle
22. Savoury taste, in Tokyo cuisine
23. **Donald Trump's edict on *The Apprentice***
25. Pecs anagram
26. Mythological giant
27. PEI recreational area: _____ Shore Provincial Park
28. **Judy Carne's catchphrase on *Rowan & Martin's Laugh-In***
30. iPod plug (var.)
34. Hospital care provider (abbr.)
36. Pitches
37. Places, to Augustus
38. Noxious atmospheres (var.)
42. Grandmother, for short
43. Notable Massachusetts uni
46. Canadian Hargreaves who played for Manchester United
47. Some yellow-skinned fruits
48. Hoosier State
50. **Ed McMahon said this nightly for 30+ years**
54. Glazier's sheet
56. Healthy cereal fibre
57. Montreal CFLers, for short
58. Subterranean Pueblo rooms
59. You might see one near NL in spring
60. Window rims
61. Regina's previous name: _____ O' Bones
62. Some sty animals
64. With a cool attitude
65. **Jeff Probst's *Survivor* catchphrase**
70. Despise
72. Spreads for breads
73. Thirteen species of these grow in Canada
74. Apple centres
75. Like a triathlon's first leg
76. Hindu sage
78. TGIF word
81. 1985 Juno-winning band: Parachute _____
82. Shape on Canada's Walk of Fame
83. **Siskel and Ebert's classic rating**
86. Equestrian competition prize
88. Interment
90. Italian pronoun for singer Fitzgerald?
91. Burning cigar end
92. Gun the engine
93. Bobbin holders
96. Place trust in (with "on")
97. Ambulance's warning sound
99. Long dashes, in punctuation
100. Origins
102. ***The Price Is Right* invitation to contestants**
106. Second-largest city in Portugal (var.)
109. Rounded, like an egg
110. Had debts
111. **Tim Gunn's advice on *Project Runway***
116. African nation: Sierra _____
117. Not common
118. Elizabethan and Victorian periods
119. 51-D might drink this after a day on the slopes
120. Puts money in the poker pot
121. Ogled
122. Ex-NHLers from Canada Emery and Whitney
123. Giddy, at the hair salon?

DOWN

1. Lad
2. Ode anagram
3. Former French coin
4. 1981 Go-Go's hit: "_____ Lips Are Sealed"
5. Rover's reward
6. Rock climbing belay device
7. Birds' cliffside perch (var.)
8. Celt's kin
9. Old name for a male City of Calgary councillor
10. Tomato purée
11. Event in Vancouver (1986) and Montreal (1967)
12. Vote in your MP
13. Dead _____
14. Illegally jab in a Flames/Jets game
15. Gives off light
16. Canada joined this military alliance in 1949 (abbr.)
17. Islamic religious leader
18. Canadien Maurice Richard wore this jersey number
24. Shania Twain hit: "_____ This Moment On"
29. Ridiculous
30. Greeting in 69-D
31. Carpentry peg
32. Some laptops
33. Alberta's official tree: Lodgepole _____
35. Admiral's shade of blue?
39. Tribal leader title in Kurdistan (var.)
40. Edmonton and Vancouver newspapers
41. Swedes' trees?
43. *Mutual of Omaha's Wild Kingdom* host Perkins
44. Completely
45. Invasive yellow perennial
49. Wild goats of Eurasia (var.)
51. They enjoy schussing at Blue Mountain

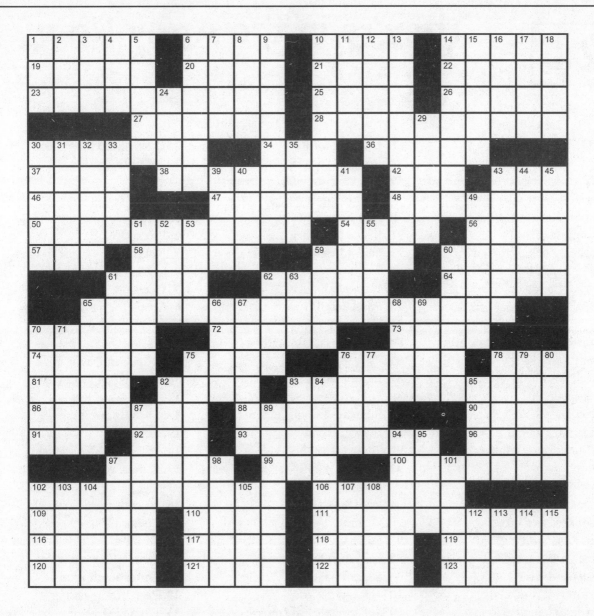

52. Ditch the groom at the altar
53. 1965 Canadian #1 hit: "Shakin' All _____"
55. Bellicose Greek god
59. Prejudice, at the dressmaker's?
60. State in northeastern India
61. "Poetry Man" singer Snow
62. Give the impression of
63. "Hand Me Down World" group: The Guess _____
65. Spotted songbird
66. Des Moines state
67. Dust jacket promos
68. Like an elegant ex-Spice Girl?
69. Hawaiian island
70. Ghanaian capital

71. Cops' notifications of wanted suspects (abbr.)
75. BC port worker, for example
76. Yellowknife landmark: Ragged Ass _____
77. "_____ be a cold day…"
78. Wight and Man
79. Sheer fabric for veils
80. Helps control the pet population
82. Austere, on the boat?
83. Groom a beard
84. More charming
85. Waterway in Nunavut: _____ Bay
87. Vacuum tube types
89. Turned topsy-turvy
94. One way out?
95. Org. on *The X-Files*
97. Fishing net used in Paris?

98. 1987 Kevin Costner movie: _____ Out
101. Belt hole
102. Coca-_____
103. Restaurant kitchen appliance
104. Like a point not worthy of consideration
105. Adele co-wrote this hit with BC's Tobias Jesso Jr.: "When We _____ Young"
107. Prefix with normal or graph
108. Word of approval
112. Tribulation
113. Trillium province upper court (abbr.)
114. Singer Stewart
115. Canadian fantasy fiction author: Guy Gavriel _____

SOLUTION ON PAGE 163

24 They're in the Army Now

At CFBs

ACROSS

1. Theologies, in brief
5. Early pregnancy procedure, for short
10. Top of Grouse Mountain
14. Mouthed off?
19. Biblical second-person pronoun
20. 1963 Beach Boys hit: "Little _____ Coupe"
21. 1981 Anne Murray hit: "It's _____ Can Do"
22. Famed violin-making family from Italy
23. Dealt with head-on
25. **Alberta CFB**
27. Pro dancers, colloquially
28. Biden or Obama
30. Acronym on Trump campaign merch
31. Opposite of yeses
32. Breakthrough brainstorms
34. Gathered as a group
36. The *Concorde*, e.g.
37. One type of child?
38. Oaks and elms
40. Smoothed rough edges, in the carpentry shop
43. Hassle, in a hair salon?
45. Green growth on bread
46. "_____, foh and fum"
47. Scout's garb
49. "As Seen on TV" advertiser: K-_____
52. Desiccated
53. Like a horse or zebra
55. Stage name
56. Rum-based cocktail: Mai _____
57. Stimpy's cartoon pal
58. Stage of enlightenment, in Buddhism
59. Brussels country (abbr.)
60. Cricket match segments
62. **New Brunswick CFB**
64. Smiled smugly
68. Jazz standard: "_____ It Romantic?"
69. Julie Christie played her in *Doctor Zhivago*
70. **Manitoba CFB**
71. Bridal veil fabric
73. Tabloid writer who gets the chop?
76. Nazareth citizen
78. **Ontario CFB**
82. Sailor's "Stop!"
84. *Rosemary's Baby* author Levin
85. Used a stencil
87. European predacious fish
88. Our, in Rimouski
89. Blue Jays initial game of the season: Home _____
92. Tents with rounded tops
93. Former Winnipeg Blue Bomber Stegall
94. Wildebeest's kin
95. Gizmos
97. Some Queen's University degs.
98. Fails to come first
99. Superficiality
101. Ocean bottom
103. Old maple leaf coins
104. It empties into the North Sea
106. Tennis court shot
108. None
109. Cleat anagram
111. Canadian singer Geddy and poet Dennis
112. They precede twos
114. Wood for the fire
116. Some deaf people do this
120. **Quebec CFB**
123. 6/8 time musical piece
125. Relative by marriage
126. Gothic-style moulding
127. Former BC premier Christy
128. US actors Arkin or Alda
129. Set of steps over a fence
130. Where robins reside
131. Northern Manitoba river
132. Minus

DOWN

1. Seven-year malady?
2. "Scram!"
3. Not stereo
4. **See 25-A**
5. Dotes on
6. Group for a brainy bunch?
7. Filbert fan?
8. Frosted over
9. Dropsy, in Devonshire
10. Appendage with claws
11. Hollywood westerns actor Jack
12. 55-A, for example
13. **See 78-A**
14. Marmalade container
15. Culinary seasonings: Liquid _____
16. Horse-drawn carts
17. Lucy's TV neighbour
18. Dumb blonde description (var.)
24. Counselled, old style
26. Gruel description
29. Restaurant reading
33. Put a new _____
35. Credibleness
38. Criticized: _____ strip off of
39. Regretting (var.)
41. Ogle
42. Money, colloquially
44. Bullets, e.g.
45. Actress Helgenberger of *CSI*
46. Islamic law rulings
48. Early genre of Joni Mitchell
50. Generate income
51. HGTV Canada show: *Love It or _____ It*
53. Some New Zealand people
54. Dampen a suitor's ardour?
58. Union, in downtown TO
61. Watch Whoopi and Joy?
63. BPOE word

65. $1,000,000, for short
66. Chooses an MLA
67. Middle Eastern fruit export
70. Ranees' garments
72. National currency code (abbr.)
73. Dangle
74. River name in Nova Scotia and Ontario
75. Justification for a war, to Justinian
77. Jewellery piece
78. July event in Calgary: Stampede _____
79. Discriminator against grandmother (var.)
80. Cardiff is here
81. Milieux of 97-A
83. Garb for Gaius
86. Bumpkin
90. Sitting room, in Rhode Island
91. See 25-A
93. See 120-A
96. Depart on a yacht
98. Vaulted (var.)
100. Tequila kin
102. Ink spot
103. Jails, colloquially
104. Singer Presley
105. Tilted, in Coventry
107. Light brown shade
110. Western Nova Scotia municipality
113. 1984 mystery from Canada's Howard Engel: Murder _____ the Light
115. Canadian-grown apple variety
117. That gal, in Gatineau
118. Word of woe in olden days
119. Former Canadian NHLers Boyle and Ellis
121. Sense of astonishment
122. Soften flax
124. Former Governor General Hnatyshyn

Colourful Comestibles

They share the same shade

ACROSS

1. Heap
6. Lea sound
11. Reach across, like Rainbow Bridge
15. Pith of the matter
19. Quarrel
20. Jouster's spear
21. State in Brazil
22. Odd, in Glasgow
23. **Indian cuisine spice**
25. Once _____ a time
26. Curly coif
27. Labrador and Beaufort
28. Pimples
29. Title for a lady
31. 1991 Stompin' Tom Connors song: "_____ Canadian Girl"
32. Canadian icons Bobby (hockey) and Marion (aviation)
34. Seed covering
36. Sail rigging supports
38. Injured with a sword
41. Andalusia city and province
43. Charged particle
44. Adam's partner
45. US writer Ephron
47. Sound of a contented kitty
48. **Fruit for a brandy**
52. Periods of 1,000 years (var.)
55. Spruce (up)
57. Canadians' tax deadline mo.
58. Unoccupied
59. **Fruit used in chutney**
61. Courts
62. Poker stake for Dorothy's kin?
63. Sheet for a philatelist
65. Brouhahas
68. Friendly international alliances
70. Pet's annoyance?
72. BMO might do this if you can't pay your mortgage
75. Incites
76. Musician's quick sequence of notes
78. Pre-nuptials party for the guys
79. Dirt
80. Sharp bites
81. Fans' sounds
83. **Fuzzy fruit**
86. Edmonton or Edmundston, properly?
89. The Leafs play on this
90. Burger sauces, in Boston
93. Hold spellbound
95. **Bugs Bunny's staples**
97. Potato salad sauce
99. _____-B personality
100. Bear's appendage
101. Victoria, in DT Regina
102. YWG departure areas
104. Artists' stands
106. Toronto Symphony Orchestra performance piece
110. US singer: Meat _____
111. Nearly silent summons
112. Middle Eastern alcoholic spirits (var.)
113. Outfit
115. Mannheim missus
117. Abroad
121. Increase, like prices
122. Too complacent
123. **Yam alternative**
126. Mountain mammal in Alberta
127. Gemstone mined in BC
128. Some Greek letters
129. To-do
130. 1970 Neil Young song: "_____ Love Can Break Your Heart"
131. Feel sorry for
132. Like a squalid garden?
133. Lady of Lachine

DOWN

1. Bursae
2. "The _____ North strong and free"
3. Tourists' destination in India
4. Computer screen pointer
5. C sharp or B minor
6. Quebec voting groups?
7. Outdoor bowling surface
8. Make yourself beloved
9. Unreturnable serve from Canada's Bianca Andreescu
10. End of the line
11. Yukon Gold tuber, colloquially
12. **Ingredient in some salsas**
13. Your nose notices this
14. Tir-_____-Og
15. Indigenous South American people
16. Use your deductive powers
17. Take off, eh!
18. Home Hardware purchases
24. Apologetic phrase
30. Fire _____
31. Decorate
33. Former Quebec premier Lévesque
35. Juno Awards category
37. Most ready for picking
38. Frequent Canada–US border crossing vehicle
39. Enthused
40. **Fruit that can spice up a salad**
41. Profit from a TSX transaction?
42. Even-steven game result
46. Health clinic aide (abbr.)
48. Right your wrongs
49. **Melon type**
50. Chose
51. Rests anagram
53. Steps outside to rake?
54. Lab culture jelly
56. Some deer
60. Some Coleridge compositions
62. Perform unction, in church

64. Not pos.

66. Women's History mo. in Canada

67. _____ on the back

69. I, to Ovid

70. Extreme fear

71. Former CBC show: *Being* _____

72. Decrees

73. See 81-A

74. S-shaped moulding

77. Kitchen gadget

79. Gets fit

82. Big sport in Tokyo?

84. Formicary insects

85. 2010 Michael Bublé single: "_____ Me a River"

87. Russian river or range

88. CTV airs this nightly

90. Peggys and Hacketts, in Nova Scotia

91. Catherine the Great's successor

92. Summary

94. Saskatchewan crop

96. Very noisy

98. Ontario Geothermal Association (abbr.)

102. **See 59-A**

103. Morally weak

105. There's one of Sir Galahad on Parliament Hill

106. Boatload or truckload

107. The Hunter, in the sky

108. Decongestant variety

109. Largo and lento (var.)

111. 1970s Juno-winning singer Gallant

114. Opposite of pretty

116. Peruse the *National Post*

118. Cozy

119. _____ bomb

120. Long ago times

122. Absorb liquid left on your plate

124. Grief

125. Carol who hosted *As It Happens* for 16 years

SOLUTION ON PAGE 164

26 Canada Cornucopia 4

ACROSS

1. Get fresh: Make _____ at
6. You might buy one at Leon's
10. Calgary-made alcohol: Alberta Pure _____
15. Does some math
19. Southeast Asian street food
20. Duelling weapon
21. Milieux
22. Tuber from the Tropics
23. "Be-Bop-_____"
24. Cartoon Road Runner's sound
25. Innocent
26. Geometric shape
27. Canadian ombudsman: Commission for _____ for Telecom-television Services
29. Open a bottle of Labatt Blue
30. 1983 Bryan Adams album: *Cuts _____ a Knife*
31. In this place
32. You see this in your mirror
34. Diacritical language marks
36. Canadian Brass instrument
39. Mechanize
42. Canadian Iraqi Dental Society (abbr.)
43. Furious
45. *Citizen Kane* mansion
46. European freshwater fish
47. Bar's amateur night show: Open _____
50. End of an eclipse
52. Neighbour of France (abbr.)
53. Sis or bro
54. _____ acid
56. Red Chamber pol
57. Carpet fasteners
59. Pretend
62. They follow alphas
63. East Coast port city
64. Fruit-filled open tart
65. More advanced, in age
68. Injures
69. Canadian pros DeLaet and Weir
71. Assist in a felony
72. Canadian middle-distance runner Phil who won five Olympic bronze medals
74. "_____ pray"
75. 100-year celebrations
77. Simple
78. US crime-fighting org.
81. Fills a cargo hold
82. 1972 Neil Young hit: "Old _____"
83. Palindromic buddy
84. Bats hang out here
86. European river
87. Corvette roof option
89. Groucho Marx quiz show: _____ *Your Life*
92. Indented, say
93. Look like
94. High-pitched flutes
96. Some Rockies bighorn sheep
97. Body shop's temporary provision
100. Unoiled hinge sound
101. Whitewater activity float
103. Anise-flavoured liqueur
104. Country life description
106. Nominates for a Giller Prize
112. "Do _____ others as…"
113. Skirt around
114. HGTV Canada airs this: _____ *Town*
115. Oak fruit
116. Decorated cupcakes
117. Discontinue
118. Not shut
119. He scored the '87 Canada Cup winner (with 6-D)
120. Bitty bits of time, for short
121. 1958 novelty song: "Purple People _____"
122. Campground shelter
123. Kananaskis Country river in Alberta

DOWN

1. Rhyme scheme
2. California place: _____ Alto
3. Grad of U of T
4. Polyatomic anion
5. Hackneyed
6. See 119-A
7. "With the stroke of _____…"
8. Robert DeNiro movie: _____ *the Parents*
9. Cola sold in Canada from 1994–2002
10. South Pacific islands area
11. Colourful California county?
12. Clear jet wings in winter
13. Polynesian beverage
14. Sterile
15. Lagoon islands
16. Former Governor General Johnston
17. Grammy-winning Canadian rapper
18. Bottoms of shoes
28. Southern constellation
33. See 43-A
35. Concept of perfection
36. Hit sitcom for Michael J. Fox: *Family _____*
37. Basic instinct
38. Farm building
40. Speaks
41. Heavy burden
42. Kohlrabi and kale
44. Type of 4-D
46. Nickname for a 1960s Canadian PM
47. High-end appliance brand
48. Iron/nickel alloy
49. US filmmaking brothers
51. Glossy fabric
53. Enjoys a day at Blue Mountain
55. Annoys
58. Mother's favourite spice?
59. Motel room cleaners

60. Slam anagram
61. Rare or unusual
62. Southern Alberta town: Picture _____
63. Tortoise's nemesis
65. Twinned crystal
66. Crosswise, to a ship's mate
67. Has an inclination to
68. Winnipeg landmark: Portage and _____
70. 20th-C. Canadian composer Clarence
73. Tim Hortons sandwich type
74. Garment tag
76. Cosmetics giant: _____ Lauder

77. Tuberculosis nodule
78. Greek cheese
79. Edge of a sombrero
80. Small hotels
83. Long-time Calgary children's TV cowboy host
85. Upright
88. Northwestern BC city
89. He cedes
90. Ontario Chiropractic Association (abbr.)
91. Violent rush of water
93. Hairnets
94. Laud

95. It precedes Sun.
97. Famed Quebec strongman Cyr
98. Shot of Canadian Club
99. Montezuma or Itzcoatl
100. Zagreb citizen
102. Jarome Iginla was one for almost 16 NHL seasons
105. Eye membrane
107. Ontario place: Port _____
108. Sign of bad things to come
109. Fruit of the service tree
110. Canadian rockers Triumph, for example
111. Canadians shovel a lot of this

SOLUTION ON PAGE 164

27 Their Cups Runneth Over

Players who've won the most Stanley Cups

ACROSS

1. Disfigure
5. Wearing footwear
9. They brought gifts, in the Bible
13. Benedick and Beatrice's brouhahas?
17. Arm bone
18. **Lowe, with the Oilers and Rangers (6)**
20. Elder brother of Moses
21. Corporate emblem
22. Cough medicine component
23. Pretty silly
24. Three-note chord
25. Lacklustre
26. "_____ No Business Like Show Business"
28. Adapts
30. Performed a diagnostic scan
32. Contemporary of Ravel
33. Amsterdam Olympics golden Canadian relay sprinter Cook
34. Provide relief from pain
36. Mrs. White game
38. Alone, on the stage
40. Tense
45. From birth to death
49. Canadian ex-NBAer Steve
50. Piste competitor
51. Every bit
52. Hitches
54. "Don't count _____!"
56. Moon, in Magog
57. Homeopathic condition, in olden days
60. One end of a needle
61. Tex-Mex meal serving
63. Crags on hills
64. African omnivores
66. Toupée bug?
68. Popular servings in Russia
70. Defensive ditches
72. Molson Canadian container
73. Bodily organ opening
75. Not in class, say
78. Nevertheless
81. Erases
85. Team that won the women's eight in Tokyo, for example
86. Open a bottle of bubbly
88. Bonisteel who hosted CBC's *Man Alive* for 22 years
90. Treatment for Parkinson's patients
91. Asian servant
92. Military prog. for US college students
93. Barbecue briquettes
95. Cdn. gov. department
96. Onomatopoeic snare drum sound
98. See 91-A
101. Griddle cake for Sprat?
104. Fashionable magazine?
105. Hamilton Philharmonic conductor Brott (1969–90)
107. Inspiration
108. Double-summit massif in Alberta: Mount _____
110. Like a guy with prophetic powers?
112. Swindlers' schemes
116. Sounds similar, in a poem
120. Lake Superior area Indigenous people (var.)
122. Fruit used in jellies
123. Lifted
124. Wraps a gift
126. Put fears to rest
128. _____ Major
129. Important historical periods
130. High-rise structure girder
131. **Anderson, with the Oilers and Rangers (6)**
132. Winnipeg is this vis-à-vis Portage la Prairie
133. *Black Beauty* writer Sewell
134. _____ on the cob
135. Canada's Gowan joined this US band in 1999
136. Gets a glimpse

DOWN

1. Curs
2. Kauai greeting
3. Inuit hamlet in Nunavut: Rankin _____
4. **Richard, with the Canadiens (8)**
5. Alpine activity gear
6. Octopus mama
7. Female reproductive organ
8. Some truck stops
9. **Messier, with the Oilers and Rangers (6)**
10. Come to the surface
11. State in India
12. Impossible to doubt
13. TV *M*A*S*H* actor Alan
14. **Harvey, with the Canadiens (6)**
15. Lustful look
16. MaxWell Realty sign word
19. Cookies for Sir Isaac?
20. Father of Agamemnon and Menelaus
27. Underwater wrigglers
29. Spanish stew: _____ podrida
31. Ration (with "out")
33. Most nasty
35. Inspect accounting records
37. Parcel delivery co. since 1907
39. Japanese screen
41. Poorly executed, at the track meet?
42. Particle that binds quarks
43. **Richard, with the Canadiens (11)**
44. Plait
45. Mary had a little one
46. Parts of the pelvis
47. A bit of extra flesh
48. Dissenting vote
53. Word of wonder

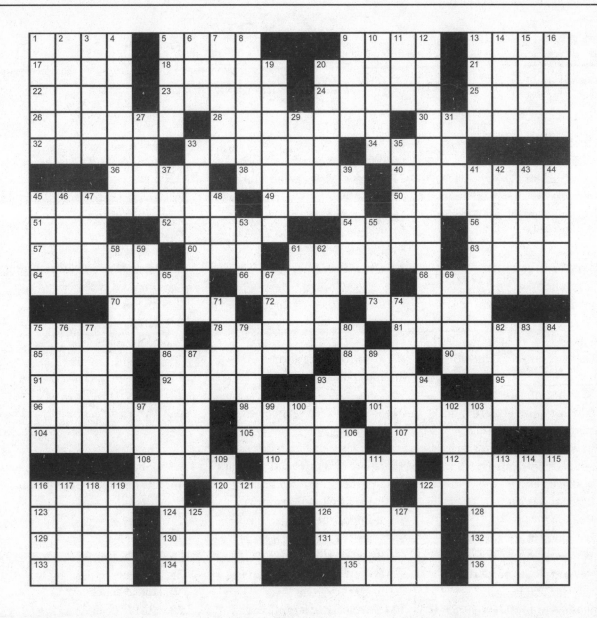

55. "…'til morning is _____"
58. To an extent
59. Source of light in the night
61. **Mahovlich, with the Leafs and Canadiens (6)**
62. Plant bristles
65. Lifelike, in the wild?
67. Popular laptop brand
69. Period of calm
71. Ecclesiastical splinter group
74. Pleasantly serene
75. Mites and ticks
76. **Trottier, with the Islanders and Pens (6)**
77. MPs chairs?
79. Some elementary students' learning, for short

80. Gold, to a Spaniard
82. 1970s TV cop
83. Massive
84. Dropped to the bottom
87. Took down information
89. Bumbling one
93. Gossip while shaving?
94. Unhappy
97. Child
99. Excessive adulation by a parent
100. Resident of Riyadh
102. Coin used in Cuba
103. **Lemaire, with the Canadiens (8)**
106. Stable sections
109. Stupid drug user?
111. Bit of land in the sea

113. Saints' surrounds (var.)
114. Swimmer Kylie who won three medals at the Tokyo Olympics
115. Flames' figures?
116. Canadian Caroline who starred in *Sabrina the Teenage Witch*
117. Rhino's weapon
118. **Cournoyer, with the Canadiens (10)**
119. Arizona city
121. **Béliveau, with the Canadiens (10)**
122. Canadian wildcat
125. Hematological classification system letters
127. "_____ takers?"

SOLUTION ON PAGE 164

Y Not...

28

Decipher this letter pattern

ACROSS

1. Title for a Hindu teacher
6. Bit in a bucket?
10. Fireplace remains
15. 2008 single by 90-A: "Workin' _____ Angels"
19. Red colouring
20. Peter Mayle bestseller: *A _____ in Provence*
21. Squadron of sea boats
22. Had on
23. Hilltop
24. Canada is one of 30 members of this (abbr.)
25. Bookish staffers?
27. Nation's export/import differential
29. Duplicate, in a genetics lab
31. **Canadian wildcats (var.)**
32. **Thesaurus entry**
33. Sideshow weirdo?
34. Zesty spirit
35. Most tangy to the taste
37. Licorice-flavoured liqueur
41. Show happiness or hatred
45. Lone Star State
46. Yugoslavian president (1953–80)
47. Blah
48. Hyperbolic function
49. Secure a new tenant
50. Setting one's sights on
52. Canadian inspirational fiction author Janette
53. Submit (to)
55. Earthquake, colloquially
57. Popular name for a pooch
59. Banned substances for sports pros
61. 1993 song from Blue Rodeo: "Hasn't Hit Me _____"
62. Distinguished
64. Boundary
65. **Electronic keyboard, for short**

67. Male sheep
68. Sandwich meat
71. Bygone New Zealand bird
72. Winnipeg _____ Orchestra
76. Sheep related
77. Admiral's vessel, in 21-A
81. Illinois city
82. Canadian singer: Stompin' _____ Connors
83. Orange juice/champagne cocktail
85. Awry
87. Woodworking shop file
88. International advertising award
90. Long-time Canadian rock band
91. Southwestern Quebec city: Sorel-_____
92. Real Canada Superstore sections
93. Oliver and Osoyoos, during BC summers?
95. Navy SEAL, for example
97. Compos mentis
98. They run in the streets of Pamplona
99. **Powerful clan with staying power**
104. **Pessimistic people**
107. Donated
108. No-cost computer programs
109. Start something up again
111. UN aviation org. headquartered in Montreal
113. Loblaw Companies chairman and CEO Weston
114. Frequent footnote abbr.
115. Raise a concern
116. Sedate
117. RBC GIC, for example
118. Okanagan or Niagara region product
119. Disgorge
120. Qualified to do a task
121. Dog breed: _____ Apso

DOWN

1. Splinter cliques
2. Fret
3. Canada partners with this Asian economic org.
4. Bungle
5. Passionate
6. **Alfred Nobel invented this explosive**
7. Bring in the barley
8. Granola flake
9. Make babies
10. Buoyant
11. Move furtively
12. Daughter of Zeus and Hera
13. Always, to a sonnet writer
14. Walter Farley literary classic: *The Black _____*
15. Coupled together in the womb?
16. 2009 Balloon Boy incident, for example
17. Osprey kin
18. Shambles
26. Stockholm rugs
28. Defraud
30. Not so much
33. HGTV Canada airing: _____ *to Fabulous*
34. The whole shebang
36. Iron Age Europeans
37. Like, in Lachine
38. Treasure cache
39. Already spoken for
40. Siskel's long-time critique partner
41. Pearson airport postings (abbr.)
42. U of A advanced communications degree (abbr.)
43. _____ upon a time
44. As a consequence, old style
46. Land that's been cultivated
49. Rule
50. Help to commit a crime

51. Old name for influenza
54. UK bumper car trademark
56. Chatty birds
58. Next to Lake Nipissing?
60. Helen Keller overcame being this
63. Swollen glands malady
65. Powerful shot from Canada's Denis Shapovalov
66. Downward Facing Dog practice
68. See 4-D
69. Architectural moulding
70. Cap
72. Limb bandage
73. Uttered aloud
74. *Decree _____*
75. Yammers

78. Edmonton Elks defeat, say
79. Mouth organ
80. Mosque officiants
84. TV role for BC-born Raymond Burr
86. Medical condition
89. Bone in the ear
91. Ripped
92. County in Ireland
94. International agreement
95. Description of some ops by 95-A
96. 19-A, for example
98. Shakespeare tragedy: _____ *Andronicus*
100. Inundated, in the laundry room?
101. Taco chips dip

102. Canada yews, e.g.
103. Yiddish gossipmonger
104. Air North flight group
105. Alleged Himalayan beast
106. Indian bread
107. Hockey is Canada's national this
108. 1979 Anne Murray hit: "I Just _____ in Love Again"
110. Spud or cuke
112. You might travel in one to YYC

See solution page for letter pattern.

SOLUTION ON PAGE 164

63

Who Am I? 1

Meet Canada's newest Governor General

ACROSS

1. Fragrant essential oil
6. Canadian telecommunications firm
10. Parisian priests, say
15. Dace anagram
19. Sucre mate, in Quebec
20. Mother, for short
21. Deceit
22. Opulent
23. **La Belle Province bestowed this honour on her**
27. Leered, lasciviously
28. Greek god of war
29. Hibernia structures
30. Set up house after moving
31. Plant fungi
33. Tent window fabric
34. Oldest synagogue in Edmonton: _____ Israel
35. Skedaddle from the health spa?
39. Knee cartilage disc
43. Cape Dyer NU airport code
44. Seek a seat in the Ontario legislature
45. Have an _____ to the ground
46. Chop into fine pieces
47. JFK and RFK are buried here (abbr.)
48. _____ Gritty Dirt Band
50. Eager attitude
52. Gate or door part
53. Not taken in by
54. Sliding steps, at the National Ballet of Canada
56. Robust perennial
57. Preface, for short
58. _____ jacet
59. Guarantee
61. Rugby set piece
63. Deli purchase
66. **She was Canada's ambassador to this country (1999–2001)**
68. Kisses, on Calgary Transit?
69. Photographers' stands
71. Corncob, in the Horn of Africa
72. President Eisenhower's nickname
73. Ruhr Valley city
74. Downtown Vancouver description
76. Like sparrows and crows
81. 1972 Stampeders single: "_____ Eyes"
82. Piece of celery
83. Penguins star Crosby has won this twice: _____ Smythe Trophy
84. 1971 Olivia Newton-John hit: "_____ For You"
85. Moose Jaw-to-Regina direction (abbr.)
86. Timberwolf Falls component, at Canada's Wonderland
87. Coward's dog?
88. Tennis match surface (abbr.)
90. American author Levin
91. Abandons hope
93. Ignore bursitis pain?
96. Canada's Alex Gough won singles bronze in this at the PyeongChang Olympics
97. Family pet, in Pierreville
98. Fencers duel on this
99. Significant export of Saskatchewan
102. Jet wing part
103. Bottom of the foot
104. Now's partner
108. **She was president of this Indigenous organization (2006–12)**
112. Make a right at a light
113. Squeezing (out)
114. For girls and boys
115. Abate
116. Requests
117. Caribou, in Northern Alberta
118. Carvey who starred with Canada's Mike Myers in *Wayne's World*
119. News agency founded in 1917: Canadian _____

DOWN

1. Teens' skin condition
2. Server's salver
3. Head, in Hochelaga
4. In the thick of
5. Olden days Oldsmobile
6. Spruced (up)
7. Most healthy
8. Hebrew Bible prophet
9. Ottawa cenotaph: National _____ Memorial
10. Biased against seniors
11. He sang "The Lady in Red": Chris de _____
12. Life story books, for short
13. Tolkien Middle-earth being
14. Serial arrangement
15. Initial Hebrew letters
16. Caribbean island
17. VP or CEO
18. House adjunct
24. Yaren is the de facto capital of this Micronesian island
25. Dismal, to a poet
26. Loosen bows
32. **She is…**
33. Like a nasty miser?
34. Tiger type
35. Gretzky won this NHL trophy five times: Lady _____
36. Dastardly doings
37. Against
38. Put back together
39. Breath freshener
40. Long poem components
41. False

42. Moves quickly on a minibike?
46. Ledge beneath a choir stall seat
49. Like porterhouse steak bones
51. Manage a group
52. Every 60 minutes
53. Reflexive pronoun
55. Uric _____
56. 1983 Michael Jackson hit: "_____ Nature"
57. **One language she speaks**
60. Underhanded person
62. Heron's cousin
63. Braised
64. Flammable, poisonous gas
65. Strong, fine threads
67. Adjust spacing between letters, in typesetting

70. Operating room stitch
75. Aries animals
77. An entire Mexican meal?
78. Northern Oklahoma city
79. Achy
80. Canadian daily: *Toronto* _____
82. More delicate, in build
83. It precedes classic or following
86. Goethe play or Gounod opera
87. Kinkajou's cousin
89. Montreal-born artificial intelligence pioneer Charles
92. Canada's prairies are part of this: Great _____
93. Use your Mastercard
94. Uttered aloud

95. X, Y or Z
97. Static _____
99. Holder for hummus
100. Burden
101. Nestlé Canada confection: Big _____
102. Sit or camel, in figure skating
103. Portico
105. Despise
106. Big Aussie birds
107. Beagle bites, say
109. Alias abbreviation
110. Canadian business association: Institute of Corporate Directors (abbr.)
111. European mountain

30

All In...

At the movies

ACROSS

1. Camel's back bump
5. NAFTA and USMCA, for example
10. Iced tea brand made in Canada
15. Small songbird
18. Mr. T's TV squad (with "The")
20. Eclipse shadow
21. Golden rings (var.)
22. 2002 Austin Clarke Giller winner: *The Polished* _____
23. Rodeo rope
24. Uncommunicative state
26. Meadow mama
27. **1979 Bob Fosse film: *All* _____**
29. Conseil européen pour la recherche nucléaire (abbr.)
30. Deposit in the desert
32. Online information service: _____ Canada Inc.
33. Small marsupial
36. Has a craving for
37. Small fry
40. Solitary person
42. In the heat of the action
44. Buddy Holly hit: "Peggy _____"
45. Satisfied sigh after dinner
46. BC-born former Buffalo Sabre Paul
47. Insect in a colony
49. *The National* anchors deliver this
51. Nurse a drink
54. Canopied House of Commons seat: Speaker's _____
56. Program for Canadian backcountry skiers: Avalanche Skills Training (abbr.)
58. Indonesian currency unit
61. Bliss Carman poem: "Low _____ on Grand Pré"
62. Community service program type
64. Smash 2009 Beyoncé single
65. Cryptanalyst
67. Annoying inconvenience
68. RRSP or GIC
70. Least common
71. Opponent
73. **1983 Tom Cruise hit: *All* _____**
76. Maximum, in math
77. Medical diagnostic machine
79. Calf without a cow
80. Order of Canada children's author Munsch
82. Las Vegas citizen
84. Wedding cake layer
85. They help stars look chic
88. Middle years?
89. Swamp that bogs you down?
91. King of Quebec?
92. Acknowledge
93. Computer connection network (abbr.)
94. Saps anagram
95. Hugh MacLennan CanLit classic: _____ *Solitudes*
97. Groom's promise
99. Green Bay-to-Sault Ste. Marie direction (abbr.)
100. CIBC money machine
102. Wickedness
105. Common Colorado tree?
107. 2002 Céline Dion single: "_____ Day Has Come"
108. Frost poem ender: "And miles to go before _____"
111. More spartan, on the Prairies?
113. Blasting crew's supply, for short
115. Montreal mayor Plante
117. National charity: Canadian _____ Association
118. **1950 best picture Oscar winner: *All* _____**
123. ON museum for art aficionados
124. Disbelief
127. Bay of Fundy component: Minas _____
128. "Immediately!"
129. South American shrubs
130. Change a security code
131. Burn with water
132. Donkey's brethren
133. "This is only _____"
134. Abrade earth
135. Subtle shades

DOWN

1. Cease
2. Beehive State
3. Flat landform
4. Ravioli and rigatoni
5. Idiot, in Israel
6. South American river
7. It aired *Mr. D*
8. US Revolutionary War-era hat
9. Satisfies
10. _____ & Bailey Circus
11. Whistler skiing trail
12. Early spring flower
13. Grilled meat on a stick
14. Like some ignitions
15. **1976 Hoffman/Redford film: *All* _____**
16. Des Moines resident
17. *Degrassi Junior High* stars
19. Charisma
25. This precedes Minor
28. Friend of Canada
31. Greek letter
34. Mossy matter
35. Short skirt
37. Franchise in Canada: _____ Bell
38. Waikiki Beach place
39. **1955 Wyman/Hudson romance: *All* _____**
41. Delphi seer
43. Genie-winning 1988 film: _____ *Ringers*

46. Stopped rising, like a river
48. Like the most tawdry novel?
50. As a result of which
52. That is, in Latin
53. Tay River town in Ontario
55. American's retirement plan (abbr.)
57. Artifact piece (var.)
59. Northern Ireland overcoat?
60. Coleridge or Keats creation
61. City of 123-A (abbr.)
63. Hindu spiritual retreats
64. Ontario-born Oscar-winning writer/producer Paul
66. Future attorneys study this
69. Rib cage locale
71. Last CFL game of the season, say

72. See 31-D
74. See 31-D
75. Squat candle
78. Old CTV comedy: *Corner* _____
81. Purged (of)
83. Slangy turndown
86. Antler point
87. Hearty supper serving
90. Reply to an invitation
91. Alberta moniker: Wild _____ province
94. "Ventura Highway" band
96. Manipulator
98. Latch _____
101. Start of a hole at Glen Abbey
103. Most sickly
104. Extol

106. Chattered excessively
107. Staple
108. One of Donald's exes
109. Some pudding bases
110. _____ noir
112. Condition to
114. Gists
116. Behold the man: _____ homo
119. Computing unit
120. Sibling of Jacob, in Genesis
121. Loathsome
122. Finales
125. _____ in "rabbit"
126. Global national standards organization (abbr.)

31 They All Fall Down

Where are these Canadian cascades?

ACROSS

1. Kelly of Crowbar
4. Sneaky
7. Infant's parent
11. Trillium province government grp.
14. Take an oral DNA sample
18. *Star Trek: Deep Space Nine* shape-shifter name
19. Karachi is this airline's hub (abbr.)
20. Bakery appliance
21. 1978 Alice Munro offering: _____ *Do You Think You Are?*
22. Redo a roadway
23. **Grand Falls Gorge**
26. **Churchill Falls**
28. Skinny street in Victoria: Fan Tan _____
29. Half-sister of Kim, Khloé and Kourtney
31. Ogling
32. British WWII entertainer Myra
33. Bride's facial covering
34. Large African wildcat
36. Uses a change room at Winners
39. Cut across
44. Fairies' kin
47. Important woman's title
49. Archaeologists' workplace
50. Electrical overload
51. **Kattimannap Qurlua**
53. Noted Canadian historian Gwynne
55. Musée _____ beaux-arts de Montréal
57. Canadian thespian Elliot
58. Analogous to a sibling?
59. Assists
61. 1990s Paul Gross CTV show: _____ *South*
63. Fixed shoe bottoms
65. Soaking
66. "…and to _____ good night"
67. Complained, like an oenophile?
69. Illness
70. **James Bruce Falls**
73. Phony
76. Crocheter's purchase
77. Domtar has one in Dryden and Kamloops
78. "The Beeb"
81. Rough up?
83. Japanese money
84. "Every cloud _____ silver lining"
85. Tree trunk growth
86. Tackle box supply
87. Furrow
89. Wash oneself
91. **Kakabeka Falls**
93. Discriminator against grandpa, say (var.)
95. Advanced U of A degrees, for short
97. Tie-in
99. Bamboozled
100. Religious beliefs?
103. Farthest orbital points
105. '50s waiters on wheels
107. Makes some mistakes
108. Bryan Adams chart-topper: "_____ of the Night"
112. Contaminated water can cause this
116. Remedy for any ill
118. Papyrus, for example
119. **Kwasitchewan Falls**
121. **Hunt Falls**
123. *Beetle Bailey* pooch
124. Hoary
125. Play charades, say
126. Narcissist's trip type?
127. ER drips
128. Garish green colour
129. Nancy Drew's beau Nickerson
130. Winter coaster
131. Take a small drink
132. Melania Trump, _____ Knauss

DOWN

1. Inspirational character for "Jack Was Every Inch a Sailor"
2. She released "Hello" in 2015
3. Caterwauls
4. Nimble
5. 2000 *Charlie's Angels* star Lucy
6. Bronx MLBer
7. Obtains new computer software
8. Extremely enthused
9. Laced anagram
10. Short sock
11. Quebec's official bird: Snowy _____
12. Small New Guinea marsupial
13. Comes off a bender: _____ up
14. Ship's pole
15. Dry African riverbed
16. Cosmetics giant that came calling in Canada in 1914
17. The Pursuit of Happiness singer Moe
24. Wedding party member
25. Volcanic activity shaking
27. Counsels, old style
30. George Harrison song: "My Sweet _____"
33. Document camera, for example
35. Settled an invoice
37. Short minister?
38. Horse's refusal?
40. There's one atop Canada's Library of Parliament
41. Musical refrain beginning
42. Pelted a house on Halloween
43. Industrious, in old England
44. Munch on like a beaver
45. Microwave, colloquially
46. "Put a lid _____!"
48. _____ marijuana
52. Lean
54. Very long sentence description
56. Misleading outward appearances
60. Platform in a throne room

62. Sushi fish
64. Go on a yacht
66. Milieux for Carr and Colville
67. Long-time game show: _____ of Fortune
68. Russian legislative body
70. Least ornate
71. The wild blue yonder
72. Japanese cuisine paste
73. Fame
74. Red, in Rimouski
75. Goa ladies' gowns
78. Char
79. Soft white cheese
80. Compact mass of mud

82. Capable of being counted
84. Nagged the chicken farmer?
85. Wailing folklore spirit
88. Trig function
90. Canadian transporter: _____ Rail
92. From head to _____
94. "Shh," on a musical score
96. "Quit it!"
98. _____ Veterans Association of Canada
101. Abandon
102. Tics
104. Prepares Parmesan, say
106. Escargot

109. Starr who sang "War"
110. Tropical American plant
111. Past, present or future, in grammar
112. "Gimme a break!"
113. Abhor
114. "You might be _____ something"
115. BC CFLer
117. American Society of Mechanical Engineers (abbr.)
118. Make a trip to The Brick
120. Tally up
122. Moviemakers use this special effects software (abbr.)

SOLUTION ON PAGE 165

69

Come Sail Away...

On these watercraft

ACROSS

1. **Pleasure craft**
6. Beethoven classic: "Für _____"
11. Ali _____
15. *Exodus* actor Mineo
18. Daisy variety
19. Natural skin lubricant
20. Shoshone tribe members
21. Mama horse
22. Neuters a colt
23. *Dancing with the Stars* dance
24. Spicy food type in Phuket?
25. Original first name of Danny Thomas
26. Banned pesticide
27. Craze
28. Souvenir for sale at the Vancouver Olympics
30. Big musical work?
31. Comply with instructions
33. Wild West bars
34. Delete files, on a computer
35. Factory-built house description
38. Average hole score, at Toronto Golf Club
39. *Olympic* or *Titanic*
41. Folklore cowboy: _____ Bill
42. Pictorial symbol in magic
44. Land-owning peasant in old Russia
45. Loblaws store section
46. Matured, like tomatoes
48. Whitechapel mother's moniker
49. Colorado venue: _____ Verde National Park
53. Ontario ex-premier Frank
55. Radiate
57. Makes seawater drinkable
59. Verve
60. 1987 Canadian film: _____ *of Singing Birds*
63. Exclude
65. Gothic-style mouldings
66. Info on an Indigo door

67. **Large carrier for cargo**
71. Season opener?
72. Lithe, like a tumbler
74. Mongolian dwelling
75. Geological time period
76. Belonging to a man
77. Real Canadian Superstore sells this type of product
80. Root you can eat
82. Famed French mathematician Blaise
84. Advantage
85. Doze (with "off")
87. Nickered
90. "Don't bet _____!"
92. Canada's Ian Bagg was a 2015 finalist on this show: *Last _____ Standing*
94. Former Toronto Maple Leaf Ron
95. Passover bread ball
96. **This vessel is featured in an annual Vancouver festival**
101. Scold the Boy King?
102. Throbbed
103. Showed again, on HGTV Canada
104. Cirque du Soleil troupe member
106. Impervious to pain
107. Highest spot
108. Skillet kin
109. Backyard storage building
110. Like old cheddar
114. Swiss Chalet purchase
115. Leaning tower town
116. Nancy Greene or Ken Read
118. Quebecers might put this in their coffee
119. Appends
120. Some Rds. and Sts.
121. NWT and NU
122. "Encore!"
123. Irish _____
124. Tent netting

125. Having irregular notches
126. **Mainland-to-Vancouver Island transport**

DOWN

1. Meditative exercise regime
2. Canada's Brian Orser was first to land two of this triple in one competitive program
3. Canadian Environmental Law Association (abbr.)
4. **Speedboat that skims over water**
5. Yours, in Quebec City
6. Assignment for a U of A English major
7. Maintain first place in a race
8. "Big Blue" corp.
9. **Underwater warship**
10. Message sent via Shaw, e.g.
11. Fleshy flank?
12. Reading room, in Indiana
13. It contains green and yellow legumes
14. With warts and all, in a store
15. **Flat-bottomed Chinese boat**
16. Stimulate interest
17. Alberta body of water: _____ Slave Lake
21. Some Auckland residents
27. Black History mo. in Canada
29. 2004 hit from Canada's Terri Clark: "Girls Lie _____"
32. Some Carleton graduates' degs.
33. Spice rack bottle label
34. Half of Canada's population of this lives in BC
35. New mom's blues (abbr.)
36. Came out again
37. Overshadowing the moon?
38. Beat at the post?
40. Christen
42. Greek mythology seductress
43. This evergreen yields a yellow fruit

46. Loverboy singer Mike
47. Canadian coin that features the *Bluenose*
49. *Chatelaine*, e.g.
50. Large African animals
51. Prepare surgical instruments
52. Beasts of burden
54. She tightens your corset
56. Canadian _____ money
58. Former froshes
59. Parasitic virus, for short
61. Swine shelter
62. Not slack
64. Baking soda meas.
68. Middle Eastern country
69. Has optimism

70. International Civil Aviation Day (abbr.)
73. Rush singer/bassist Geddy
78. Privy to
79. Like a soldier's abrasive attitude?
81. **This carries crude**
83. **This transports a natural resource**
86. Bishops' jurisdictions
88. Overabundance
89. Wallop
91. *The Fox and the Hound* fox
92. Hoodwink
93. Petro-Canada station section
95. Alternative to 48-A
96. Some CTV shows

97. Ebb
98. **Naval fleet**
99. Highlanders' kin
100. See 107-A
102. Top ten Ocean hit: "_____ Your Hand in the Hand"
105. Moisten during cooking
106. Hospital employee
108. Send unwanted emails
109. Opposite of 76-A
111. Kit or caboodle?
112. Rime anagram
113. Withhold authorization
117. Interest Rate Option (abbr.)
118. HS lunchroom

SOLUTION ON PAGE 165

33

Murder, She Wrote

Canadian mystery authors

ACROSS

1. Member of some sects
8. Candle flame extinguisher
15. 1984 Kim Mitchell hit: "Go For _____"
19. Practical (var.)
20. Take the spoils
21. Getting every last bit (with "out")
23. **She created Detective William Murdoch mysteries**
25. Hag
26. Feline's foot
27. Coming up, at the dance competition?
28. Canadian resources company: Imperial _____
30. Speedy serves from Canada's Milos Raonic
31. Quickly depart
34. 1991 hit from Canada's Boomers: "Love You Too _____"
35. 1999 Sarah McLachlan hit single
37. Allow
38. Fire a logger?
39. KFC serving
42. Negative response
43. It runs, but doesn't fly
44. Lo-cal, in advertising
45. Singular thing?
46. Atop
48. More cheeky
50. Relies on TD for financial services?
52. End-of-pregnancy marker: _____ date
53. Trophy won multiple times by Gretzky and Lemieux: _____ Ross
55. Ireland, to Yeats
56. Street name in Montreal?
57. To the _____ degree
58. Barcelona buddy
60. Gets Fifi fixed
61. Sleep _____ (var.)
63. Evergreens
64. Logical Internet search type?
66. **She wrote the Camilla MacPhee series**
69. Yielding of rights
70. Wisp of smoke
71. Caribbean music instrument
75. Torment
77. Public demonstration of discontent
79. Liable to
80. *Schitt's Creek* actor Levy
81. Honoured an RSVP
82. Hallucinogenic drug in the '60s
83. Pembroke's prov.
84. Coming down in pellets?
86. Technique for colouring fabric
88. Two-time Oscar winner Penn
90. Expectorated
91. Saltimbocca meat
92. Jalopy description
93. And more, for short
95. First aid pencils
97. Pull the wool over someone's eyes
98. US law enforcement org.
99. Shoulder wrap
101. Baseball icon Aaron
102. Combined ingredients
103. Royal Alex theatre attendee
105. Plumb of *The Brady Bunch*
106. Northern India chickpeas dish
108. Battery type: Lithium-_____
109. Held title
111. **She writes cozies set in Wales**
117. Thick
118. Parasitic worm genus
119. Brisk tempo, musically
120. Fixtures on 112-D
121. For that reason, old style
122. Measurement standards in Canada?

DOWN

1. Summa _____ laude
2. Canadian neighbour (abbr.)
3. Romanian money unit
4. It's used on 54-D
5. Construction site girder
6. Big bunch of stuff
7. Purple Canadian bill
8. Canadian boxer Mary who won 2011 Pan Am Games gold
9. Beethoven's musical chords?
10. Forearm bone
11. HGTV Canada airs this: _____ or Flop
12. Supporter of the Senators
13. Prod a poultry farm owner?
14. Call it quits at work
15. Wine label word
16. Gumbo ingredient
17. Roman emperor from 284 to 305
18. **Her series features a lawyer and priest**
22. Hand signals
24. Electrical energy units
29. Jumped off a springboard (var.)
31. White part of the eye
32. Horizontal bar exercise
33. Spoiled _____
34. January or July
35. Amazement
36. Strong janitorial product
39. Canada's Katic and Fillion were this on *Castle*
40. **Chief Inspector Gamache scribe**
41. Hails from 17-D
47. Eloped or drained
49. Patch trousers or a tire, say
51. Anxious
52. Patch a knitted garment
54. Housetop
58. Krall and Cummings play this
59. Toward the back of the boat

60. Parliament Hill government group
62. Foreshadowed, old style
63. Norwegian inlets
65. Some gastropods
67. High-pitched puppy cries
68. Is obligated to
69. Profession of 100-D
72. Farewells, in Frontenac
73. Hors d'oeuvres item
74. Tilted
75. Natural disaster of biblical proportions?
76. **Her Joanne Kilbourn series is set in Saskatchewan**

78. Suit _____
79. Old-style word of woe
82. River in Hades
84. Petite piano
85. Boob tube viewing meal?
87. Affirmative answer
89. Short course for a BC immigrant?
90. Least fresh
94. _____ emptor
96. Fear of flying or needles
100. Order of Canada actor Kenneth
102. Shed feathers or fur

104. Quick sleep
106. Former Winter Palace resident (var.)
107. Aesop fable race participant
108. Not busy
110. Montreal entertainment venue: Place _____ Arts
112. Bell Centre game surface
113. Glazed meat serving
114. Software for cinematic special effects (abbr.)
115. Circle's curve
116. Our, in Repentigny

34

Canada Cornucopia 5 Challenger

No three-letter answers

ACROSS

1. Famed humanitarian: Mother _____
7. Somewhat wet
11. Singer's scale exercise
16. Ennui
17. Cops catch speeders using this
18. Radio antennas
20. Fee for flying on Flair
21. Merino descriptive
22. Knick-knacks shelf
23. One who alleges
24. The earth's shape, hypothetically
25. Nefarious serf?
26. Canadian coin that had a maple leaf
27. Amiable city in France?
29. Ho Chi Minh City used to be this
31. Shot the puck too far at Rogers Arena
32. Ottawa venue: National _____ Centre
33. Glaswegians
35. Lays potato chip quality
37. Like Jack Sprat's dinner?
38. _____ acid
41. "_____ we forget"
42. Trash can, in Torquay
46. Topper for a princess
48. Ration resources (with "out")
50. Molson and Labatt libations
51. Accessory that wraps around a bicep
53. Intense dislike
58. This illustrates the lay of the land?
60. Golden Horseshoe city in Ontario
63. Mecca pilgrim (var.)
64. Like a pre-owned car
65. Pub in your Newcastle neighbourhood?
67. Suspicious
68. Some Shelley poems
69. Painful twinge
70. See 2-D
72. Courses of study at 71-D
74. Canadian actress Shannon, et al.
76. Trampled underfoot
78. One of the five senses
79. Louisiana cooking staple
82. Easily understand a concept
83. Ottoman Empire VIPs
84. Certain
87. Some Chapters purchases
89. It's NNE of Santa Fe
91. Hide damage to walls?
93. Foals' feet
95. Spreadsheet contents
99. National charity: The War _____
100. Debark
103. Yearning
104. It follows Dutch or microwave
105. Reddish rash
107. French _____
109. Former YTV music videos show
111. Gospel, old style
112. Tummy trouble
113. Flatter to excess
114. These trucks travel Canadian roads in winter
115. Female family member
116. Makes music?
117. Destroys, in Devon
118. Sleep cheap
119. Got accustomed to

DOWN

1. Hard worker
2. Off the mark
3. Rigs a ship again
4. Netherlands dairy product
5. Global TV's senior national affairs correspondent Eric
6. Country that's south of Canada, for short
7. *SCTV* star (with 54-D)
8. "So long," in Seville
9. Mood disorder
10. Forecast the future
11. Protests for those not standing?
12. Libran's birthstone
13. Brief *TV Guide* program summary
14. Rips off a sheep farmer?
15. Most ethereal (var.)
16. Cranberry or grape, in old Rome
17. Man of many words?
18. Pronounce without vocal cord vibration
19. Transmits
28. Binding agreement between businesses
30. Bleak
34. Granite chunk
36. "Guilty," for example
37. Deputy premier of Quebec Bacon (1985–94)
39. Iraqi, for one
40. Rideau or Welland follower
42. Sudden
43. Park toy for a pair
44. 1960s CBC kids' program: *Chez _____*
45. Montreal landmark: Jacques Cartier _____
47. Share helpful information
49. "I thought _____ never leave!"
51. US cookie brand since 1975: Famous _____
52. Fears
54. See 7-D
55. Red-and-white slice in a salad
56. Volcano output
57. Badmouths
59. Thermos
61. Sensory organ
62. Canada's Ken Taylor served as ambassador here (1977–79)
66. Bogart/Bacall classic: *Key _____*

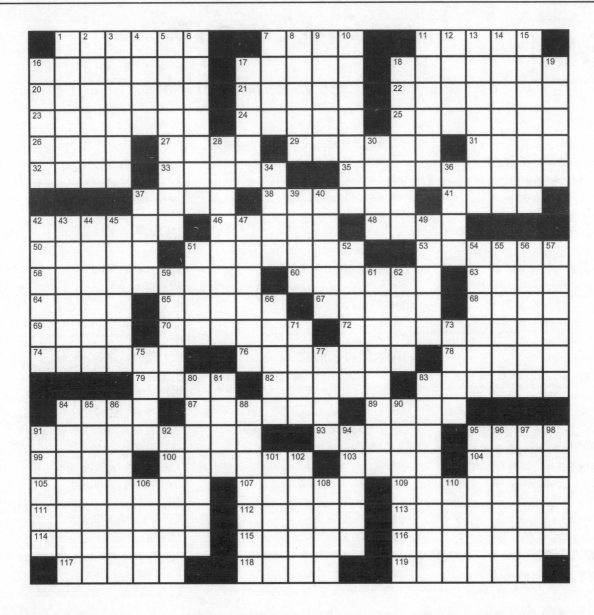

71. Toronto university
73. YYZ postings
75. 10-year Manitoba premier Gary
77. DeHavilland Canada turboprop: _____ 8
80. Unveils
81. Assist a lawbreaker
83. This god had an underwater adventure?
84. Russian tea-making device

85. Swedish city
86. Holds a grudge
88. Pretentious
90. Currency for a Kabul resident?
91. Preps the spuds
92. Lecherous lookers
94. Besides, in Baie-Comeau
95. Loonie denomination
96. Fly WestJet?

97. Tried someone's patience?
98. Puts money in the kitty
101. Large book, in olden days
102. Joanne Woodward movie: *The Three _____ of Eve*
106. Gothic-style moulding
108. Mini moments
110. Royal Winnipeg Ballet stage attire

SOLUTION ON PAGE 166

35 Gastronomie

Celebrating foods from France

ACROSS

1. Enjoy a winter's day at BC's Panorama resort
4. Long-jawed fish
8. Deadly snakes
12. Create the first row of a knitting project
18. Twelve-month span
19. Came down to earth?
20. Wicker hive
21. Be absorbed, gradually
22. US poet and author Angelou
23. Clare Boothe _____
24. Canadian Medal of Bravery honouree
25. Game in which iron rings are tossed
26. **Hot ham-and-cheese sandwich**
29. Pool player's computations
30. Allocate a task
31. *SCTV* character: _____ Floyd
32. Sound of impact
34. Before, of yore
35. Tie down a sail
37. Moosehead product
39. Former Ontario premier Ernie
41. Like a weighty roast?
45. Diminutive detective?
47. Like something that can be fixed
52. With 43-D, a Labatt product
53. Understand the ocean's depths?
56. Alberta's Lake Louise, for example
57. Past participle of "lie"
58. Very much
60. AB mediation group: Utilities Consumer Advocate (abbr.)
61. Belleville clock setting (abbr.)
62. Moisten the roasting chicken
63. Montrealer Bruce who won the International Fryderyk Chopin Piano Competition in 2021
64. Cessation of hostilities
66. Highly toxic metallic element
68. Lingerie department purchase
71. **Traditional fish stew**
74. Espionage professional
75. 1986 Canadian Top 40 hit: "Patio _____"
77. Clubs for Canadian golfer Graham DeLaet
78. Posed for a photographer
80. Bar made of gold
81. Pasty-faced
83. A notable Yoko
84. Notched, like a knife
88. Emily Dickinson poem: "For every Bird a _____"
89. Dixie cornbread
90. Mythological nature maidens
92. Mid-term at U of M
93. "Hurry up!"
96. White or orange tuber
97. Hammer parts
98. Not on time
99. 1970s Leafs star Ullman
102. Facial feature
104. Chicago trains
107. Monikers for moms' moms
109. Home on the plains (var.)
111. Spinal column support
116. 1980 Olivia Newton-John movie
118. **Savoury pie filled with cheese and bacon**
121. Cdn. kids collect money for this org. on Halloween
122. Strange, in the Highlands
123. Irritate
124. Sidney Crosby's hometown: _____ Harbour
125. Baby's noisemaker
126. Djibouti abuts this gulf
127. Words of understanding
128. Israeli airline
129. West African country: Guinea-_____
130. Victorian Whitechapel lodgings: _____-house
131. YWG postings
132. It follows Canada and Victoria

DOWN

1. Singes
2. Knocks out, in boxing lingo
3. Basra citizen
4. Bluish-grey mineral
5. U of C reunion attendee
6. Carom
7. Office stationery item: _____ pad
8. Take _____ to
9. Summertime biter, colloquially
10. Lima nation
11. Department of Canadian Heritage branch: _____ Canada
12. **Braised chicken dish**
13. "Let no man put _____"
14. Sometime air quality issue in Southern Ontario
15. Pastoral scene fabric
16. Blender brand
17. Thuringia river
18. In 1851, this charitable org. opened its doors in Montreal
27. Nursery rhyme duckling description
28. Canadian sandwich shop: Mr. _____
33. Fireplace surrounds
36. _____ of execution
38. Bodily nerve network
40. Evergreen shrub
41. Miles Per Gallon (abbr.)
42. A lobe here has a hole for a stud
43. See 52-A
44. Blue-green shade
46. Uncouth one
48. Anise-flavoured aperitif
49. Foundation
50. Made brighter

51. Someone to keep closer?
53. Engineering/procurement company: _____ Canada
54. Round windows
55. **Meringue-based sweet**
59. Lhasa is its capital
62. Go out of focus
64. Herbal drink
65. Wood from an Asian tree
67. Nincompoops
68. Ostentatious jewellery
69. Saree-clad royal
70. Feeling of unease
72. Coming apart at the seams?
73. Collapse of societal standards (var.)

76. Bottom line figure
79. Ash or oak
82. 1990s CTV show: _____ Rider
84. Ordinary guy (var.)
85. Chopping tool
86. Catch some sun
87. Paramedic's jacket acronym
89. **Classic beef stew**
91. Canadian jury member (var.)
94. Iconic South African Nelson
95. Observes
97. British noble
100. Exploratory excursions, for short
101. Driving speed (abbr.)

103. West Edmonton Mall shopping trips
104. Bedroom community
105. Molokai patio
106. Hissy fits
108. Flames or Jets, say
110. Rather uncanny
112. Like spiked punch
113. Her image graces Canada's $10 bill: _____ Desmond
114. Porcelain filling
115. Eels anagram
117. Play parts at Stratford
119. Nullify
120. Olive genus

36

C-A-N-A-D-A Sixpack

Find your country here

ACROSS

1. Hellos from Hadrian
5. Fell to the depths
9. Dalai _____
13. Mexican adobe hut
18. *Schitt's Creek* actor Eugene
19. Swiss artist Paul
20. Visit: Drop _____
21. Dissonant
23. Advantageous TSX transaction result
24. Creating a mental picture
26. Excursion along BC's coast
27. Notification that the danger's done
29. Corporate correspondence
30. Sue Grafton's PI Millhone
31. **1916 US legislation that created an eight-hour workday for some**
33. Derbyshire dads, colloquially
34. Cancel a janitorial job?
38. Gratuity at 8-D
39. Wily
40. Cup at Glen Abbey
41. Lira anagram
42. Alberta winter mecca: Marmot _____
44. Runway walk, say
46. Former Buffalo Sabre from Canada Lindy
50. Smarties manufacturer in Canada
52. Taos colonnade?
54. Japanese food fish
55. Quebec: La _____ Province
56. Disapproved of weeping?
58. Business Council of Canada (abbr.)
60. **Holt Renfrew retails this: _____ Rose Facial Treatment**
62. Rocky's big screen love
65. American civil rights org.
67. Tack on
68. Rose stalk
71. Barrel shaped
74. Annoys
75. Thin plate of rock
77. Tim Hortons tea choice
78. Smoothly, to a musician
80. **South American snake**
82. Space between teeth
84. Enya's song about a river: "_____ Flow"
88. Kilt, for one
89. Prairies oil field structure
91. Cancelled mission at NASA
94. Somewhat
95. Saint's shiny circlet
96. Short summary?
98. _____ Secord
100. Ontario-born Lockhart who acted in 300+ films
101. Eject, forcefully
103. _____ & Perrins
105. American Indigenous group
106. Passover meal
107. Digital device for the Net
110. **Ornamental table setting piece**
113. Gully, in the SW US
114. Of base eight
115. Driver's licensing requirement
120. Camera stand
121. Upholsterer's chosen weapon?
123. *Gilligan's Island* actor: Alan _____ Jr.
124. Mentally infirm
125. Slightly colour
126. Wood preservative oil type
127. Julia Roberts movie: _____ *Brockovich*
128. Sticker
129. Canadian pilot Billy Bishop, et al.
130. Hand over the reins
131. *Desire Under the* _____

DOWN

1. Pond surface particle
2. Wiener schnitzel meat
3. Diabolical deeds
4. Harmonize, say
5. Enjoyed a day at 42-A
6. Old capital of Kazakhstan
7. Close call
8. National eatery: The _____
9. Former US retailer in Canada: _____ 'n Things
10. Three of these appear on Ontario's coat of arms
11. White blood cell type
12. Dread
13. Lotto 6/49 prize
14. Heart trouble: _____ fibrillation
15. Spying on spies
16. Biscotti flavouring
17. Eye surgery beam
22. Livestock graze on these in Lincolnshire
25. 1917 Halifax explosion ship
28. Scientists' workplace
32. Rotisserie
34. Community on the Ottawa river: _____ Point
35. Canadian Indigenous group: Woodland _____
36. Reduced Instruction Set Computer (abbr.)
37. Super small
40. Maui dance
42. Labatt Blue container
43. Upper-class Englishman
45. Cut down on
47. Inflammatory gastric condition
48. _____ steak
49. Wards (off)
51. Pan topper
53. **Early resident of today's Maritimes**
55. Soft bun type

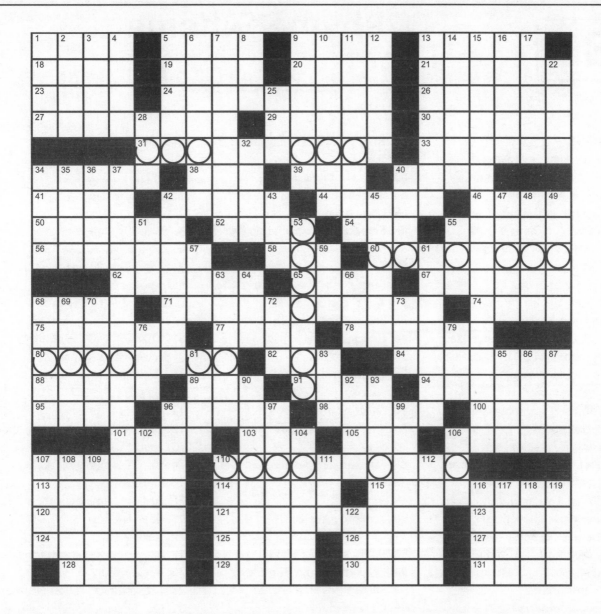

57. Canada's Bryan Baeumler hosted this show: *Disaster* _____
59. "Lodi" band, for short
61. Infectious disease
63. Greek and Roman verse form
64. National Institutes of Health (abbr.)
66. US rapper: _____ Kim
68. Punctuation mark
69. Japanese poetry form
70. Message sent via TELUS, e.g.
72. Hound a spouse
73. In times gone by
76. "_____ so fast!"
79. Tuna container
81. A *Property Brothers* brother
83. Kraków nation (abbr.)

85. Had arrears
86. Christmas confection: Candy _____
87. _____ and terminer
90. Out of this world?
92. Ancient European citizen
93. Win a debate
96. Modernize a bathroom, say
97. Hydrocarbon type
99. Bounce, in a Leafs/Habs game
102. Corrupt music business practice
104. Builds a better mousetrap?
106. Down
107. Thai temples
108. Made a mistake
109. Liquid for pickling

110. _____ Rica
111. House adjunct
112. BC's Coast Mountains, for example
116. Rankin Family hit: "Fare _____ Well Love"
117. Camembert played by 18-A on *SCTV*
118. Delicate in build
119. The Royal Canadian Mint produces these
122. And more, briefly

What do the theme answers have in common?
(Answer on page 166)

37

Rhyme Scheme

Unlock the letter pattern

ACROSS

1. College type in Quebec
6. 1985 Ian Thomas album: _____ *Water*
9. Academy of Canadian Television & Cinema honour
14. Hardwood floor component
19. Eocene, for example
20. Juno-winning band: _____ Lady Peace
21. Forearm bones
22. Canadian country singer Sean
23. **Thingamabob**
25. Drain blockages
26. Lively, in Laval
27. "Money _____ object"
28. Cereal grain
29. Ancient Persia ruler
30. Get another *Canadian Living* subscription
31. Unspecified amount
32. GoFundMe beneficiary
33. Sound of the crowd at Commonwealth Stadium
35. Negligent
39. To this point
40. Former mining hotspot in Yukon
41. "See ya!"
44. Botanical angles
45. 1999 Bryan Adams album: *The _____ of Me*
46. Slunk like a snake
48. **Annual Canadian prize: The _____ Metcalf Award for Literature for Young People**
49. Old-style prov. abbr.
50. Whale constellation
52. Launching civil litigation
53. Edmonton CFLer
54. This encases Gouda
56. Ike or Honest Abe
58. Snug, in Sussex
59. Sail management technique

61. Saint Petersburg landmark: Winter _____
62. Shade of blonde
64. Singer Bob
65. **Über fussy**
66. Real Canadian Superstore buggies
69. Chemical suffix
70. Burps
71. Not brand name
73. Stiletto or slingback
76. Comments
78. Poet
79. Unhealthy
80. Assegai
82. *Jolly Roger* hand
83. Last _____ not least
84. **See 65-A**
86. Transferable, on a UFO?
88. Move carefully
89. Vexed
90. Triple-decker sandwich (abbr.)
91. In _____ straits
92. Like a steamy Sarnia day
94. US comedienne Boosler
95. Silent films star Theda
96. Groups in the 'hood
97. Amaze
98. Morning, in Châteauguay
101. Like a torrid glance
103. Thoroughfare, in Thetford Mines
104. Helper
108. "It's _____ Way to Tipperary"
109. The PCs and Canadian Alliance did this in 2003
110. **Highball cocktail**
112. See 109-A
113. Travels on GO Transit
114. To the utmost, for short
115. Push
116. *The Maltese Falcon* star Mary
117. Put yourself out?
118. "I agree"

119. Ecclesiastical assembly

DOWN

1. Accra currency
2. Long poem form
3. Thug
4. Reverberation
5. _____ Beta Kappa
6. In perfect condition
7. Barbra and Céline sang one in 1997
8. Canada _____ ginger ale
9. Secrets of a sect
10. New Brunswick-born actor Pidgeon
11. Cherish
12. Latvia's capital
13. Censure a minister?
14. Egyptian rulers of old
15. Hermit
16. Anti, in some dialects
17. Baptize
18. Realized
24. They oppose Libs in the House of Commons
29. Like a downy pillow
31. Old Mesopotamian language
32. Query from Juliet: "_____ thou love me?"
34. Oral Rehydration Therapy (abbr.)
35. Dance party ranter?
36. Banished from a nation
37. **Famous Disney mouse**
38. Variety
39. Email button
40. Erratic (var.)
41. Verve, musically
42. Cravings in Tokyo?
43. Avant-garde, in fashion
45. Doper's pipe
46. Kindling material
47. Trick-taking card game
50. **Irritable infant description**

51. Passes, on Parliament Hill
55. Empress Hotel location: _____ Harbour
56. Garden fertilizer
57. Canadian Grand Prix participant
60. Anorak lining fabric
61. Plagiarize Blackbeard?
63. Kids' play place
65. 1992 thriller: *Single White* _____
67. **Wily**
68. Canadian rowing great Laumann
71. Green Park entrance in London: Canada _____
72. Former NL premier Wells
73. Generous slice, colloquially
74. Toronto entertainment venue: Massey _____
75. "Step _____!"
77. Battlement slot
78. Occupied
81. Put in peril
83. Satchels
85. *Son of Rosemary* author Levin
87. _____ Canada
88. Like a Christmas season beverage
92. Have importance
93. Insomniac's strife?
94. Decor piece
95. You might play this at a Royal Canadian Legion
96. Parasail
97. Some of your parents' siblings, to you
98. Papa's partner
99. Molson and Moosehead products
100. Legal wrong
102. Operating system developed at Bell Labs
103. Make mad
104. Like sore muscles
105. Greek church art piece (var.)
106. 1980 "Whip It" band
107. Stared at
110. Former Canadien Lafleur who wore #10
111. Skylab successor (abbr.)

SOLUTION ON PAGE 167

Beijing Bonanza

38

Canadians shone at the 2022 Winter Games

ACROSS

1. "Golly!"
5. "Scars to Your Beautiful" Canadian singer Alessia
9. Big Smoke pollution problem
13. On a hot streak, like a Calgary NHLer?
19. It precedes formaldehyde
20. US singer Tori
21. Scholarly book
22. **Marie-Philip who won her third Olympic hockey team gold**
23. Canadian icebreaker: _____ *Grey*
24. Picks up a pickup?
25. Take _____ view of
26. Lengthen
27. Stocking _____
29. Burrard _____
31. Most sere (var.)
32. Deep-fried veggies and fish dish
33. Nerve
34. National Crossword Day mo.
35. Cork country
37. **Canada won bronze in this inaugural mixed team event**
44. Stunned state
47. Cause disfigurement
49. Playing surface for 22-A
50. *Royal Canadian Air Farce* star Abbott
51. Aspirant
52. October zodiac sign
53. _____-tac-toe
54. Regional trees (var.)
55. Whitesnake hit: "Here _____ Again"
56. Richard who played "Jaws" in Bond films
57. *Fiddler on the Roof* setting
60. Turndowns
61. **Christine de Bruin slid to bronze in this inaugural event**
64. English exam components
66. Canada's Shatner, et al.
68. Health-care worker
70. Pose a question
71. Income offering to a church
73. Globe or orb
76. Scenic views
79. **Speed skater Hamelin who capped his career with a gold**
83. Attention-getting interjections
84. Buddhist principle of non-violence
86. Old CBC show: _____ *30*
88. To the utmost, briefly
89. Supplement
91. Pal anagram
92. Spacious
94. Inane
96. Paddock mamas
97. Blue jeans brand
98. Waterproof canvas
99. Employ incorrectly
100. **Snowboarders Parrot and McMorris won gold and bronze in this**
103. Verse form used by Petrarch
105. Tiny, in Troon
106. Nocturnal insect
108. Preferred coffee in Cairo?
112. Not as light
116. Plaster of Paris
117. Checked a garment for fit
118. Beer brand: _____ Extra
119. Astronaut-turned-politician Garneau
120. A law _____ oneself
122. Fluffy bit from the dryer
123. **Nickname of ski cross silver medallist Thompson: _____ Mar**
124. 1970s gymnastics queen Korbut
125. Visionary
126. Theatregoers' box
127. Porcine guffaws
128. Duke or duchess, in the UK
129. Corn cobs
130. Medical care charitable org: _____ Canada

DOWN

1. Empress Hotel visitor
2. Give a speech
3. Truth _____
4. **Sharpe and Karker won silver and bronze in this freestyle skiing event**
5. Party food provider
6. Unethical
7. Massey Hall ticket info
8. Like ownership that can be legally transferred
9. Stable compartment
10. Famed catwalk Canadians Rocha and Harlow
11. Leave out
12. Agate or amethyst
13. Clever insight, in Quebec?
14. Like a vixen?
15. Early stringed instrument
16. Pub potables
17. Royal Canadian _____
18. "I'm at the _____ of my rope"
28. Hue and cry, say
30. Low point
31. Lower someone's spirits
34. Most risky, in craps?
36. Gaspé girlfriend
38. Pet for C&W star Wells?
39. *The Marvelous _____ Maisel*
40. Dog breed: Canadian _____
41. Domed dwelling in the North
42. 1960 movie: _____ *on Sunday*
43. Backyard ground cover
44. Thin wedge of wood
45. West African country
46. Fairy tale phrase preposition

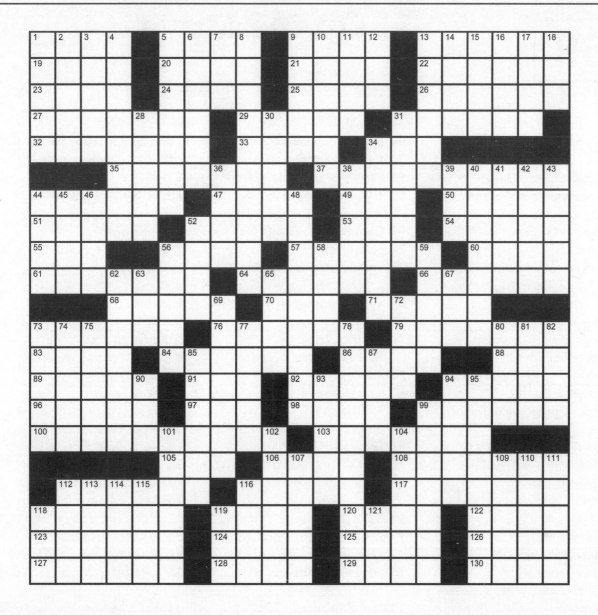

48. Ivanie Blondin raced to speed-skating silver in this

52. Justin and Chrystia, politically

56. Canada won 29 medals at this nation's 2018 Olympics: South _____

58. Traditional Maori dance

59. Wood shop machine

62. Foxtrot precursor

63. Prickly seed (var.)

65. Impertinence

67. Canada Health Act (abbr.)

69. Hag's malevolent stare

72. Disgusting

73. Pillowcases

74. Propel a bike

75. Electricity giant: _____-Quebec

77. Motivate

78. The Bay depository?

80. Second-most populous island in BC

81. Elbows in pipes

82. Eyelid irritant

85. Skimpy top type

87. Rush roadie's gear

90. Sugary suffix

93. Kilns for hops

94. Toronto hospital: Mount _____

95. Triple medallist Weidemann who carried our closing ceremony flag

99. These cause you to reflect on you?

101. Cusses

102. Come to light

104. Small piece of cloth

107. Mary Pickford was the first Canadian to win this acting award

109. Canuck or hoser, e.g.

110. Latin line dance

111. Ponies up, in poker

112. Exhaust

113. BMO Field home player

114. Lion's sound

115. Interwoven fabric

116. Strong wind

118. *60 Minutes* network

119. Swabbing implement

121. Nuclear Energy Agency (abbr.)

SOLUTION ON PAGE 167

On the Move

39

A little fun with puns

ACROSS

1. U of L living quarters, for short
4. Michel's mate
7. There's one named after W.A.C. Bennett in BC
10. Swindler's scheme
14. Later on
18. ArriveCAN, e.g.
19. Glass of red, in Chicoutimi
20. Central Netherlands municipality
21. Soda
22. Canadian Triple Crown event
23. Body of water near Canada's North: Labrador _____
24. Federal program for seniors (abbr.)
25. Book by Canada's Sara Gruen: *Water _____ Elephants*
26. Ovule husk
27. Medical misfortunes?
28. Apiece
29. Heavy hydrogen, e.g.
31. **Handsome sailor?**
33. Tot or tyke
35. Edward and Anne, in Nova Scotia
36. Medicinal salves
37. Tchaikovsky ballet: _____ *Lake*
39. Least refined
40. Asparagus piece
41. Butt heads, like bucks?
43. Dust particle
44. Culinary chopping device
49. Soft palate lobes (var.)
50. They ogle
53. Married lady, in 13-D
54. Adjusts clocks for DST
55. Simple sugar with six carbon atoms
56. They might work at a CP facility
57. **Motorcycle passenger's cocktail?**
58. Excessively emote, during a Royal Alexandra performance?
59. Skeet shooter's balderdash?
65. They ask odd questions?
66. Scoring play for a Blue Jay
67. **Commuter's reading material?**
72. Belittling
73. Spanish cuisine stalwart
74. Putting cargo on board
80. Snare drum sound
81. Eat at The Keg, say
82. Speaker
83. Canada's Triumph, et al.
84. Scourge
85. Completely wipe out
87. Maliciousness
89. Just a precautionary phrase?
91. Feline's weapon
92. Backcountry skiing adjective
96. MLB pitcher's perfect game description
97. Sushi fish
98. **Hertz, for an old bike rider?**
100. Having scalloped edges
102. Old Canadian game show: *Cash _____*
105. South American birds
106. Hairstyle
107. Have bills to pay
108. *Porgy and Bess* co-writer Gershwin
109. Phrase repeated five times in a 1975 ABBA song title
110. Rate of movement
111. Indirectly suggest
112. More, in Mexico
113. BC nature area: Pacific _____ National Park Reserve
114. Alberta attraction: Edmonton Valley _____
115. Categories
116. Loonies, say
117. Hurricane's centre
118. Aunt in *The Wizard of Oz*, et al.
119. Timmins time setting (abbr.)

DOWN

1. Croak, vocally
2. Fencer's blade
3. Starring role for Kirk Douglas in 1960
4. Eschew
5. Actress Farrow, et al.
6. To such an extent (with "as")
7. Removed trees
8. Gets a pet from the SPCA
9. Least
10. Fish type
11. Subverts software?
12. Property receiver, in olden days
13. Costa del Sol city
14. First Nations group
15. Fire-extinguishing gas
16. Conspicuous public success
17. Fledglings' homes
30. **Where the captain lives onshore?**
32. 1939 James Mason thriller: *I Met a _____*
34. This connects your leg to your foot
37. Epithet
38. Laboured over a loom
39. In 2007 and 2014 Sidney Crosby won this: Art _____ Trophy
40. More achy
42. Southern Alberta place: Medicine _____
43. Flat tableland
45. Madagascar lemur
46. Prolonged periods of unconsciousness
47. Straight up
48. Tirades
51. Chop

52. Rest Of Canada (abbr.)

53. Charitable organization: _____ the Children Canada

56. 1995 Annie Lennox hit: "No More I Love _____"

57. Emulated Sarah McLachlan

59. Medical history recording document

60. Type of pneumonia

61. Pricey old violin

62. Basil-based sauce

63. Mesozoic-era period

64. Smallest litter member

65. Engineer's preferred poem?

67. Express your point of view

68. Bison's hair mass

69. Previously named, in French

70. International Labour Organization (abbr.)

71. Caronzola dairy product from Quebec

74. Miners' "jackpot"

75. Tycoon Onassis, for short

76. Dhaka was this before

77. Use slanted type

78. _____ care in the world

79. Expanded

81. Canada's Keith Morrison is a correspondent on this NBC show

84. Digital currency

86. Noted American hoofer Fred

88. 1960 classic Hitchcock film

89. CERB provided this for some Canadians

90. Scandinavian country

92. Giraffe's cousin

93. Last Rogers Cup match

94. Film, colloquially

95. Models

97. Alouettes and Argos

99. Little amphibians

101. Use fingernail clippers

103. Fusses

104. Inuit mukluk, for example

SOLUTION ON PAGE 167

40

Illustrious Alumni

From the University of New Brunswick

ACROSS

1. Dump rodents
5. Canadian prime minister Macdonald, by birth
9. TO CFL team member
13. Hungarian, to a Hungarian
19. Brothers Grimm villain
20. Scarlett O'Hara's homestead
21. Ooze out slowly
22. Northern Canada phenomenon: _____ borealis
23. Form letter computer program
25. Singing style for Ella and Mel
26. Remain at one's post
27. Perfunctory, to Julius Caesar
28. *Common Sense* writer Thomas
29. Tyrone Edwards, on *etalk*
30. College head's office
32. Basaltic rock
34. **Two-time Oscar nominee Walter**
38. Justin Bieber, e.g.
40. Stuff things into a suitcase
41. Love affairs, in Laval
42. Jack's bird?
43. West Indian magic
45. American lyricist Gershwin
48. Heathen
49. Grey who was the first Reform Party MP
50. Archaeologist's discovery
52. Sheer fabric for curtains
54. Our southern neighbours
56. Final Greek letters
58. Idle mollusc?
59. Musical compositions for one instrument
60. Georgian _____
61. Peacock's pride, for example
63. Former Greek city state
67. **Former New Brunswick premier Frank**
71. Respond
72. Jokers-are-wild rummy game
74. *On _____ Majesty's Secret Service*
75. *Pieces of a Woman* actor LaBeouf
77. "It Came _____ the Midnight Clear"
78. Canada's Ryan Reynolds learns lines from this
80. Ghosts
85. This flower is highlighted at an annual Ottawa festival
87. Leases
88. One of your limbs
89. Ontario landmark: Bruce _____
90. Self-Addressed Envelope (abbr.)
91. Patton quote: "_____ of sweat will save a gallon of blood"
93. Margaret Atwood novel: *Life Before _____*
94. Skinny, in Saguenay
95. Attach (onto)
96. Specific areas
99. **Author Alistair**
100. Some fuel delivery fellows
103. On the QT
105. C.S. Lewis series: *The Chronicles of _____*
106. Important Arabic personages
108. Weapons storage facilities
113. Install a new software package
114. Mixed breed dogs: Shih _____
115. Related to a judge's duties
116. *Jane Eyre* scribe Charlotte
117. Wings (Lat.)
118. Norwegian king (1957–91): _____ V
119. Accra cash
120. Chars
121. Extend credit to
122. *Private Practice* star Diggs
123. Semi-hard cheese

DOWN

1. Cavort
2. Laboratory gelling agent
3. Group of three
4. Psychotherapy subject
5. Hi-fis
6. **20th-C. poet Bliss**
7. Keyboard instrument
8. Edison's initials
9. Lash out at
10. Cookbook inclusion
11. Wild cherry
12. Picked a preference
13. "Great Lash" cosmetic
14. German expressway
15. **Former New Brunswick premier Shawn**
16. Walk-the-Dog trick toys
17. Neil Young wrote this Ronstadt hit: "Love Is _____"
18. Diatribe
24. Artists who break with the past
28. Sigh of relief interjection
31. Crusty wound coverings
33. Ellesmere Island is covered by one
34. 1986 Madonna hit: "_____ Don't Preach"
35. Mosque officiant
36. Former Venetian magistrate
37. Food thickening gum
39. This Anne lost her head
42. Blue jeans material
44. Tom Cochrane & Red Rider hit: "_____ League"
45. Relative by marriage: Father-_____
46. Quebec place: Rivière-_____
47. Fury
49. Lentil or split pea
50. **20th-C. poet Charles G.D.**
51. Intergovernmental group in Canada: Ecological Monitoring and Assessment Network (abbr.)
53. Basic beliefs, informally
55. Parkas and anoraks

57. Murdered
62. Not connected, romantically?
63. Animal tails
64. _____ New Guinea
65. Tropical America lizard
66. Hindu princess
68. Brightly coloured fabric
69. Retained
70. Grey in the face
73. 1986 Sade hit: "Is It _____?"
76. She might be evil
79. *The _____ & Stimpy Show*
80. Water dropping noise

81. Liar anagram
82. Wise mentor
83. Picasso contemporary Joan
84. Children's coaster
86. Provide pain relief
92. Hairstyling products
93. Pickle or predicament
94. Huge
95. **Long-time chocolatier family scion David**
97. Akron resident
98. Took care of the sick
99. **Singer Anne**

100. Italian isle
101. Synthetic fabric
102. Kathmandu country
104. Vancouver Island junk removal firm: _____ Day
105. Central points
107. Double agent, in spydom
109. Pleasant
110. Did well, colloquially
111. Russian-made car
112. _____ pickings
115. Quickly scribble down

SOLUTION ON PAGE 167

41

What's the Tea?

For the grannies out there

ACROSS

1. Canadian comedy show: *Trailer Park* _____
5. Stay away from
10. Prelim races for Andre De Grasse
15. Ensnare
19. River that starts in Shakespeare ON
20. You can buy one at Second Cup
21. Two cents' worth, say
22. Long-time Canadian band: April _____
23. Echo's boyfriend's problem?
25. Canadian writers Guy Gavriel Kay and Charles de Lint, for example
27. Saanich BC lake
28. Canadians Koffman and Norman
29. Annual tour in Canada: Stars _____
31. Operating room knife
32. Reminders of wounds
34. African antelope
35. Japanese straw matting
37. Greek goddess of wisdom
39. New Brunswick port city: _____ John
41. Compound that binds to a receptor
45. Stain
46. See 34-A
48. Story about a knitting shop?
51. Share the same opinion
52. Canadian Critical _____ Society
53. Put seeds in the ground
54. Goat-like
57. Very dry
58. That is, to Octavia
60. Deceive or defraud
62. Fire-breathing mythological monster
64. Ottawa Senators season ticket holder, say
65. More chic
67. Chief Operating Officer (abbr.)
68. Gordie Howe, to Marty
69. Increases
70. **Canadian tea brand since 1892**
73. **For years, this Canadian tea came with china figurines**
76. **Largest tea company in the UK and Canada**
78. Sweet _____
79. You can do this in or out
81. Tourtière, for example
82. MLBer from Baltimore
84. _____ Farmers of Canada
85. Sodium chloride product
87. Took a load off
88. _____ a sour note
92. It precedes "-do-well"
94. Rained relentlessly
96. Condiment in Quebec
98. Scotch _____
99. Lesser Antilles Amerindian
101. Peppard's '80s show: _____ -*Team*
102. Excessive bodily swelling
104. Greetings in old Rome
105. Tie up traffic?
107. Bob or Doug McKenzie, on *SCTV*
109. Starts
111. Watery porridges
114. Take an oath
115. Sank a putt at Victoria Golf Club
116. Regency-era writer Jane
119. Relating to pond scum
121. Genre of 7-D
122. US gov. stock market overseer
125. Diabetic's concern
127. In a markedly different manner
130. Erelong
131. Grammarian's milieu
132. Bullies do this
133. They wriggle underwater
134. Canadian actors Aykroyd and George
135. Velvety-petalled flower
136. Pass through a doorway
137. Archaic past-tense verb

DOWN

1. Cause of misery
2. Egg shaped
3. **UK "county" tea launched in 1977**
4. Canadian company: _____-Lavalin
5. Foot race losers?
6. These display flowers
7. Singer Redding
8. 1985 duet from Bryan and Tina: "_____ Only Love"
9. Like Regan, in *The Exorcist*
10. LP player
11. Legislate
12. Sleep _____
13. Carter opened his tomb in 1922
14. Holden film: _____ *17*
15. **English tea brand since 1706**
16. Computer architecture acronym
17. Penny _____
18. Bothersome bug?
24. She hosted *Project Runway Canada*
26. Fiji neighbour
30. She wears a wimple
33. Glockenspiel kin
34. Woman
36. Bronzed by the sun
37. Spore enclosures
38. Leaping amphibian
39. Rush hit: "Tom _____"
40. **UK tea brand since 1903**
42. Angry
43. Mexican shawl
44. Like small adolescents?
47. Baseball great Berra

49. Operatic passages
50. Vancouver lodgings: Fairmont Pacific _____
55. Grow together, like plants
56. Sister of Terpsichore
59. Fusses
61. Get ready
63. Wiseman who won a Governor General's literary award in 1956
66. Backs of necks
70. Hepburn's moniker for Tracy
71. Sea close to Crete
72. Some Molson products
74. **Internationally sold Sri Lankan tea**
75. One end of an HB pencil
77. Encampment

80. Spill the beans
83. Big ticket purchase?
86. Fifth scale note (var.)
89. **Canadian-based specialty product retailer**
90. 1994 Alice Munro book: _____ Secrets
91. Kevin Costner played this Eliot in 1987
93. **English tea business founded in 1907**
95. Grieving
97. Manual worker
100. Revealed one's soul
103. Dawn moisture
106. Incurs debt, say
108. Gametes
110. 2004 film: _____ Enchanted

112. Northern Ireland river
113. Criticizes, in Coventry
115. Canadian Rockies landmark: Kicking _____ Pass
116. Bon Jovi hit: "You Give Love _____ Name"
117. Wrist–elbow connector
118. Imminently
120. The CFL trophy is named after this earl
121. 12D on a WestJet flight
123. House annexes
124. Bump under your skin
126. NAFTA participant
128. Canadian sprinter Johnson who forfeited Olympic gold
129. Recent

SOLUTION ON PAGE 168

42

Canada Cornucopia 6
Superchallenger

No FIBs

ACROSS

1. Canadian drag racing pioneer Ken
5. Places, to Probus
9. Skin or plant transfer
14. Allude to
19. Wrestling match
20. Rowboat paddles
21. Old film spools
22. Dim
23. Miniature whirlpool
24. Old Grecian portico
25. Sunny lobbies (var.)
26. Not erect
27. Canadian McFarlane whose pen name was Franklin W. Dixon
29. Edmonton Oilers role filled by Connor McDavid since 2016
31. Actresses Lane and Ladd
32. Pronoun for us?
33. Alberta town north of Lethbridge (with 72-A)
34. Daytime TV fare, colloquially
35. Web page for adorers of an idol
38. Assistance
39. Racing vehicles at an annual Nanaimo event
43. Ontario Municipal Board (abbr.)
44. Under, in Umbria
47. Casual tops
49. It screws to a bolt
50. Pack of paper
52. Like a crude landscaper?
54. Biggles books character, for short
55. School bus driver on *The Simpsons*
56. Laundromat appliance
58. Elizabethan instrument
59. Ocean land mass
60. He said, "You had an option, sir," in a 1984 Canadian political debate (with 93-A)
61. Mumbai money
63. Tattered, to an exterminator?
65. 1960s Canadian skiing star Nancy
66. Clicked send, say
69. Sight or smell
70. Frothy desserts
71. Put the tail on the donkey
72. See 33-A
73. Passerine songbird
74. Hodgepodges
75. Spending money in Mexico
76. Former New Brunswick premier Bernard
78. Some tides
82. Steals, old style
83. Walkway
84. Off the beaten track, to actress Sally?
86. Atlantic waters fish
87. Positive response
88. Zealous devotion to a sect
90. Prevaricating
92. Make a mistake
93. See 60-A
95. PC's "brain"
97. Very slightly
99. Some McGill majors
100. Quintessentially Canadian cheese curds fare
103. Girl's counterpart
104. Adheres
107. Mentor's apprentice
108. After-effect of long Air Canada flights
111. Ballerina or gymnast description
112. Regional fauna and flora
113. Tardy
115. Famed Danish toy maker
116. To go, in Terrebonne
117. Like expectations not yet realized
118. Elevator manufacturer since 1853
119. British scribe Bagnold
120. Water sources
121. The Bay or The Brick
122. Physics resistance units
123. Hankerings

DOWN

1. Offspring of Eve
2. It's encrypted
3. Canadian inland sea
4. Engraving tool
5. Come in last
6. Granola bar grain
7. Floral signs of spring (var.)
8. Ontario's Brock University is named for him
9. Waiter's tip, at The Keg
10. Impedes progress
11. Nest on the cliffs
12. Manitoba city (with 16-D)
13. Toronto Soccer Association (abbr.)
14. Indonesian banknotes
15. Captivated, old style
16. See 12-D
17. German language article
18. Some rural roads (abbr.)
28. Tennessee's official flower
30. School fundraising grp.
31. A bit senile
33. In bloom, in Baltimore
34. Military rank nickname
35. Ontario premier Doug
36. USA part, for short
37. Piggy, on the foot
39. Canadian WWI flying ace Bishop
40. Loosens one's laces
41. Lighter fluid
42. Pebbles
45. It precedes "patriot love" in "O Canada"
46. Rideau Hall city (abbr.)
48. Hurriedness

51. Sheep known for their fine quality wool
53. Until now, in legalese
55. Euripides play
57. Regulations of play
59. Third-person pronoun
60. Canadian ex-NHLer Neely was one for 10 seasons
62. Children's doctor (abbr.)
64. "Carpenter" insect
65. Political grp. of Presidents Bush
66. Tesla or Shirley Temple, for example
67. Environment
68. Newfoundland pine marten, for one
69. Edo Japan offering

70. Kind of crisis
72. Oliphant who co-founded the National Ballet School of Canada
73. Fly, to the spider?
75. Loses colour
77. Canadian resource
79. Type of torch
80. Knitter's stitch
81. Light on your feet
83. CFL kickers' kicks
84. Remove a limb, in the OR
85. Crime labs test this
88. Fantastic vintners?
89. Minibike
91. Barbed remark (var.)

94. Former Alberta premier (with 98-D)
96. Western US Indigenous group
98. See 94-D
100. Movie trailer
101. Home made of snow in the North
102. Bard's "below"
104. Shredded cabbage serving
105. Rectangular backsplash piece
106. Contraction with "do"
107. Pub order
108. Falconry strap
109. Opposin'
110. Aeolus and Odin
112. TransLink vehicle in Vancouver
114. Horton of donut franchise fame

43

A Star Was Born Here

Name that city

ACROSS

1. Hawaiian hello
6. Has title to
10. Jack and Rose embraced here in *Titanic*
14. Shopper's Drug Mart bottles
19. Poisonous
20. Hammer or tongs?
21. Canadian impressionist Little
22. Make sense, in math class?
23. More than plump
24. Fishy flavour for a feline
25. Engaged in no good doings?
26. Emma Roberts, to Julia Roberts
27. **NHL icon Mario Lemieux**
29. Former Montreal Expo Martinez, et al.
31. Dried coconut meat
32. Rather ribald
34. Type of tide
35. J.K. Rowling created him: Harry _____
36. Desert description
40. Most mentally sound
42. Middle Eastern rice dish (var.)
44. Townhouse renter
46. South American animals
48. Infiltrated, like cinematic body snatchers?
53. **Young adult fiction author Sigmund Brouwer**
55. Puerto _____
56. Impala
57. Smiley face, for example
59. Professor's term at Trent
61. Cow's stomach section
62. Eucharist vessel
63. Went back on one's word
65. Shaving cream lather
67. Event for Canada's Andre De Grasse
68. Racing vehicle in Yukon
69. Fermented mare's milk beverage
71. Slope, to a Scot

74. Hibernian
75. Intensely analyze a frog?
76. US narcs' org.
79. Opera viewing boxes
81. Trees used for deck wood
83. Making very mad
85. Saves corncobs for supper?
87. Swiss Chalet menu choice: _____ Chicken Dinner
89. **Rapper Drake**
90. Old-style golf club
91. Apparatus for Canada's Yousuf Karsh
93. Moon indentation
94. Mild curry dish
96. "Be it _____ humble, there's no place like home"
98. Neighbour of Draco
99. Privileged Persian owner?
103. Footnote citation (abbr.)
105. Adulterers' assignation
107. 1970s Canadian band: _____ in Coldwater
108. Fake name
110. **Actor Michael J. Fox**
115. Gerussi who starred in *The Beachcombers*
116. Get _____ a good thing
117. Dhofar Mountains country
119. Pacific Ocean island
120. _____ 6/49
121. Info on 14-A
122. Elders' tales
123. Looked on in amazement
124. Cloppenburg municipality
125. Porcelain pitcher
126. Peter Fonda film: _____ *Rider*
127. Sambuca flavouring

DOWN

1. Canadian Egoyan of film directing fame
2. Wolf, in Mexicali
3. Farm working pair

4. High school subj.
5. Tart
6. **Singer Paul Anka**
7. Beach Boys classic: "_____ It Be Nice"
8. Negative response, in Neuville
9. _____ on the wrist
10. Fuddy-duddy person, say
11. These protect against erosion
12. Eight-legged cephalopods (var.)
13. *How the Grinch Stole Christmas!* villagers
14. **TV home show stars Drew and Jonathan Scott**
15. Dumdum
16. Accomplished at
17. Dirty money?
18. As far east as you can go in Canada: Cape _____
28. Colourful find on a special spring Sunday?
30. Lured
33. Calendar span
35. Puff or huff
36. Take _____ down memory lane
37. Like oboe sounds
38. Consumer Price _____
39. Wainscot part
41. Behaved maliciously
43. Distinctive facial feature, for example
45. Black, in Barcelona
47. Newfoundland folksinger Hynes
49. McGill grads, for short
50. BC Place roof feature
51. Fencer's sword
52. Fender-bender damage
54. Pillager
56. Create interest, say
58. Free-for-alls
60. Strange sightings in the sky
64. Desex a stallion
66. Miniature model
68. Considers to be

69. Hanukkah begins in this month
70. One of the Fab Four
71. Little bubble
72. Crowd sound, at Winnipeg's Canada Life Centre
73. Taj Mahal place
75. TV genre of *House* and *Scrubs*
76. Beef stew brand: _____ Moore
77. Go inside
78. Plaza for Plutarch
80. Golden Olympian Catriona Le May Doan
82. "Gotcha!" interjection
84. Aim of a Canuck?
86. Civil disobedience event
88. Tie yourself up in knots
91. Little red railcar
92. Debt trouble
95. *Gilligan's Island* boat: S.S. _____
97. Sportscaster Scott Oake
99. *The Ant and the Grasshopper*, for one
100. Bushy hairstyles
101. Promotes
102. Old Italian nobility title
104. Kingston neighbourhood: _____ Harbour
106. See 119-A
108. Politician's wingman or -woman
109. Subterranean mammal
111. Bangladesh bakery product
112. Brazilian indigenous group
113. Strata discoveries
114. *Au naturel*
118. *Dinornis novaezelandiae*

SOLUTION ON PAGE 168

44

X Marks the Spot...

In this rule-breaking grid

ACROSS

1. Data storage device
10. Bull that's beyond criticism?
18. Condemn
19. Pertaining to farming
21. Canadian classical violinist: Lara _____ John
23. Stubborn, in Sacramento
24. Serving trolley
25. Greeting word
26. Sue Grafton mystery: _____ *for Evidence*
28. Have a yen for
29. Purchase an RRSP
30. Neither's partner
31. WestJet inflight employees
33. They claim to have second sight
34. Frighten
35. This might come back to haunt you
36. Change the boundaries
38. Sexy skirt opening
39. _____ like a glove
40. Conservative former MP Turner
41. Prepared *Chatelaine* articles for publication
43. Worships as a god
45. Calgary venue from 1950–2020: Stampede _____
46. Court technique for Canada's Milos Raonic
48. Revenue source at The Source
49. Freight transportation fee
50. Spanish or Swiss
52. Managed the troops
53. Lethal weapons
54. Alberta town: _____ Plain
55. Former Saturn model
57. RCMP Red Serge, for example
58. **Sauce base, in cuisine**
59. **Dental office procedure**
60. Like the most committed neo-con?
67. Female reproductive cells

68. Mourning hymn
73. Oxygen-eschewing organism
74. You no longer roll up this to win at Timmies
76. How closely linked couples stroll?
78. Jerusalem resident
79. Sounded like a sheep?
81. Soldier who's conscripted
82. Fool, in Folkestone
83. Winces
85. Specialized roofing installer
86. Some indigenous Canadians (var.)
87. Rile up the waters?
88. _____ reflux
90. Glances over
91. CIBC and RBC do this
92. Where a ship docks
93. Runs from the law
95. Little South American monkey
96. Tiny table scrap
97. Reduce in rank
98. Automobile safety device
100. Sign that precedes Virgo
101. Sarah McLachlan hit: "Don't Give Up on _____"
102. Kneecap
103. Come apart, like sweater threads
105. "_____ apple a day..."
106. 1990s ABC drama: *My _____ Life*
107. Tidied up
109. Navigational reference points at sea
110. Emphatic declaration

DOWN

2. Short commercial?
3. Make a quilt, say
4. Authors Blyton or Bagnold
5. Bob and Doug McKenzie, for Rick Moranis and Dave Thomas

6. Edible seaweeds
7. Rogers Centre playing surface
8. Hightails it
9. Heavenly
10. Sated
11. CRA and CBSA, for example
12. Ascots
13. Yukon Quest competitors
14. Clean a chalkboard
15. Gardeners' gossip?
16. Siamese or Abyssinian
17. Supremes hit: "You Keep Me Hangin' _____"
20. Devoid of merriment
21. Hides
22. Pooped
25. They're held captive
27. Not in the big leagues yet
30. Tell a tale
32. Sometime *This Hour Has Seven Days* host Patrick
35. Formal room, in Florida
37. Brimming with vim
40. Squash or pumpkin
42. 2012 Justin Bieber song: "_____ in Your Arms"
44. **Show off your muscles**
45. Astronomer Sagan
47. Kenya's capital
49. Rope that raises a ship's flag
51. Hangman game rope
53. Tree native to Mexico
56. Crackpot
57. To's opposite
60. Sign in the sky of an upcoming storm
61. Intact and Great West Life
62. Article of clothing
63. Made a pile
64. Old-style weight allowances
65. It follows holy in a phrase
66. **One of China's oldest cities**
68. Radio knobs
69. Actually

70. Exterminator's preferred hairstyle?
71. Colourful beverage?
72. Submarine's surfacing, for example
74. Ends of the lines?
75. Elephants and giraffes, for example
77. _____ Mila Mulroney

79. More prone to breakage
80. Turns down an invitation
83. Popular Toyota model
84. California/Nevada mountain range
87. Make a new candle from leftover wax
89. House of Commons activity
92. Some Greek consonants

94. Desktop option: Screen _____
97. Carp's kin
99. Chap
102. Whales' group
104. Polynesian floral garland
106. Former CTV show: _____ *You Think You Can Dance Canada*
108. 1985 Ian Thomas track: "All I _____"

Places for positive people

ACROSS

1. US-invented garden salad name
5. Nimbus
9. Dines at East Side Mario's
13. Urbanologist Jane who received the Order of Canada
19. Arab world VIP
20. Trebek who hosted *Jeopardy!* for 37 seasons
21. Dirty reading material
22. Noah landed on this mountain
23. X-ray department
25. Filipino meat serving
26. Larvae do this
27. Sgt. Joe Friday show
28. **Village for kindly folks?**
31. Hot drink in Drummondville
32. Charlton Heston movie: *Ben-_____*
33. Make a stack
34. Ablan who founded a major Canadian furniture retailer
35. Ontario region that includes Mississauga
36. Considers
39. Where Timbits teams practise
40. Subatomic particle
41. Expands: _____ on
42. _____ Domini
43. Autumn mo.
44. Tegs' mothers
46. Winged Persian spirit
48. Support for a ship's primary sail
50. No score, in soccer
51. Former Toronto City Council electees
55. CBA member
56. Emotionally distant
58. October star sign
60. Lady's crown
61. To-do
62. In a discourteous manner
64. Submit your CRA forms, say
65. Poi source

68. **Town for vigorous folks?**
71. Actress Rowlands who received an Honorary Academy Award in 2015
72. 1983 Police hit: "Every _____ You Take"
74. Negates
75. Actress Gardner, et al.
77. Bingo kin
78. Abbreviated beginning?
79. Carpentry fastener
81. Canadian Psychological Association (abbr.)
84. 1979 Jane Fonda film: *The China _____*
86. Request
88. Some endocrine glands
90. Campbell's tinned product
91. Not closed
92. "_____ whiz!"
93. Moonfish
94. Crunchy Mexican meal serving
97. Kitchen furniture piece
99. *Toronto Star* columnist's POV piece
101. Black hardwood used for piano keys
102. Magnum _____
103. Dirt chunk
104. Waver in the wind
105. Lass or lady
106. Dog or cat
107. **Locale for happy people?**
109. Risk averse
113. Stoa adjunct, in old Greece
115. Footnote abbr.
116. Engine duct
118. Influential economist: John Maynard _____
119. Chromosome component
120. Twelve o'clock
121. Miners' finds
122. Analyzes 121-A
123. Sacred chests and biblical boats

124. See 9-A
125. Home for a heron

DOWN

1. Funny faro player?
2. Persian poet Khayyam
3. _____ fond farewell to
4. **Town for sharp thinkers?**
5. More fit
6. Plenty
7. Triathlon segment
8. We can't live without this
9. Prohibit, in court
10. *Diary of _____ Housewife*
11. Some Mississippi trees?
12. Ogles
13. Coated with lacquer, in Tokyo?
14. Calla family flower
15. Labatt bottle top
16. Spoke from the podium
17. Took a turn in the tub
18. Braces (oneself)
24. Big burden
29. Made from a certain wood
30. Blatant hype
33. 1986 Huey Lewis and the News hit: "_____ Be Square"
35. A couple of waiters' suggestions?
36. Female parent
37. Go _____ length
38. Defer a decision: Sleep _____
39. Banff Sunshine Village, for one
40. Justin Bieber's third album
43. BC/WA sea
45. **Place for a crazy good time?**
47. Bodily network
49. Picture frame insert
51. Benzene compound
52. Old CBC sitcom: _____ *in Canada*
53. Poetic name for Ireland
54. *Peter Pan* dog
57. Union Station street in downtown Toronto

59. Rapture
61. Jerks
63. Take down curtains?
64. Harsh
65. Recedes
66. Where squirrels sleep
67. *Rebel Without a Cause* star James
69. Olden days alphabetic symbol
70. Exaggerated, like the pastry chef?
73. Bullring beast
76. Overwhelm
78. African savannah antelope

80. Wily, at the Edmonton Valley Zoo?
81. Mob boss
82. CPP word
83. Pallid
85. Best a schoolmate?
87. Not obscure
89. **Community for dignified people?**
91. Hip golden ager?
94. Kansas city
95. Summits
96. Darling children, say (var.)
98. Señor's shop?

100. Songs of praise
101. Near anagram
104. Former *Take 30* host Paul
105. Puts on weight
107. Coveted CFL trophy: _____ Cup
108. Military machine
109. Potatoes, in PEI
110. WestJet seat price
111. Luau guitars, for short
112. For fear that
114. Part of 119-A
117. Note that guarantees repayment

46

Wanna *Stay* Here?

Saintly places

ACROSS

1. Tool that gets to the point?
4. At the pinnacle
8. Strait between Cape Breton and Newfoundland
13. Lozenge
19. Sign that follows Cancer
20. Kill a bill in the Oval Office
21. Honolulu hello
22. Some Western Canada tycoons
23. Greek letter
24. Moniker for 48-A: The Botanical _____ City
25. Book of Ruth mother-in-law
26. Transfer a computer file
27. Air Transat pilots do this
29. Parcel of land
31. Provides grounds for arrest?
33. Say "Alaska" again?
35. Noah's transport
36. Gymnastics great Comăneci
37. Dublin country
39. It surrounds Earth
44. Some U of T tests
47. "I cannot tell a _____"
48. **Wild Rose province city: St. _____**
49. Genus of olives
50. Brood
51. Terrible
53. His, to a Quebecer
54. Gratuities
55. Direction from Hull to Montreal
56. Whitehorse and Winnipeg, for short
57. Visibly stunned
59. Toronto Santa Claus parade vehicle
60. Recent right wingers?
62. Armadillo's armour
63. Equality
65. Queen's Plate, for one
66. On the ocean
67. Stuns
68. Emergencies
70. Bribed, say
71. Exterminator's rundown digs?
75. East Flanders capital
76. Capital of France
77. Not his
78. _____ ideal
79. Canadian business journalist Amanda
80. An iconic hockey Bobby
82. Buttercup plant
84. Jann Arden won a Juno for this: "Could I Be Your _____"
85. Canadian Willie who was the first black NHLer
86. **New Brunswick town: St. _____**
88. Umpire's call at a Blue Jays game
89. Canada's Donovan Bailey did this twice at the Atlanta Olympics
90. Colour for a Vancouver band since 1978?
92. Type of antiseptic acid
94. Prove as false
95. Calgary Transit rider's option
96. Tetanus trouble
100. Writes a song
104. Moons, in Mirabel
106. "Excellent," in hippie-speak
107. Egg-shaped objects
108. Frosting
110. Faux pas
112. AB legislation: Health Information Act (abbr.)
113. Small sofa
114. Old enough to vote or drink
115. Omani or Iraqi
116. The Rock time zone (abbr.)
117. Radial patterns
118. Sip slowly, like an RN?
119. Walk back and forth
120. Frequent toper

DOWN

1. Bachelor's final stop?
2. Use a loom
3. **Missouri city: St. _____**
4. Hindu deity manifestations
5. Tapered, in botany
6. Royal Canadian Mint city (abbr.)
7. Prairie paper: *Regina Leader-_____*
8. Duck, in Drummondville
9. Old-style word of regret
10. The shape of Italy
11. German physicist Georg
12. From a certain Asian island
13. Many Banff visitors
14. Fortify a breakwater, like Canada's Drake?
15. Mexican pottery piece
16. "Time's a-wastin'!"
17. Warm up the oven
18. Finishes
28. Sloping
30. Rajah's spouse
32. Love like crazy
34. …at the ends of sentences
36. Luxe San Francisco neighbourhood: _____ Hill
38. Broadcasts on CTV
39. Uncomfortable while sick?
40. Health Canada advisory tool: Cosmetic Ingredient _____
41. "The Waste Land" poet T.S.
42. Settle a CIBC loan
43. Compass point
44. Unseal a jar
45. Valentine's Day flower
46. Civic or Corolla
48. **Northeastern Florida city: St. _____**
51. Old CTV show: *So You Think You Can _____ Canada*
52. Payment to a Scottish property manager

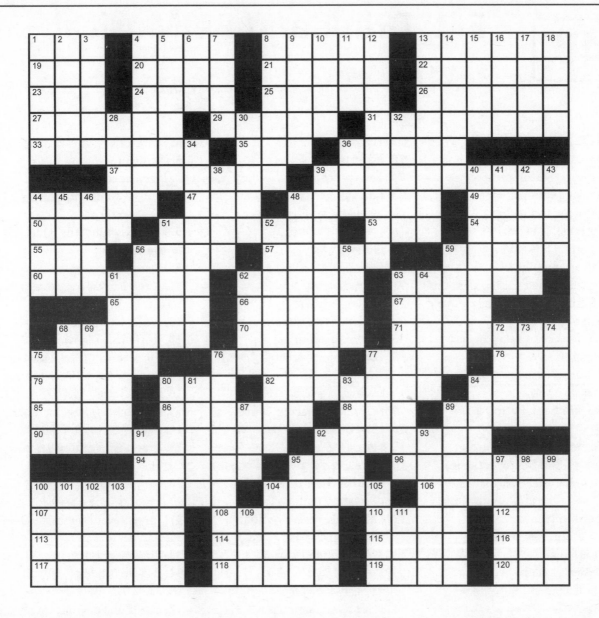

56. BC area: Sunshine _____
58. _____ moss
59. Guitar components
61. Winced
62. Trilogy of novels, say
63. Pertaining to mom or dad
64. Cognizant
68. Spain-born "Cuchi-cuchi" entertainer
69. Subscribe to more *Maclean's*
72. Angus _____ Institute
73. Raga might be played here?
74. Service conducted by 72-D
75. Gooey food

76. Preliminary discourse, old style
77. Clock increment
80. Mythological man-eaters
81. Hasidic community leader
83. Mammal not found on Vancouver Island
84. Tropical lizard
87. You might be stuck in this
89. Bacterium
91. Washed away, like a levee
92. Cord for a daring jumper
93. French brandy
95. Cask closers
97. **Newfoundland and Labrador capital: St. _____**

98. French navy vessel
99. Wild West lawman Earp
100. Price
101. 2016 Drake track: "Summers _____ Interlude"
102. Scintilla
103. Flatbread with a pocket
104. Perjurer synonym
105. Crackle and Pop's companion
109. Canadian Freelance Union (abbr.)
111. "Are you a man _____ mouse?"

47

Eat, Drink and Be Musical...

With these Canadian bands

ACROSS

1. Former Canadian reality show: *Til _____ Do Us Part*
5. Popular 1970s hairstyle
9. Belonging to that guy
12. Extremely abundant
19. "Pretty maids all in _____"
20. Unvarying in pitch
22. Contact lens cleaning solutions
23. **Multi award-winning country band**
25. Symbols of societal shame
26. Make lace
27. Brazilian city: _____ Paulo
28. Whistler run
30. Hockey book by 36-A: *The _____*
31. **Toronto synth-pop group**
35. Footnote space-saver (abbr.)
36. Famed Canadiens goalie Ken
38. Russian country home
39. Exert influence
42. 1979 Triumph song: "_____ It on the Line"
44. Yemen port city
45. TV Clampett: _____ May
46. Inference
48. Lost, in Laval
50. European Medicines Agency (abbr.)
51. Manitoba town: The _____
52. Irish lads
54. Changed gears
58. Pilot
60. Liveliness
61. Underwater Location Transmitter (abbr.)
63. *Canadian _____ Dictionary*
64. Geometric measurement
66. Unemotional
68. _____ bran
69. **This band notched a 1980 hit with "Echo Beach"**
76. Shipboard journal
77. Windy day description
78. Utopian
79. Tel Aviv country
83. Litigate
84. 2009 Drake single: "Best I Ever _____"
86. Fluffy fabric
89. Office supplies chain in Canada
91. Staircase post
93. Tonic's partner
94. Rock concert stage equipment
96. Harmful, odourless gas
98. Brought forth a baby
100. Troops' bullets, briefly
101. Whirl
103. Former Canadien Gainey
105. Lower abdomen part
106. Polished
107. Canadian skater Stojko won gold at these three times
109. Private eyes, for short
111. **Multiple Juno-nominated rock band (with "The")**
113. 2002 Céline Dion album: *_____ Day Has Come*
114. KFC bucket piece
116. Contented sigh
118. Capture a con, say
119. Arterial linings
121. **Pacific Northwest indie–folk band**
127. Newborn
128. McGill and McMaster, e.g.
129. Old-style wizard
130. Scattered seeds (var.)
131. Website feed letters
132. Ontario, vis-à-vis Quebec
133. Often

DOWN

1. Skip stones, say
2. Make a miscue
3. S. Amer. snake
4. Antsy
5. Strike down, in earlier times
6. Gardening tool
7. Inability to smell
8. Spanish Romantic painter Francisco
9. Loverboy hit: "The Kid is _____ Tonite"
10. Bumbling
11. Canadian banknote component: _____ number
12. Quiet interjection
13. Reviewed a movie
14. Ontario Land Inventory (abbr.)
15. **Former NL folk-rock band**
16. Like a messy bed
17. Some ships' crew members
18. City close to Cologne
21. It performs at Roy Thomson Hall (abbr.)
24. _____ *avis*
29. Wound on the wrist?
31. Innovative thought, in Quebec
32. Pacifies
33. Positive publicity
34. Bits on bristles
35. See 4-D
37. Ten in the decimal system, for example
40. Central European river
41. Circlet of thread
43. Ouija board word
46. Cry of exasperation
47. _____ Criminal Justice Act
49. Greek consonant
51. Caged (with "up")
53. Wild plum
55. *The Flintstones*, for short
56. Significant epochs
57. The US banned this in 1972
59. Head part
60. Peace Tower tolls
62. Shy
65. Chemists' milieu
66. Pen for pigs

67. Ruminant's mouthful
69. Just about all
70. City in Uttar Pradesh
71. Oakville or Ottawa, properly?
72. Uncool one
73. Foul smelling
74. Pointy-eared mythology creature
75. Under the weather
76. Scenic Cape Breton route: Fleur-de-_____ Trail
80. **This band has released 30+ singles since the '70s**
81. African antelope
82. Showed the way
84. Mannheim gentleman
85. Saxophone type

87. More enfeebled
88. Colony insect
90. Cry
92. *Canada's Drag Race* contestants' accoutrements
93. MacLellan who wrote Anne Murray's "Snowbird"
95. A little slow
97. Reply to the Little Red Hen
99. Strike a chord, at Rogers Centre?
100. Neighbour of Florida
101. Shakespearean poem
102. Old Roman magistrate (var.)
104. Panhandler
106. Shadowbox
107. Old-style farm wagons

108. Aver
110. Purdys box bits
112. Feeling of dread
115. Obey advice
116. Tack insult onto injury?
117. Famous lyric written by Paul Anka: "Regrets, I've had _____…"
120. Mom's mouth?
122. 65+ federal program for Canadians (abbr.)
123. Dorm at Dalhousie
124. Close friend
125. _____ trip
126. Workplace for Canada's Tatiana Maslany

48 Cinematic Spectres

Haunting movie characters

ACROSS

1. Breeding time, on the farm
7. The North Star
14. Regina Pats league type: _____-junior
19. Commands, in olden days
21. Inferior copycat
22. On the ball
23. *Beetlejuice* spirit
25. Trent–Severn Waterway features
26. Pivot abruptly (var.)
27. Lamb's mama
28. "..._____ o'clock scholar"
29. Source of mother-of-pearl
31. Tibetan dog breed: _____ Apso
33. Vietnamese New Year
34. Command to a corgi
35. Antwerp is here (abbr.)
36. Popular pen brand
39. Editor, for one
41. Went on the lam
42. Angina pain relief drug: _____ nitrite
43. Old-style theatre employee
45. Blue Jay's fielding flub
47. Famed American espionage org.
48. *Ghostbusters* ghoul
49. Children's song lyric: "..._____ my spout"
51. Match attire for Canada's Denis Shapovalov
54. Rock garden stonecrop plant
55. Old Global TV show: _____ Will They Think of Next?
57. Tree type
58. Annual Ontario visitor: Wiarton _____
59. Teensy
60. "_____! The Herald Angels Sing"
62. Like a prominent point
63. Marry in the middle of the week?
66. **Hogwarts haunter**

69. Bachman-Turner Overdrive song: "You Ain't Seen Nothing _____"
70. House of Commons speech, say
72. "See you later," in Salerno
73. Gardener's weeding tool
74. Enzyme type
75. Cul-de-_____
76. Not at all speedy
78. Cowboy's circlet
83. Expert marksman
84. Sly, at pottery class?
86. **The Friendly Ghost**
87. Corncob
88. Old-style strumpet
89. Update a product's appearance
92. Snowy birds of Quebec
94. New Mexico artists' community
95. Generally
97. Pronoun used in Chibougamau
98. Scrap of cloth
99. NB has a heritage lighthouse here: _____ Point
100. Shoshonean, for one
101. Northernmost Canadian settlement
103. Attack from above during WWII
105. Singers Redding or Rush
106. Gabrielle Roy's first novel: *The _____ Flute*
107. Middle Eastern religious officiant
111. Spike on a soccer shoe
112. *Blithe Spirit* spirit
116. Like many supermodels
117. Bone marrow tumour
118. Old French dance
119. Lawn trimming gizmo
120. More placid
121. Most unusual

DOWN

1. Recedes, like the tide

2. Canadian coastal waters mammal
3. Show that highlights heavy rescue in BC: *Highway _____ Hell*
4. Social nonconformist
5. Hockey rival of CDA and USSR
6. Long, tapered flag
7. Thick fog event: _____-souper
8. Morphine, for one
9. Law-breaking trash tosser
10. Shoelace tip
11. Equine colouring
12. Airbnb alternative
13. More dignified, in the OR?
14. Kuala Lumpur language
15. Missing from a CFB
16. *A Christmas Carol* spectre
17. Scottish archipelago
18. Put on the market once more
20. Blade sharpening tool
24. 2008 single from BC's Theory of a Deadman: "Not _____ to Be"
30. Not good
32. Concubine group
34. Spill over the top
36. Kiss, on a TTC route?
37. Capri or Skye
38. Censured (var.)
40. Indian caste
41. Playful, like a pussy cat
42. Zesty sandwich spread
44. Big bird
46. In the very back of the back
47. South American coastal country
50. Deriving from a particular culture
51. Marshy area
52. Trident point
53. Badgers' lair
55. Go from bottle to cup, like baby
56. Chicken coop bird
59. Man who goes to court?
61. Edmonton art mecca (abbr.)
62. Put away gear
63. Stir-fry vessels

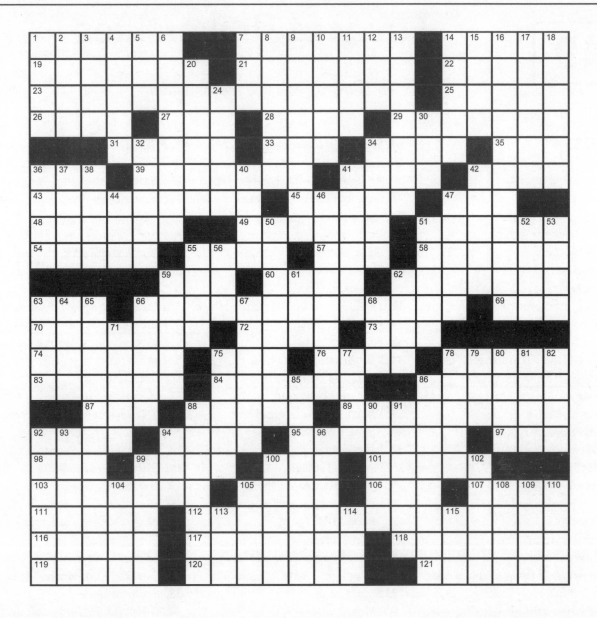

64. O'Toole of federal politics
65. Captain in *The Ghost and Mrs. Muir*
66. Parsimonious person
67. He flew too close to the sun
68. Greek letter
71. Ibiza bar plateful
75. Young haddock
77. Aryl anagram
78. He spikes the punch
79. 1989 Eurythmics hit: "Don't _____ Me Why"
80. Time interval
81. Lily type

82. Canadian Shield minerals
85. Monopoly game token
86. Day-timer component
88. Bicycles built for two
90. Greek poetry Muse
91. Whimpering, like a kitten
92. 1976 Margaret Atwood novel: *Lady* _____
93. Keened
94. Fruity cocktail: Mai _____
96. Bert and Ernie sometimes appeared on this CBC kids' show: _____ *Park*
99. Woodland mythological deity

100. Very handy
102. Indonesian island shared by two nations
104. Fashion frenzy?
105. Shania Twain blockbuster album: *Come On* _____
108. Child, colloquially
109. They start marching one by one
110. Gathering of athletics athletes
113. Caustic cleaning product
114. CN train component
115. Ontario Volleyball Association (abbr.)

SOLUTION ON PAGE 169

49 Eminent Universities

Early schools still teaching today

ACROSS

1. Very fast, musically: Allegro _____
6. Pierces
11. CRTC's US counterpart
14. 19th Hebrew letter
18. Straitlaced
19. FDR's malady
20. Cue sport
21. Pupil membrane
22. Scientist who studies rocks
24. "To Sir, with Love" singer
25. 1961 Gene Chandler hit: "Duke of _____"
26. Flat piece of concrete
27. Reluctant (to)
28. Bullet diameter
30. Coats invented in Canada's North
32. Speaks like a windbag
34. Pass legislation in the House of Commons
38. Sleep stage acronym
39. Full of thorns
40. Eric Braeden played this tycoon in *Titanic*
41. **Sackville school (since 1839)**
46. Port of Vancouver boats
48. A Grey Cup game can't end in this
49. 19th-C. boys' fiction scribe Horatio
50. Brain scan (abbr.)
51. Chinese gambling game: _____ bo
53. 1970s chart-toppers: Loggins and _____
55. Some Esso gas, for short
56. Montreal Notre-Dame Basilica instrument
58. Rest your eyes
60. Pit or seed, for example
61. Good, but not excellent
63. "Yikes! I saw a mouse!"
64. Petro-Canada competitor
66. Some chords
67. **Antigonish school (since 1853)**
71. Landlocked African country
74. Stations, in Saguenay
75. Zip
76. Staircase riser
80. Darwin work: *On the _____ of Species*
81. 1973 Constance Beresford-Howe novel: *The Book of _____*
82. Scatter seeds
84. *This American Life* host Glass
85. Broke a promise
87. Archery bow wood
89. Flake on a multi-grain bun
90. Savoury entree jelly
92. Lawn covering
93. Food, colloquially
95. **University now with campuses in Fredericton and Saint John (since 1785)**
98. Incense resin
100. They hang over babies' cribs
102. Bride of a Beatle
103. Burst a boil
104. Mixes
105. Great game result for Flames fans
109. Adding adornment
111. Eagle's claw
113. Wrangle in the boxing ring
115. Places (Lat.)
118. 1995 Bryan Adams movie song: "_____ You Ever Really Loved a Woman?"
119. Layer surrounding the sun
121. Illegally absent, in the military
122. "Don't count _____!"
123. Encouraged
124. Nosy neighbour, in a kibbutz
125. Unprincipled shoemaker?
126. Affirmative vote
127. Snarls
128. Tabulated

DOWN

1. Horned vipers
2. Inscribed stone pillar
3. Prince of Darkness
4. Like WestJet jets in the sky
5. Altar vow
6. Scare a spy?
7. Some college party costumes
8. Landed
9. **University in Lennoxville (since 1843)**
10. Drunkard
11. Most disgusting
12. 2010 Olympics skating venue: Pacific _____
13. Whisky brand: Canadian _____
14. **Ontario university (since 1841)**
15. Roe, to Romans
16. PSI word
17. 1990s Ontario Lieutenant Governor Jackman
20. Ancient Athenian philosopher
23. Camel's South American kin
28. Astute attitude, say
29. Offer comfort in stressful moments
31. Canadian TV channel: Stingray _____
33. Rivers, to a Spaniard
35. _____ the Hun
36. Made money, like the Royal Canadian Mint?
37. Picks up the tab
39. Omen
41. Red planet
42. Margarine a.k.a.
43. Sheepskin boots brand
44. Canadian polling firm
45. Fluid discharge
47. Non-Jewish, to a Jew
52. Powdery mineral residue
54. See 104-A

57. Smeltery employee
59. _____ wart
62. Tree or shrub name: _____ orange
64. Toronto International Film Festival premiere event
65. Hurry
68. Built more like a British supermodel?
69. Our fleet: Royal Canadian _____
70. *Objets d'art*
71. Tidbit for Fido
72. This surrounds a nipple
73. Former Vancouver Canuck Trevor
77. Indigenous dwelling (var.)
78. Canadian Olympic medal-winning showjumper Lamaze
79. Get ready to move house
82. Bawls
83. 1980 (Irish) Rovers hit: "_____ That a Party"
86. Poisonous tropical plant
88. Fuse metals with a torch
91. Made a rustling sound
94. South American country
96. **Ontario university (since 1878)**
97. Proper parts of speech
99. **Montreal university (since 1821)**
101. 1944 Pulitzer Prize for Poetry winner: Stephen Vincent _____
105. More cunning (var.)
106. Kitchen fan enclosures
107. Overturn
108. Dessert favourite in Quebec: _____ au sucre
110. Hello from a ship's helm
112. Gala anagram
114. Crazy Canuck Ken
115. _____-di-dah
116. Have a mortgage with BMO
117. Canadian ex-LPGA pro Dawn _____-Jones
119. Clasp in your arms
120. Myanmar coin

SOLUTION ON PAGE 170

105

50

Canada Cornucopia 7

ACROSS

1. Necklace fastener
6. Noted anthropologist Margaret
10. Gather at Toronto's St. Michael's Cathedral Basilica?
15. BC's Pacific geoduck, e.g.
19. Big cat crossbreed
20. Gross
21. Welland _____
22. Mair who wrote *Canada, is Anyone Listening?*
23. Get _____ start
24. "Whatcha _____?"
25. In an appropriate manner
26. Calgary speed skating facility: Olympic _____
27. 2021 Nobel Prize winner from Canada (with 31-A)
28. Chronicles
30. Hayworth/Mature movie: *My Gal _____*
31. See 27-A
32. Best-case _____
34. Spots
36. Legendary story
38. Wood-devouring insect
40. It precedes omega
42. Céline Dion movie song: "My _____ Will Go On"
46. This stage musical had its Canadian premiere in 1993: *Miss _____*
50. The Personal product (abbr.)
51. Posed for a painter
52. Kitty _____
53. It's sometimes bliss
55. Stipends for Canadian babies?
57. Oat anagram
58. Goad
59. River in Eastern Ontario
61. Light source
62. Beach wriggler
64. Yolk sheath
65. Sun, in Seville
66. Lineage of some early explorers of Canada
67. Kidney locale
69. Like a sultry voice
71. There's one on the back of this book
74. Sunbathe
75. Make romantic overtures
76. Like lamb chop bones
80. Lemon peel
81. Deliberate display of overt emotions
84. Social gathering on Oahu
85. South African political party (abbr.)
86. Concert bowl ticket info
87. Philosophical concept of Plato
89. Southern BC city
91. Have a meal
92. _____ and don'ts
93. Country singer Brooks, et al.
94. Gloomy, in poetry
95. www.nightwoodeditions.com, for one
96. Hand-held recording device, for short
98. End of a hammer
100. Croat or Czech
102. Bounces a ball like a Toronto Raptor
107. Bangkok citizen
110. BC place: Salmon _____
112. Peggy Parish kidlit character: _____ Bedelia
114. Serving spoon
115. Icy coating
116. Respond
118. Mob scene?
119. Wear away the shoreline
120. Sacred religious image (var.)
121. Okay, legally
122. Not false
123. More soft, like a tomato
124. Shampoo brand
125. Park plaything
126. Cheekiness
127. Reminders of surgeries

DOWN

1. Covers with siding, say
2. Fragrant spring blossom
3. Plant sourced for tequila
4. Ensconce in stone?
5. Canada's Shea Weber spent 10 years as an NHL this
6. Where trapeze artists cross
7. Discipline of prize won by 27-A/31-A
8. Similar to
9. They inherit kingdoms
10. 1971 Joni Mitchell track: "_____ of You"
11. Navigator's document
12. Picnic pests
13. Real Canadian Superstore deli purchase
14. In a sneaky manner
15. Make an afghan
16. Mount Vesuvius flow
17. Victoria, vis-à-vis Victoriaville?
18. Lay down cards, in canasta
29. Monroe's role in *Gentlemen Prefer Blondes*: Lorelei _____
33. Gave a new moniker
35. Córdoba cooking bulb?
37. 2006 Diana Krall album: *From _____ Moment On*
39. Things that don't really matter?
41. State of near unconsciousness
43. Rose oil
44. Lots and lots of paper?
45. Rhetorical figure of speech
46. Small mouthfuls of liquid
47. Agar anagram
48. Get _____ the ground floor
49. Long-time Canadian music journalist Peter
51. Captain's call for help

52. Necklace worn at 84-A
54. Of Cleopatra's river
55. Degree from U of C
56. Stain
60. *The National* newscaster Hanomansing
61. More steadfast
63. Wane
66. Utmost, in math class?
68. U of M program: _____ of Fine Arts
69. Likewise
70. Spear for a Bantu
71. Canadian Club, for example
72. Canadian frozen foods producer: High _____
73. Male of the family

75. The Eskimos (now Elks) did this on 11/29/15
77. Third down option in the CFL
78. Per person
79. Annual club fees
81. Barnyard bird
82. Spoil
83. Subtly dangerous
86. Like an achy loser?
88. Wordy walkers?
90. Insightful
92. Sidetracks
95. Release a fishing line
96. Mother, in Manchester
97. Wooden boxes
99. Canadian dining chain founded in 1982

101. Tim Hortons beverage option
103. Containing element #56
104. Drug for people with Parkinson's
105. Canadian Indigenous tribe leader
106. Prophetic people
107. Stumble
108. You might go for one on the Bruce Trail
109. Love, to a Spaniard
111. Biblical visitors to Mary and Joseph
113. Currency used in Turkey
117. Valencia conqueror: El _____

SOLUTION ON PAGE 170

51

Ready for the Runway

Famous fashion houses

ACROSS

1. Cross, like the Capilano Suspension Bridge
5. Sign of a scrape
9. *Charlotte's* _____
12. Cut the grass
15. Frenchman's vineyard
18. It's beside the radius
19. Turned up as requested
20. Australian bird
21. Some US attack helicopters (var.)
23. Greek letter
24. Mineral formerly mined in Quebec
26. Go back over your steps
27. **Yves co-founded this French fashion house in 1961**
29. Outdoor living space: _____-in porch
30. Toronto museum: Hockey _____ of Fame
31. Party attendee
33. Passionate
34. Multi-headed mythological monster
38. Some calendar components
41. Much, in music
42. Tippet-Richardson helps with this task
44. Links
45. 1970 Carpenters hit: "(They Long to Be) _____ to You"
47. This puzzle's got your number?
48. National award established in 1967: _____ of Canada
50. Like some alibis
55. 1974 BTO hit: "Takin' _____ of Business"
57. Valuable personal skill
59. Canada's Catherine O'Hara played the mom in this: _____ *Alone*
60. **Luxury fashion and perfume house since 1952**
65. "In other words" alternative
67. Prize won by Alice Munro in 2013
68. Lack of motivation
69. Lazes
70. Astilbe (var.)
72. Twilled fabric
73. Annual CBC Radio competition: Canada _____
74. **British house known for its trench coats**
75. Fog
76. Pretentious sort, in Swindon
78. Russian car
79. Sultans' footstools?
81. Himalayan creatures, supposedly
84. They give to the Canadian Cancer Society
90. Numbskull
92. Select
93. Water protozoa (var.)
94. Trades
98. IOU holders
101. On _____ and a prayer
102. Fish with sharp teeth (var.)
104. Udders
105. Georgia neighbour (abbr.)
107. Scraps or dregs
109. **French fashion house since 1854**
115. Energy sapping malady in Manchester
116. Grieved
117. Positivity about the future
118. Most on edge
119. Shipboard affirmative
120. Cost of riding Calgary's CTrain
121. Fencing weapon
122. _____ Lanka
123. Drug Enforcement Administration (abbr.)
124. Petro-Canada retails this
125. Strata discoveries
126. Gordon Lightfoot song: "If You Could Read My _____"

DOWN

1. HMCS *Victoria*, et al.
2. Response to a judge's question
3. _____-social
4. Bread for grandmother?
5. Milan landmark: La _____
6. Famed cellist Pablo
7. Capable of walking
8. Labatt makes this
9. She's hired to breastfeed
10. Showed your true feelings
11. Coach Canada vehicle
12. Former Quebec premier: Pierre-_____ Johnson
13. Vocalists' company: Edmonton _____
14. British river workers
15. **Coco founded this fashion house in 1910**
16. Newish
17. Inured
22. Personal philosophy
25. Seamlessly transitioned
28. Express gratitude to
29. Hair salon employee
32. Pouch for a yolk
34. _____ *Pinafore*
35. Alanis Morissette smash: "_____ Oughta Know"
36. Rental from Rogers, formerly
37. Canada won three silver medals at these Olympic Games
39. Cause fatigue
40. Annoyed or angry
43. **Lady Gaga starred in a 2021 film about this fashion family**
46. Habitual imbiber
49. Three-time Grammy winner Lou
51. To-do list item
52. Pneumonia type
53. Important Muslim person (var.)
54. YYZ annoyance
56. Eureka moment exclamation

58. _____-boom-bah
60. Gadget, in Greenwich
61. Some Nunavut people
62. Old Russian distance measurement
63. Sister of Clio
64. Ultimate degree, in math
65. He fawns over a frog?
66. OAS word
67. Pen's end
69. Bucharest cash unit
70. Quebec compass point
71. **The devil wears this in a 2006 movie title**
73. Fairmont Hot Springs and Panorama, in BC
74. Deep-sea echinoderm

76. Notebook
77. Prune a rose bush
78. Some scalp parasites
80. Given the wrong moniker
82. Embodiments
83. Kleenex
85. Muscat resident
86. _____ Democratic Party
87. Sensei's attire item
88. Emulated Andre De Grasse
89. Line part (abbr.)
91. One of ten digits
94. Picky nursery rhyme pair
95. _____ schnitzel
96. **Giorgio's fashion house since 1975**

97. Glass units
99. Former southeast Asian federation
100. Storm warning word on The Weather Network
103. Pernod flavouring
106. Artists' unclad models
108. "Bye-bye," to a Brit
110. Just the facts, ma'am?
111. Those folks
112. Fast African antelope
113. 2002 Lisa Moore Giller Prize nominee
114. Impoverished condition
116. Stay behind the crowd

52

Who Am I? 2

A renowned literary lady

ACROSS

1. Not short
5. Demean
10. Guess Who hit: "_____ the Land"
15. Many
19. Black-and-white cookie
20. Rustic retreat in the Rockies
21. Puts a curse on
22. Canadian-born Perry Mason portrayer
23. Pilot who's great at golf?
25. **She won the 1996 Giller Prize for this novel**
27. **She is… (with 43-D)**
28. Compare to a summer's day?
30. Whet an appetite, for example
31. Untruthful person
32. Going out with
33. Affirmative vote in the House of Commons
34. Wool shop product
37. Crude shack
38. Plant sowing place
42. Walk in water
43. Walter Huston was the first Canadian male to be nominated for this US prize
47. Harper government cabinet minister Bev
48. Eye part
49. By way of, old style
50. We thank these Canadians for their service
51. *Around the World in Eighty Days* protagonist Phileas
52. Place to hang a pocket watch
53. Holey dairy product
57. Sponges and tortes
58. Olden-days Scottish burgh municipal building
60. Paul Brandt hit: "My _____ Has a History"
61. Neatness
62. Spending money in Spain
63. Art able to
64. Keep the car on the road
65. Like a bearded bristle
66. Glow
67. J.M. Barrie's boy who wouldn't grow up
70. Menial workers
71. Vertebrae enclosure in the back
73. Polymeric molecule (abbr.)
74. Canadian Forces group
75. Canadian actor Rubinek who starred in *Warehouse 13*
76. Make a declaration
77. Cesspools
78. US intel grp.
79. This TV reality show had 38 seasons from 1948 to 2014
83. Modernist poet Pound
84. Canine shelters
86. Some woodworking tools
87. Theft at Rogers Centre?
88. Before, in times past
89. Pancakes, in Pointe-Claire
91. "Quit that!"
93. Inactive period
96. Prolific writer of fables
97. **Her 2019 graphic novel**
101. **Her 2019 sequel to *The Handmaid's Tale* (with "*The*")**
103. Blue-eyed feline
105. Safe from gales, on ship
106. 1953 Dean Martin hit: "That's _____"
107. Slang for a TV: _____ box
108. Cucumbers grow on this
109. Happy
110. Taboo activities
111. The Brick sells these
112. Prepare to publish *Maclean's*

DOWN

1. Rich earth for the garden
2. A Canuck has one on his jersey
3. _____-do-well
4. Tricky cricket manoeuvres
5. City in Ghana
6. Farm machine
7. New Brunswick and Maine do this
8. Bro or sis
9. Bring into servitude
10. In an unsteady manner
11. Humpheys who won the Rogers Writers' Trust Fiction Prize for *Afterimage* in 2000
12. Abruptly dismissing a logger?
13. *Mens* _____
14. They try to write a term paper?
15. One woman travelling overseas?
16. Traditional Oahu gathering
17. Tolkien beings
18. The white spruce is Manitoba's official this
24. Gladly, in olden days
26. Avarice
29. Big ticket _____
32. Extinct flightless birds
34. Saskatchewan city: _____ Current
35. Semi-desert plateau in South Africa
36. **Her first novel (with "The")**
37. Exceptionally severe
38. Quell a hunger
39. **She won this prestigious honour twice (2000 and 2019)**
40. Landscaper's trimming tool
41. Hammarskjöld, et al.
43. **See 27-A**
44. Vouchers
45. Prevent a disaster
46. Alberta, directionally from Saskatchewan
51. Studio sound-mixing device
53. Skin irritations
54. Leon's or Canadian Tire
55. Reddish-brown dye

56. Canvas display tripod
57. Basket for freshly caught fish
59. Bugs _____
61. Her Ontario birth city
63. It precedes pepper and powder
64. Mexican man's title
65. Cliffside nest
66. Stompin' Tom Connors song: "Bud the _____"
67. Repairs a rutted road
68. Sinuses
69. Like a twangy voice
70. Sprain soother: Ice _____
71. Without, to a Quebecer

72. Enjoys a vacation in the great outdoors
75. Classic Miller play: *Death of a _____*
77. Akita owner's objection?
79. Compound used in glass polishing
80. Sheaths and shifts
81. Mafia head
82. State of being germ-free
85. Fit together, like Matryoshka dolls
87. Weeps
89. Printer brand name

90. Like something old that's new again?
91. Polynesian islands group
92. Shipping allowances
93. Pre-wedding guys' gathering
94. Blab
95. Out on the Adriatic?
97. Ragamuffin
98. LSD, for one
99. Indian royal
100. "Don't change," in proofreading-speak
102. Genre of moody music
104. Phrase heard twice at the altar

SOLUTION ON PAGE 170

53

Ships Ahoy!

Vessels of the silver screen

ACROSS

1. Diplomacy
5. Family pet, in Frontenac
9. Greatest Canadian Tommy Douglas, by birth
13. Scents
19. Unbleached linen shade
20. Munich Mr.
21. BC catch
22. Newbie
23. Ounce at the bar, say
24. **1975 *Jaws* boat**
25. Dismounted from a steed
26. Earhart of flying fame
27. Class at U of S
29. Far North shelter
31. **Chinese junk in 2007's *Pirates of the Caribbean: At World's End***
32. Helps an Ottawa Senator score?
33. Soft drinks
34. Attila's people
35. Most disingenuous
37. Pilfered
39. Quick
43. Ontario place that shares its name with a region in France
47. Receive a gift
48. Hesitant
50. BC community: Bella _____
51. See 33-A
53. Not ready for picking
54. Eye doctor, in olden days
56. Nursery bed
58. Uttered, in Utah?
59. Delusional
61. Graceful, like a Miss Universe Canada contestant
63. "Intrepid" Canadian William Stephenson served as this in WWII
64. **1968 Beatles movie transport**
69. Saskatchewan Minor Football (abbr.)
72. Coughs up
73. Gingerbread recipe ingredient
77. Bard's bane or boon: _____ justice
81. Lions _____ Bridge
82. Priest's cassock
83. Largest of the terriers
85. Chops veggies
89. Canada Dry offering: _____ water
90. Occurred
92. Title, in Terrebonne
93. They stand on their own two feet?
94. Some condiments, in Candiac
95. Apply chrism, old style
96. Thrifty
98. River that flows to the Caspian Sea
99. Boston resident's houseplant?
101. Scholarly
106. **"The Ship of Dreams," in a 1998 blockbuster**
110. Fragrant shrub
111. *The National* panel participant?
112. Good-looking guy, in mythology
113. Boyfriend, colloquially
114. **Mythological ship in a 1963 film about Jason and his crew**
116. Canadian Taylor who first landed a triple Axel in competition
117. Pie-eyed
118. Author Ayn
119. 2012 Taylor Swift hit: "I _____ You Were Trouble"
120. Organs for listening
121. Transformer type
122. Poker pot contribution
123. 20th-C. Canadian Governor General: _____ Grey
124. Louvre board

DOWN

1. Popular plug-in car
2. Sore spots?
3. Foam clogs brand
4. Little Richard classic: "_____ Frutti"
5. Laugh softly
6. Unorthodox belief
7. Joan of _____
8. Walked around aimlessly
9. Top of the head
10. Massive statues
11. State south of Ontario
12. Little tater bit
13. Patient's medical history
14. Easy victories
15. Anne Murray hit: "Talk It _____ in the Morning"
16. BC place: 100 _____ House
17. Alberta Climate Information Service (abbr.)
18. Caribbean and Celebes
28. **Destroyer–minesweeper in a '54 film about a mutiny**
30. Early Bee Gees single: "I've _____ Get a Message to You"
31. 18th-C. Swiss mathematician
34. Birch family tree
36. I, to an old Roman
38. Actual adage?
39. Parasite on a Pekingese
40. Some female relatives
41. Brew some oolong
42. A Kennedy, for short
43. 1987 Burt and Liza thriller–comedy: *Rent-_____*
44. Ricky Martin #1: "Livin' la Vida _____"
45. Tart
46. Assuage concerns
49. Make a choice
51. Fence-crossing steps
52. Searched for a Cub pack?
55. Costa del _____

57. Swiss Chalet entree choice
60. Funny verse about a mutt?
61. Whispered interjection
62. Stelco smelting waste
65. Mink's cousin
66. UN labour standards agency (abbr.)
67. **Captain Nemo commanded this in a '54 Disney adventure**
68. Prohibit, to an attorney
69. Petty disagreements
70. Wavy-patterned silk
71. Not tamed
74. Of rational mind

75. British kidlit scribe Blyton
76. Minute bits of time?
78. These bills are purple in Canada
79. SIN no. cards, for example
80. Horse's protective covering
84. Linear accelerator, for short
86. Down below, to Diocletian
87. Type of fritter
88. Green eggs layer
91. Rebellious
93. Farm rodent catcher
97. Radiation detection device: _____ counter
98. Harmonious agreement

100. Evade
102. Plunges into the pool
103. Perfect
104. Canada's most easterly national park: _____ Nova
105. Bond films baddy Blofeld
106. Indents
107. Bone _____
108. RONA purchase
109. Colony builders
110. Like meat without much fat
113. Bikini's top half
115. Ribonucleic Acid (abbr.)

SOLUTION ON PAGE 171

54 Whoo Are They?

A letter pattern leads the way

ACROSS

1. Defendant's courtroom utterance
5. Old Venetian judge
9. Meadow bleaters
14. United States Marine _____
19. Warmth
20. It abuts Afghanistan
21. With regard to
22. Cleaned your plate
23. Mentally unstable
25. Spicy meat and rice dish
26. Move obliquely
27. Story
28. Biblical plague insects
30. **Former federal Conservative Party leader Erin**
31. Samantha Stevens did this on a sitcom
34. Abate
35. Former flyer: TransCanada _____ Lines
37. Top Rogers Cup entrant
38. Stratford ON theatre name
39. Danson of *Cheers*
41. Burkina _____
43. Most friendly
45. Area's plant and animal life
47. Rajah's mate
49. Eye operation tool
51. First Nations teachers
53. _____ Angeles
54. Spicy cuisine option: Tex-_____
55. Jousting weapon
59. Long-running Discovery show: *Canada's Worst* _____
61. Fermented milk liquor
63. Jump-start a jalopy
65. *A Nightmare on* _____ *Street*
68. Do as you're instructed
69. Sparkling wine description
71. 2007 Diana Krall cover song: "You _____ My Head"
72. **April Wine front man Myles**
74. Senior diplomat, say

75. **Crazy Canuck Todd**
77. Stravinsky or Sikorsky
78. Finds
80. Look like Tom?
81. Blunder
82. Pancake topping, in Taos
84. Imitated Marcel Marceau?
85. Not awake
87. Monarch, in old Ethiopia
89. U of M teaching aides
90. Canadian Crown corporation: _____ Rail
91. Serengeti lion families
95. Pierre and Justin
97. Nonsensical
99. First Hebrew letter
100. Become overcast, archaically
103. Laotian currency units
105. Desecrate
107. Architectural arch component
108. Canadian cell service company
109. Off-roader's ride, for short
111. Chaotic street disturbance
113. Medical facility: Canada Diagnostic _____
115. **Award-winning Canadian author Margaret**
117. Narcissist's sojourn?
120. Marco's preferred shirt?
121. Victor, for short
122. *Corner Gas* star Butt
123. Like a middle-class mentality?
127. Suggestive of the supernatural
128. Sensibly use resources
129. Facts or figures
130. Male deer
131. Maples and magnolias
132. Hour for mid-morning prayers
133. Commotions
134. Transmitted

DOWN

1. Advanced deg. from McGill
2. Necklace for a luau

3. *Material World* actress Jayne
4. Shamed, to Shakespeare
5. Alberta power provider: _____ Energy
6. Rob anagram
7. Highlander or Hibernian
8. Give to Queen's University
9. Gaps in old manuscripts
10. Maltreats
11. Canadian-born comic Sahl
12. Joint sac
13. Hogs' home on the farm
14. CBC *Strays* ensemble
15. Lethargic
16. Changes decor
17. Frying chicken
18. Calgary Olympic Oval activity: _____ skating
24. Final (abbr.)
29. Bistros
30. Window seat spot
31. 1995 family film about a pig
32. _____ *Under the Sun*
33. That gal
36. Intact offering (abbr.)
40. Jim who coached several CFL teams
42. Hydrocarbon type
44. Scurry like a crustacean?
46. 1950s Canadian plane: Avro _____
48. Scandinavian country (abbr.)
50. Earth "spins" on this
52. Delphi oracle
54. Viral online images
56. Cancellation
57. **00's Vancouver Canuck Matt**
58. Glyceride, for one
60. Rattlesnake's toxin
61. Excited (with "up")
62. Insurrectionist
64. Barometric pressure unit
65. Patronage (var.)
66. Computer access code

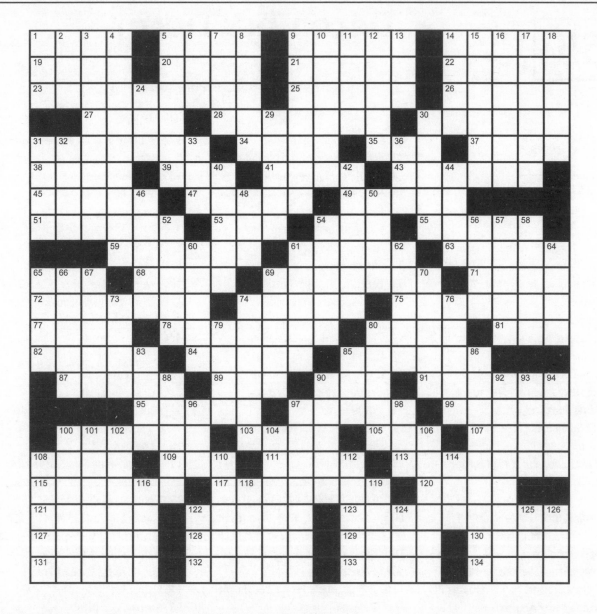

67. **Three-time Giller Prize nominee Lisa**
69. Lavishes with affection (with "on")
70. Lecherous looker
73. Shoppers _____ Mart
74. Serviette fabric
76. BC performance group: Pacific _____ Victoria
79. List references
80. Sacred song in church
83. Young ruffian
85. Have a bug
86. Drone description

88. Caesar's light lunch?
90. Golfing hat part
92. **Business and philanthropy magnate Michael**
93. Thrust-and-parry sword
94. Anka wrote this Jones classic: "_____ A Lady"
96. Gathered for a conference
97. Saliva
98. Cat Lake ON airport code
100. Hesitate
101. This pops up on websites
102. U of T dorm sharer
104. Sarcastic 1996 Alanis Morissette single?

106. Xeroxes, for short
108. Gem surface
110. Gusto
112. Leg bone
114. Yuletide quaff
116. Unlocks, to a bard
118. Neutral or reverse
119. *On Golden* _____
122. Cricket match club
124. Aliens' craft
125. "Painted Ladies" singer Thomas
126. CFB staffer

SOLUTION ON PAGE 171

55

December Decor

Adorning abodes for the holidays

ACROSS

1. Swindles
6. Cathedral areas
11. Recipe measurement (abbr.)
15. "Let it stand," to a proofreader
19. Not spoken
20. Local official in some provinces
21. Pearl Harbor island
22. Canadian *North of 60* star Keeper
23. French naval craft
24. **It might be a star or an angel**
26. Pismires
27. GOC bureaucracy, say
29. Wealthy ones, in Britspeak
30. Quits harping or haranguing
32. 1976 Burton Cummings hit: "Stand _____"
33. The Queen held one on June 2, 1953
35. Aim at a woodcock?
37. 1971 Poppy Family single: "_____ Evil Grows"
38. Red eye source
39. International environmental accord signed by Canada in 2002
41. Fodder on the farm
44. Guided
45. Manitoba town: _____ Pas
47. Grandmothers, for short
49. Swimming
51. "Vamoose!"
53. He wears shining armour
55. Sobriquet, in Sherbrooke
56. Equipment for Canada's golden Tokyo women's eight crew
60. Connects
62. Ilk
64. **Jewish home candelabra**
66. CBC reality program: *Dragons' _____*
67. "Give him _____ of his own medicine"
70. Top part of a house

72. Bring good cheer
73. Not modern
74. **Biblical figures tableau**
78. Falsehood for Canada's Brooke Henderson?
79. Gather, bit by bit
81. Perv, perhaps
82. Cords anagram
83. Brett, to Bobby Hull
84. **Banister decoration**
87. Bring in the crops
89. Out of bed for the day
91. Estimate phrase
92. Ontario Association of Broadcasters (abbr.)
94. Traps
97. Air Canada arrival times, for short
98. Like many major streets
101. Tiny tipple in West Lothian
102. Dave Thomas, to Ian, for short
103. Former union for Canadian car factory employees (1985–2013)
106. Shoe component
108. Friendship
110. Picturesque Nova Scotia place: Peggys _____
114. Wall hanging in a French town?
116. Muslim household living quarters for women
118. Fall into decay
119. Singer Chaka
120. She interprets oracles
123. Italy's capital
124. Draw boundaries
126. Snakes that constrict
127. **Popular plant**
131. Foolish
132. Anne Murray's vocal range
133. _____ of Capri
134. Like the square kid in school
135. Inconsequential one: Ham-and-_____

136. Chemistry Nobel Prize winner Otto
137. Tattled
138. Put on a party gown?
139. Dopers

DOWN

1. Begins
2. Buyer beware word
3. In a mordant manner
4. **You might kiss under this**
5. Oats anagram
6. Blood vessel
7. _____ capita
8. Get the picture?
9. Later afternoon Anglican church services
10. Determined to
11. Tennis stroke technique for Canada's Leylah Fernandez
12. Protestant denom.
13. Backyard hut
14. Sound of a well-oiled engine
15. Kind of bacterial infection
16. **Glistening thread**
17. Completely whole
18. Sampled a bite
25. Geishas' belts
28. Prod
31. Long-time Canadian filmmaker Don
34. German city on the Rhine
36. Liveliness
40. Clavell novel: _____-*Pan*
42. 1960s cartoon: _____ *Ant*
43. *HNIC* airing
46. Church cry of praise
48. Secretarial skill
50. You might buy one at Ace Hardware
51. Out of this world, to Roberta Bondar?
52. Prevents progress

53. Ship's speed measurement
54. Mythological Helen's town
57. Uzbekistan body of water
58. Soldiers' MREs, say
59. Sateen shine
61. Ontario pharmacy chain
63. Throw a pitch
65. More penurious
66. Hidden, by the Saint Bernard owner?
68. Polite phrase in Plessisville: _____ vous plaît
69. Veer anagram
71. Canadian agricultural business lender (abbr.)
75. Treats a sprained ankle
76. Stats for MLB pitchers

77. Lillehammer Olympics nation (abbr.)
80. "Thanks _____!"
85. Ross CanLit classic story: "The Lamp at _____"
86. Eurasian crows
88. Quantifiable characteristic
90. **They're hung by the chimney with care**
93. Soothing soak
95. Dodge truck type
96. Arabic world VIP
99. Astute
100. Had a craving
102. It follows giga
103. 1982 single from The Clash: "Rock the _____"

104. Pupil surround
105. **Door decoration**
107. Canucks and Oilers
109. Canadian magazine for moms and dads: _____ Parent
111. Electrical resistance measurement
112. More self-absorbed
113. Passes through a doorway
115. Firebug's felony
117. Make a revision
121. Barbecue rod
122. Somewhat blah
125. In _____ of
128. Down with the flu
129. Three, in Turin
130. Areas of exploration for Freud

SOLUTION ON PAGE 171

56

The Greatest of All...

In Canada

ACROSS

1. Type of black tea
6. "Thou _____ not then be false to any man"
11. True piece of info
15. Husky's greeting
19. Clearing in the forest
20. Spry
21. To read, in Rivière-Rouge
22. Lake Superior description
23. Credit _____
24. Summary
25. US credit card?
26. "_____ do you good"
27. Dragonfly scientific classification order
29. Oust from a rental unit
31. Opposite of a miser
33. **Insurance company: Great _____**
35. Order in the court?
37. Singer Britney
38. Ontario ex-premier Bob
39. Wild and free
41. Freshwater fish
43. Austrian river
44. Royal Air Force (abbr.)
46. Snatch hold of
48. Excessively ornamental, in furnishings
50. Barrette
52. Court calendar
54. Smidgen
55. Stage of sleep
58. Hair cleansing product
60. Actresses Arden and Plumb
62. Prickly plants
65. Photo, for short
66. Son of Cain
69. Ivy League university
71. Description of some electrical resistance units
72. 1985 Canadian legislation: Access to Information _____

73. Antenna
75. Feline sounds (var.)
78. Debtor's promissory note (abbr.)
79. Food Network Canada offerings
81. School zone driving speed
83. Outrigger canoes (var.)
84. Compass direction in Quebec
85. Interpret incorrectly, aurally
88. Asian childminder
90. Irons
92. Caspian _____
93. Arborist's adage?
95. Lagoon islands
98. Lab experiment rodents
99. Scrape or cut
102. Ardent environmentalist: _____ hugger
103. TD Bank investment option (abbr.)
104. Assassinated, old style
106. Lacklustre
108. South African antelope
110. Have a loan with CIBC
113. _____ and Hardy
115. Butcher's claptrap?
117. **Newfoundland place: Great _____**
120. Set a goal
122. Boulevards
124. Refuses to comply
125. Gangster's switchblade
126. Karate training centre
128. Dependable
130. Entreaties in the courtroom?
131. Not crazy
132. Mature
133. 1994 Céline Dion track: "Think _____"
134. Wash with a solvent
135. Yore anagram
136. Guess Who hit: "These _____"
137. Change
138. Scruffs

DOWN

1. Luminous
2. Rogers Centre sandwich?
3. Savoury turnover
4. Temporarily, to Tiberius
5. Genre of Canadian bands Triumph and Helix
6. Tim Hortons pot
7. See 132-A
8. Beach Boys hit: "Wouldn't It Be _____"
9. **NWT body of water: Great _____**
10. Lukewarm
11. CP train component
12. William Tell's skill
13. Work gang
14. Dallas state
15. **Moniker for Canada: The Great _____**
16. Won, like Andre De Grasse?
17. They keep their eyes on you
18. Chops down trees
28. Toronto International Film Festival (abbr.)
30. Butt
32. Moniker for Hamilton's newspaper (with "*The*")
34. As a result of
36. Paddock pace
40. Pendulum's path
42. Glance at 32-D
45. Mollify
47. Flock of quails
49. Bard's offering
50. Mexican restaurant chain formerly in Canada
51. _____ intolerant
52. Long-time Canadian kids show: *Polka Dot _____*
53. Oilers or Alouettes
56. Most abounding with Dutch trees?
57. Cell division processes

58. Uncontrollable muscle contraction

59. Gretzky moniker: The Great _____

61. Lingerie model's error?

63. CFL quarterbacks, for example

64. Back ends of bunnies, say

67. Canadian Ice Service (abbr.)

68. Hawaiian tree

70. Cob of corn

74. Historic Toronto attraction: Casa _____

76. Hit from 37-A: "_____!... I Did It Again"

77. Many Canadians fought in this: The Great _____

80. Quebec waterway: Great _____

82. 100- or 60-, for a light bulb

86. It's smaller than a horse

87. SWAT bust, say

89. Bird that lives in Canada: Great _____

91. Chicle gum source

94. St. John's _____

96. Felixstowe livestock field

97. _____ year

100. Pitcher

101. Northern Saskatchewan village: Pelican _____

103. Steak preference at The Keg

104. Walk with a swagger

105. Wolfish adjective?

107. *Terry Fox: His Story*, for short

109. Pantry

111. Become sager than magi?

112. Long-running CBC show: *The Fifth _____*

113. This corrals dogies

114. Windowsill

116. Fusilli or fettuccine

118. BC place: _____ Grove

119. Curvy letters

121. Small boat

123. Use a letter opener

127. Ontario-born NHLer Thornton

129. Golden Olympic sport for Virtue and Moir: _____ dance

57

Les *Liz*

Women who made their mark

ACROSS

1. Attack with a knife
5. Snaps one's fingers
11. *Sextette* star West
14. Loblaws buggy
18. Sonata's closing
19. A firehose connects to this
21. Canadian specialty channel
22. US state
23. Petri dish gel
24. Trying person?
25. **Original Boney M singer Liz**
27. Italian infant
29. Vet clinic pill
31. Preened
32. Remove, for short
34. Young Drivers of Canada students
36. **Liz of *Austin Powers: International Man of Mystery***
40. Hairstyling product
43. Pollen-producing flower part
44. Famed MA university
47. Swords for duelling
48. Hungarian tongue
50. WSW opposite
51. **Long-time US gossip columnist Liz**
53. TD RRSP, e.g.
54. Bluebell, for one
56. National economic measurement (abbr.)
58. Monty Python member Eric
59. The Travellers hit: "_____ Land Is Your Land"
60. Papa, in Papineau
61. "Just _____ thought!"
63. Belatedly
65. It ferries bricks or mortar
66. Foretell
67. Please, to a German
69. Carollers' beverage, for short
70. Commits larceny
72. Spirited stallion
74. Votes in an Edmonton city councillor
78. Sodom escapee
79. Jyoti Gondek was elected Calgary's this in 2021
80. Central Alberta lake
82. _____ and cry
83. Transportation for the manicurist?
87. Queen's Park city (abbr.)
88. Pine for a girl?
89. Lasso
90. Andean tubers
91. 28-D, e.g.
93. Lets the livestock out
95. Paddled a dinghy
96. **Liz who founded Animal Alliance of Canada**
98. Blue Rodeo performance
100. Like a zealous beaver?
101. Climb Alberta's Mount Rundle
102. Distressed vessel's call
103. Closer to
106. Exercise regime: _____ Bo
107. **Liz who played Cleopatra**
108. Body related
110. Passerine bird
112. Hard drive deletion
115. Use elbow grease
118. More dull
123. **Liz who co-wrote *He's Just Not That Into You***
125. Japanese monarch
127. 1985 Bryan Adams hit: "One Night _____ Affair"
128. Woman's vocal range
129. Swiss climber's peak
130. Entourage
131. Soprano's solo
132. Examination
133. Justin's dad's initials
134. Underwater exploration systems
135. Governor General's residence: Rideau _____

DOWN

1. Lesion covering
2. Attire for Julius Caesar
3. Dora Mavor Moore Award playwright nominee Pettle
4. Canadian pair skating icon Underhill
5. **Wyoming congresswoman Liz first elected in 2017**
6. Popular cleaning product
7. Bouncers might check these
8. Traditional seafood serving: Nova Scotia _____ Cakes
9. Knock out in a bout, colloquially
10. Nylon fishing line
11. Stay-at-home _____
12. Tire shop job
13. The Keg plate
14. West Coast salmon (var.)
15. Throat-clearing sound
16. Cause annoyance
17. Snitched
20. Makes plumb
26. Toe woes
28. That is, in old Rome
30. Satisfy a craving
33. Beverage made with milk, carbonated water and syrup
35. Pealed
36. Scrubby UK tracts
37. Skeet shooting result?
38. Live in Lillooet, say
39. Dregs
41. Canada and the US share this lake
42. _____ *Abner*
44. Noon, in Laval
45. "_____ cost you!"
46. Shania song: "We've Got Something _____ Don't"
48. Pre-owned
49. **Liz who founded a famous fashion line**
52. Gnat

55. Out of bed, say

57. *Front Page Challenge* groups

60. Address component: _____ code

62. "Make _____ double"

64. Throw the dice

66. Lucien Bouchard first led this party: _____ Québécois

67. Louisiana landform

68. CP job title

71. Roster of VIPs?

73. Kenora's old name: _____ Portage

75. Like some Handel works

76. Birthplace of Elvis

77. Farm field planting machine

81. Canada hockey rival (abbr.)

83. Captured Cdn. soldiers, in WWII

84. 1980 Martha and the Muffins single: "_____ Beach"

85. Royal's platform

86. Frivolous piece for a pianist?

88. Prefix meaning "massive"

89. A little lewd

92. Rookie (var.)

94. 30th premier of PEI Binns

95. Japanese city

97. Boredom

99. Agate and amethyst

104. Cap adjunct

105. Sieve

107. *The John Larroquette Show* co-star Liz

108. Type of tie

109. 2013 Arcade Fire song: "Here _____ the Night Time"

111. Aroma

112. *Coup d'*_____

113. Reign

114. Emulates Mike Myers

116. _____ the minute

117. Horse rider's strap

119. Uninspired

120. When repeated, a Polynesian place

121. Nefarious

122. Actual

124. Choose

126. Health care helper (abbr.)

SOLUTION ON PAGE 172

58

Canada Cornucopia 8 Challenger

No three-letter answers

ACROSS

1. Lily type
5. Loses intensity
9. Downtown Halifax landmark: _____ Parade
14. Sidewalk edges
19. Canadian celebrity chef Crawford
20. Indigenous Manitoba people
21. Handle
22. Very obvious
23. 24 Sussex Drive grounds building
25. Place des Arts performance group: _____ de Montréal
26. Former Egyptian kingdom
27. Irregularities
28. B, on a chemistry table
29. Timepiece
30. Share your point of view
31. Smooch
32. Nightclub singalong activity
34. Removes rind
37. Gulches
40. Gnats and ants
41. She starred with Kelsey on *Frasier*
42. Brings back a furloughed worker
44. Cried
46. In an otiose manner
48. Symbol of Canada
53. Marketplace issues advocacy group: _____ Association of Canada
54. Sandwich on a long bun
56. Perimeter
57. Microscope component
58. Leans (on)
59. Canadian Forces youth program participant
60. Rush's Geddy Lee, for example
64. Shoe parts
65. Become rusty
67. Provide gear

68. Domed dwellings in Northern Canada
70. Cellphone, in Britspeak
71. Bergman's role in *Casablanca*
72. Aimless, on the ocean?
73. Pelts with stones, old style
78. Stage show light
80. Scientific study of congenital abnormalities
81. St. John's is on this coast of Newfoundland
82. Gateways
84. It borders the Arabian Sea
85. Kills, biblically
88. Heartfelt
90. Fabric for gloves or shoes
91. Amazed
93. Teapot cover, in Canterbury
94. "Marry in _____, repent at leisure"
97. Former Air Canada low-cost subsidiary
98. Drenched, at the laundromat?
100. Document binding process
104. Beatles song: "Any Time _____"
105. CBC _____ One
106. Subdued colour
107. Turned off the sound
108. Jury or judge, say
109. Swamp plant
110. Sheep farm livestock
111. Nobility folk in England
112. Catch in a trap
113. Is incorrect
114. Jordan who won a most promising female vocalist Juno in 1989

DOWN

1. Bit of plankton
2. Vancouver-born *Deadpool* star (with 79-D)
3. Golden rule word

4. Techniques that improve memory
5. Cause of some food recalls
6. Canadian ex-NHLer Bourque was one for 21 seasons
7. They beg
8. Glimpses
9. Teardrop, for example
10. Rests comfortably
11. Loath (to)
12. Octavia was married to this emperor
13. Sipped
14. Tangible, on the building site?
15. Soft palate parts (var.)
16. Fire up a computer again
17. Cheese units
18. It supports a tomato plant
24. Chance occurrences, in olden days
31. Lay to rest
33. Crispy, crunchy fruit
34. Cleaning product: _____ and Span
35. Bingo alternative
36. Neighbour of Pakistan
38. Some paints for Emily Carr
39. Forging tool
42. US vocalist LeAnn
43. Before dusk times, to a bard
45. Christian _____ Church of Canada
47. Spring flower
48. But, in Bécancour
49. Shakespearean king
50. Type of tuber
51. Got older
52. It precedes "nationale" in Quebec
54. Old-style servant
55. Spaniards' hurrahs
58. *Cat on a Hot Tin* _____
59. Personal motto
60. Long-time Canadian telecommunications company

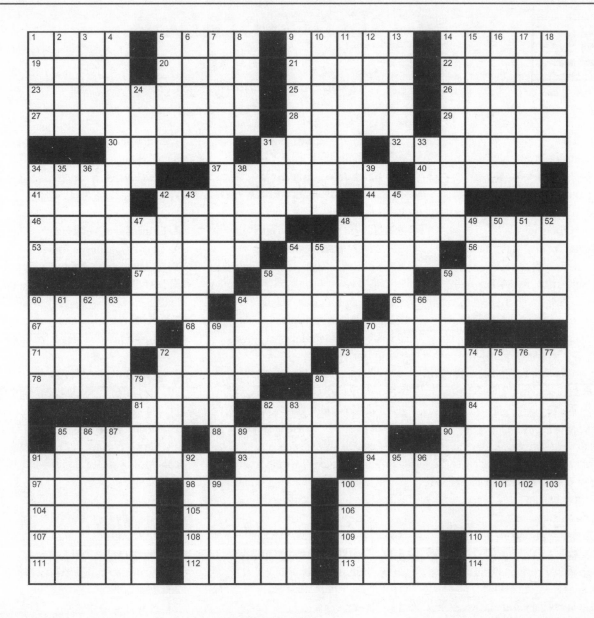

61. Watery colour?
62. Edmonton and Ottawa newspapers
63. Facet
64. Svelte
66. In memoriam notices, in brief
69. Fireplace fixture
70. Canada's Tom Longboat when he won a marquee event in Boston
72. Put down
73. 1996 Bryan Adams hit: "_____ Make a Night to Remember"

74. Montreal CFLers
75. Big book
76. Old-style interjection
77. "Auld Lang _____"
79. See 2-D
80. Deuce topper
82. More dull, in literature?
83. Beside Lake Nipigon?
85. There's one of Queen Victoria on Parliament Hill
86. Crescent shaped
87. He fools you hook, line and sinker?

89. University in Wolfville NS
90. Corner Brook weekly paper: *The Western _____*
91. McMahon Stadium home player, for short
92. Flits around the pub?
95. Rot-resistant wood
96. Toboggans
99. Advise of potential danger
100. Heal
101. Sioux City state
102. First numbers
103. Loch _____ Monster

SOLUTION ON PAGE 172

59

Echo Location

Alliterative Canadian places

ACROSS

1. Nassau country
8. John Labatt's job title
14. Exterior wall covering
20. Ancient woodwind instrument
21. Make mad
22. Formal room, in Indiana
23. Eight-line verse form
24. **Newfoundland village**
26. Belonging to that woman
27. He's too fond of Beaujolais?
29. Group of seven
30. _____-ballistic missile
31. Positive vote on Parliament Hill
33. 1982 track from The Nylons: "Up on the _____"
35. Hanoi holiday
36. Pharaohs' crosses
37. Cheering interjection
39. **City that straddles the MB/SK border**
43. Having two parts
45. Alberta Name Index (abbr.)
46. Visage
47. Burden of responsibility
49. Old Afghani currency
50. Connor McDavid has won this four times: _____ Ross Trophy
53. Medieval weapon (var.)
55. Furniture piece for 22-A
57. "Chantilly Lace" singer: The Big _____
59. First USSR/US arms agreement
60. _____ Well That Ends Well
62. Doorway component
64. Emulate Margaret Atwood
65. Saudi _____
67. Walk with a limp
69. Take home a paycheque
70. *Madame Chrysanthème* author Pierre
73. **Place name in Nova Scotia and New Brunswick**
75. Arrogant one
76. Nutmeg seed enclosure
77. Cathedral chapter priests
78. Lawn trimming tools
80. 1975 Paul Anka hit: "I Don't Like to _____ Alone"
82. "Give that _____ cigar"
83. *Airplane!* actor Robert
84. Shot of whisky, say
88. Tawdry
90. Strong Saharan wind
92. Cons and swindlers
93. The constabulary, in Ottawa (abbr.)
94. Nipigon, to a Quebecer
96. Many Canadians received this GOV benefit in 2020/21
97. "Awesome," in street-speak
99. Craven who created A Nightmare on Elm Street franchise movies
100. Device that connects computers
102. **Saskatchewan village**
104. Prefix signifying "new"
105. Monastery leader
108. KFC drumstick
110. Not sweet
111. Montreal suburb: Dollard-Des-Ormeaux (abbr.)
113. Fibre on a coconut
114. Eric, vis-à-vis the NHL's four Staal brothers
117. Beatles classic: "Back in the _____"
119. "_____ I've heard"
122. **Saskatchewan regional municipality**
125. Religious sects' skirmish?
127. Highly respect
128. *The Nutty Professor* co-star Stevens
129. Use Veet or Nair
130. Tall and slender, like plants
131. Too
132. Some Air Canada flights

DOWN

1. Joni Mitchell song: "_____ Sides Now"
2. Patch for vegetables
3. **Central Alberta hamlet**
4. "…there _____ such a clatter"
5. Metric thickness measurement
6. Turn over _____ leaf
7. Like tongue-in-cheek literature
8. Old-style advantage for the farrier?
9. Genetic info letters
10. Deviates from the straight and narrow
11. Ending for hard or soft
12. Cairo country
13. Took a siesta
14. Twosome's tiff
15. Viscous substance
16. Socially refined
17. Dull sound
18. Well-mannered
19. Root used in perfume
25. In a lather
28. Not any
32. Extramarital fling
34. They're seen off Newfoundland's coast
36. Permit
37. Sings like Drake
38. Asian animal
40. Lenient
41. North Bay's prov.
42. Eccentric employee?
44. Brighton bar
48. Porgy or scup
50. All about bees
51. Style reminiscent of the past
52. Peterborough ON university
54. Sold products online
55. Dvořák music opus: "_____ Dances"

56. Personify
58. Arm exercise, in Exeter
60. Crosswise, to a sailor
61. Tropical vines
63. Writings on the Web
66. First alphabet letters
67. Eddie Murphy movie: *48 _____*
68. Barely squeeze by (with "out")
70. Calgary Stampede competition equipment
71. Lowest deck on a ship
72. Echelons
74. Coating on teeth
79. Defeated decisively
81. WestJet employee
83. Vagabonds, in Virginia
85. **See 3-D**

86. One of Canada's largest First Nations
87. Petro-Canada competitor
89. Papa
91. Gold, in Granada
92. US terr. that was split in 1889
95. Order of Canada musician Harnoy plays this
97. See 131-A
98. More punitive
100. Tidbit
101. Snake-haired mythology figure
103. Like words for a person or place
105. Pinnacles
106. Nestlé Canada nutritional drink

107. Fungi, flora and fauna
109. Ladies' partners
112. Old CBC comedy-drama: *Republic of _____*
114. US TV award won by Canada's Kiefer Sutherland
115. Goulash or gumbo
116. Kate DiCamillo children's novel: *The _____ of Despereaux*
118. Canada Cordage product
120. Satisfy a glutton
121. Miners look for these
123. Rodent-sighting screech
124. _____-timed
126. Top for a pot

60 Big Tech

Information technology titans

ACROSS

1. Chess Federation of Canada (abbr.)
4. Bought at The Brick
9. Soldier's safety gear: _____ jacket
13. Tenement locale
17. Instrument with 47 strings
19. Car brand identifier
20. Sofia spending money
21. 1991 Bryan Adams hit: "Do I _____ to Say the Words?"
22. Competitor of 93-A
23. Nearby
24. Brightly coloured fish
25. Court hearing
26. Lauren Lee Smith played one on CBC's *Frankie Drake Mysteries*
28. Basic urge description
31. Two together
32. Support of your husband?
34. **Largest information technology company by revenue**
35. Pope a.k.a.
38. _____ *de suite*
39. Wildebeest
40. **Japanese multinational conglomerate**
41. Duplicates, for short
43. Aniseed liqueur
48. Wyatt Earp adversary Clanton
49. Throw off track?
50. British country house spread
51. He rules "safe" at Rogers Centre
53. Capital of Austria
54. Montreal subway
55. Genre of some CBC shows
57. Not liquids
60. Ewoks' Star Wars franchise planet
62. Drs. save lives here
64. Rams' mates
65. Barometer without liquid
67. **US multinational tech corp.**

68. Mechanical levers
70. Pre-Easter period
71. Canada provides this to Haiti
73. Fine sprays
76. Be a go-between
77. Love, in Longueuil
79. Fend off
81. With complete attention
83. Disabled American Veterans (abbr.)
84. Turns turtle
86. Something to pay attention to
87. Drivel
90. Nighttime matins components
92. Ontario university named for Victoria
93. **Computer company since 1984**
94. Aunt or brother (abbr.)
95. Give a shove
96. Canadian Art _____ Association
98. **See 67-A**
101. Pulsating effects, in music
105. Plate or bowl
106. Some logic theorems
108. Full WestJet flight?
112. Speed skaters' track shape
113. Dismounted
114. Ski racing governing body: _____ Canada
116. *Royal Canadian Air Farce* actress Goy
117. Jack's part of the church?
118. Upper body clothing item
119. Amend text again
120. Drove too fast on the Coquihalla
121. Espies
122. Grey in the face
123. Fathers
124. Ontario city: Sault _____ Marie

DOWN

1. Kroeger of Nickelback
2. **Social media services giant**

3. Floral cotton fabric
4. Traditional Indian garment
5. Show through evidence
6. Canada's three-time Olympic medal winner Lamaze, for one
7. *The Flying* _____
8. Boringly repetitive
9. Dental _____
10. Old Athenian coins
11. Use resources wisely
12. "It Had to Be You" lyricist Gus
13. Canada's Greg Stewart won gold in this at the Tokyo Paralympics
14. Basketball rebound shot
15. Eye part-related
16. 1930s Hollywood star Oberon
18. Show that starred Canada's Shay Mitchell: _____ *Little Liars*
19. Gymnast's landing pad
27. Greek letter
29. Pecan, for one
30. Preserved peaches
33. Shark's game?
35. See 27-D
36. Bouquet bloom
37. Boston _____
39. Small horse-drawn carriage
42. Window glass
43. AGO display
44. Denuded
45. Porky's guffaw
46. **Chinese multinational technology corporation**
47. Some ants
49. Phoenician queen who founded Carthage
50. Microbes
52. No longer trendy, in Terrebonne
53. Interest in the finer things
54. Esso sister brand
56. Settle a Scotiabank loan
57. Caesar enjoyed this meal?
58. 1970 Three Dog Night single: "_____ Band"

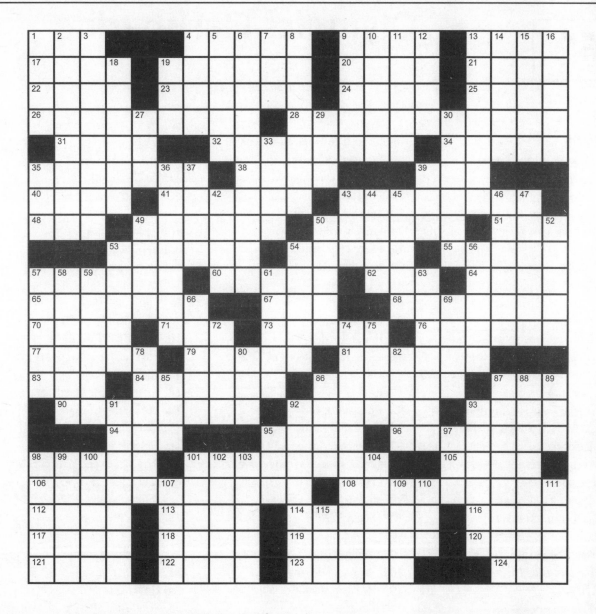

59. **Chinese–American multinational technology company**
61. These Canadian coins feature the *Bluenose*
63. Somewhat saline
66. More severe, like consequences
69. Classic Alanis Morissette album: *Jagged Little _____*
72. 2020 Oscar acting winner Laura
74. Insect that branches out?
75. Hit the spot, gastronomically
78. Repeat to Swiss archer William?

80. Liq. measures
82. Breathe heavily
85. Vancouver Ultimate League (abbr.)
86. It precedes bunny or bowl
87. Green veggie purees
88. **Google holding company**
89. Tissue layer
91. Some Louisiana folks
92. Bright astronomical objects
93. Looks for oil on the Prairies
95. _____-qualify
97. Nigerian–Canadian poet Amatoritsero

98. Terry Fox and Rick Hansen
99. Starbursts
100. Crossbeam
101. Low-lying areas
102. Long-time Canadian entertainers: The _____ Rovers
103. Wee
104. Water park chute
107. Magma
109. Glossy black birds
110. Rogers Arena ice fixture
111. Florida county
115. Greeting gift on Oahu

Olympics Flashback

61

Memories of Tokyo

ACROSS

1. Catalogue into groups
7. _____ pet
11. Bandy
15. Title for a Portuguese lady
19. **Canada won six medals of this colour**
20. Ontario-based WWII spy school: _____ X
21. Optimistic BC place?
22. Ares anagram
23. Chemical washings in a lab
24. Catriona Le May Doan won 500 m Olympic gold in this state
25. River in Yorkshire
26. Blue Jays dugout equipment
27. Machine in a BMO foyer
28. Alberta Theatre Projects (abbr.)
30. Groups of geese
32. Sore spot?
33. Teases a fisherman?
36. Eat too much pork?
37. Elon Musk's electric cars
39. **Former Olympian Marnie McBean served as Canada's this at Tokyo**
42. Move unsteadily
43. Gory film genre
44. 1960s group: The _____ & the Papas
45. Rubik's favourite shape?
46. Bread spread
47. Calgary Public Library (abbr.)
48. Winnow
49. Parliament Hill party "disciplinarian"
53. _____ *non grata*
56. Canadian actress Kidder
60. City in New York state
62. Céline Dion smash: "The Power of _____"
64. Jane's *Barefoot in the Park* persona
65. Turn
66. **Slogan for Canada's Tokyo Olympics brand campaign**
70. Consecrate
72. Forged
73. 16-D, for example
74. Guy (var.)
75. Place to thread a shoelace
77. Has a goal
82. _____ list
83. Some short abbrs.
85. Feel rotten
87. Beach bird
88. "Sunglasses at Night" singer Corey
89. Pile
92. Energy sapping disease
94. Disarm a bomb
97. **She scored the only goal in our semis soccer victory over the USA**
99. Shakespeare's village?
100. See a PI?
101. Biblical second person verb
102. Olden times pulpit
103. Kuwait, for one
105. Beatles moniker: The _____ Four
106. Nevertheless, in brief
109. Spanish greeting: Buenos _____
110. Chess piece
111. _____-crazy
113. Body of water west of Turkey
116. E.D. Smith factory bottles
117. Lymphatic knot
118. Ireland, to an old Irish poet
119. **Canada won 11 medals of this colour**
120. Like the squirt of a squid
121. Like hand-me-downs
122. Mel Tormé sometimes sang this type of jazz
123. Some gemstones

DOWN

1. On 113-A?
2. Riverbed deposit
3. Rip Van Winkle or Sleeping Beauty
4. Eggs
5. Keyboard key, for short
6. She buys a round at the bar
7. Bra size
8. Toque or trilby
9. Ezra Pound's poetry style
10. Inability to swallow
11. Former Japanese warlord
12. Young fowl
13. Notre-Dame Basilica area
14. Puts back in place
15. Corrupt, morally
16. Delphi diviner
17. **Rugby player Hirayama who served as an opening ceremony flag-bearer**
18. Beasts that bray
29. Annual festival and academy: Toronto Summer Music (abbr.)
31. Baby's first syllables
34. Curly dos
35. Single woman's final words?
36. "The Lord is my shepherd," for one
38. Before, before
39. Lamb or pork serving
40. This requires patching
41. Mythical being
42. _____-de-sac
45. Adorable people (var.)
47. South American rodent
48. Loonie or toonie
49. Propeller's noise
50. Shawn Mendes hit: "If I Can't _____ You"
51. Canadian Tire Centre surface for the Sens
52. Buddy
54. Milan's river

55. Twitter handle for a Boston university

57. 1980s beverage ad line: "Have _____ and a smile"

58. Regroupement des Organismes du Montréal Ethnique pour le logement (abbr.)

59. Canada _____ A Beef

61. Ninny

63. Cause and _____

66. 1975 Lightfoot "best of" album: *Gord's* _____

67. 2002 Disney film: _____ *&* *Stitch*

68. Former Governor General Hnatyshyn, et al.

69. Hive, for example

70. At the back of the ship

71. Right winger: _____-con

76. Like an unspoken agreement

78. Things of interest?

79. Like a fever that abates at intervals

80. *Happy Days* actress Moran

81. Setback

84. Canadian cheese producer: _____ Stelle

86. Mamie's White House mate

88. Subtle shade

89. _____ new world record

90. Sleeping sickness flies

91. Spartan person

92. Middle Eastern folk hero

93. Canadian rowing great Hanlan

94. **Decathlete Warner who carried our flag at the closing ceremony**

95. Set out on a journey

96. Ostentatious

97. Moved suddenly, at the soda fountain?

98. Food and Drug Administration (abbr.)

99. Mecca pilgrim (var.)

100. Part of LED

104. Cattle calls

105. Worry

107. Big Smoke smog, say

108. Some cardinal numbers

112. American's retirement plan (abbr.)

114. Physics energy unit

115. Panaji is the capital of this Indian state

SOLUTION ON PAGE 173

62

Keep On Truckin'

Some hauling humour

ACROSS

1. Flew on an Air Canada Airbus?
7. Nice and friendly
15. Sound of water running down the drain
19. Ontario Six Nations Indigenous people
20. He gets the goods?
21. Genus of otters
23. Put on a performance at the Stratford Festival?
24. Making a claim
25. _____ accordance with
26. **Favourite Toyota truck on the Puget Sound?**
27. Murmur like a dove?
28. Loosen a bow
29. Apprehension
30. Tropical vine
31. Repeats a theme, in music
33. **GMC truck for a trip over a CA/NV range?**
34. Alberta Foothills mammal
35. Former Montreal-born NHLer Gilbert
36. Tans anagram
37. Former CTV show: *Who Wants to _____ Millionaire: Canadian Edition*
38. Group of six
41. Poet St. Vincent Millay
42. Least harsh
47. Gran Canaria capital: _____ Palmas
48. Johnny Mathis and Dean Martin, for example
50. Brio
51. Guarantees, at the altar?
54. Atwood novels, for example: Can_____
55. New Delhi money
56. How Osoyoos folks argue in summer?

57. This Frank recorded Paul Anka's "My Way"
61. Pulls behind
62. It directs traffic at YYZ (abbr.)
63. Pair
64. **Nissan truck favoured by Tennessee NFLers?**
65. Feeling unwell
67. Chen who's hosted CBC Radio's *Ontario Morning*
68. Did up shoelaces
70. Perform a post-mortem
72. They're sometimes secret?
74. Dense books
76. Provence vineyard
77. Stealthy one's runners?
78. Lacquer resin
79. Pest that bothers a pinto?
83. Maiden name preceder
84. Settled a dispute about a crossword clue?
86. On one's guard
87. Elton John classic: "_____ in the Wind"
90. _____ in "victory"
91. Traditional Japanese seasoning
92. Enormous mythological bird
93. Mountain to scale with a pal?
95. **Ford truck preferred by Texas MLBers?**
99. Mourned
101. British–Irish singer: Chris de _____
103. Live, at CTV or CBC
104. Raised earthen barrier
105. "_____ the season…"
106. **Toyota truck for a trip towards Northern Canada?**
107. Pore on a petal
108. Tropical, iron-rich soil
110. Military forces
111. Directed toward
112. 1974 Andrews Sisters Broadway musical

113. Pay period, in foreign commerce
114. Grain farm storage structure
115. Bleeped, on TV
116. Sultry dances

DOWN

1. Push or shove
2. Necessitates
3. Château Laurier afternoon dessert?
4. Big cat crossbreed
5. Cause of swollen feet
6. Papa
7. Placed at intervals
8. Liner's lowest deck
9. **Chevrolet truck for a trip through the Centennial State?**
10. It comes in cubes
11. Like Virgil works
12. Pickling liquids
13. Provides a hand?
14. Hence
15. **Jeep truck for boxers?**
16. Filthy money?
17. Complete and _____ chaos
18. Prickly rose (var.)
22. CTV aired this sitcom: *Two _____ Half Men*
31. Decay
32. "_____ uncertain terms"
33. OTT NHLer
35. Remnants, to a Roman
37. Get up onto a horse
39. Canada Post community mailbox opening
40. Subdued a Saluki?
41. RNs work here
42. True Canadian Liberal?
43. Galoot
44. Authorize decision-making at Ontario Hydro?
45. Etna and Vesuvius, say

46. U of C grad student's treatise
48. Six-time MLB all-star Ron
49. Panache
51. Leaf stem
52. Flower parts
53. Doesn't stand up for oneself?
56. Mad milliner?
57. Drink slowly
58. Michael Bublé hit: "_____ a Beautiful Day"
59. Negative response from a Scot?
60. Farmers consult this yearly?
64. Annual cycling event: _____ de France
66. Make an analogy
69. Activity on HGTV Canada's *Scott's Vacation House Rules*

71. Walked all over
72. Big Shania hit: "_____ Man of Mine"
73. 1960s Saskatchewan Roughriders stalwart George
75. Popular Chevrolet truck in a southwest Calgary neighbourhood?
77. Artful
80. Canada's Oleksiak, et al.
81. Put one's mind at _____
82. Nissan truck for a trip to the wilderness?
85. Alt. spelling (in a crossword clue)
87. Stagnant East Coast fish stock
88. Exaggerating

89. Crete-born Renaissance artist
91. NL species: Newfoundland pine ____
92. Treat a sparse lawn
94. Stages
95. US civil rights figure Parks
96. They vote "no"
97. Canadian non-fiction author Klein
98. Hebrew letter
99. Go
100. Chemical solution strength
101. Sac in the shoulder
102. Break a guy's spirit?
104. Quebec federal political party
106. Pulled tight
109. 17th Greek letter

SOLUTION ON PAGE 173

131

63

Destination: Charlottetown

Take a tour

ACROSS

1. State that abuts British Columbia
6. Black-and-white mammal
11. World-weary
16. Buzzing bug
19. Like Montreal's Saint Joseph's Oratory
20. Fencing swords
21. Student, in Sherbrooke
22. Alberta area: _____ Island National Park
23. **Annual fall event**
26. "_____ Maria"
27. Utterances of excitement
28. Alto or baritone instruments
29. TUMS or Rolaids
31. Chicago's state
35. More adorable
37. Palm trees
38. 1992 Neil Young song: "Harvest _____"
39. Sound of a knock
42. Actor Dan, to actor Eugene Levy
43. Per person
45. Environmental science subj.
46. Early 1900s distance runner Longboat from Ontario
48. Invitation acronym
51. Group for Canadian brainiacs
52. A golden retriever is a popular one in Canada
53. Genre of Canadian writer Robert J. Sawyer
55. Distant
56. **Legislature location since 1847**
61. One of David's "Mighty Warriors" in the Hebrew Bible
62. Coral reef
65. Single digit number
66. Plant hormone
67. Trickery
69. Featured musician in a concert
71. Bacon slice

72. Releases from Millhaven Institution
73. Level of loudness
74. Handsome horse farm employees?
75. Baby's bed, in Britain
76. Quirky
77. She, in Portuguese
78. **Shoppers' mecca**
82. Ends of pens
84. Motif
85. Home repair work, for short
86. Ignited again
91. Old Greek walkway
92. Moray
93. Needs to pay a loan
95. Sugar type derived from wood
96. Raises
98. A quality of hard water
102. Singer/actress Falana
103. Rosetta _____
105. Hindu mystics
106. Christie Premium Plus crackers
108. Hobo
110. Possible name for 52-A
112. "You _____ what you sow"
113. "Where did _____ wrong?"
114. **It showcases military history on the island**
120. Marc Jordan song: "Marina _____ Rey"
121. Embryo enclosures
122. Nigerian currency
123. Christopher Columbus ship
124. Sound of 52-A
125. Canadian vocalist Ian
126. _____ a high note
127. Southeast England county

DOWN

1. Primitive instincts, in psychology
2. 1991 Michael J. Fox movie: _____ *Hollywood*

3. Org. for AB drivers
4. Munro and Montgomery protagonists
5. Cineplex _____
6. Iran's name in olden days
7. Army Post Office (abbr.)
8. Sandie Rinaldo delivers this on CTV
9. In reality, to Nero
10. One type of plant reproduction
11. Elite Air Canada travellers?
12. Will Smith starred in this 2001 boxing biopic
13. Hindu deity
14. *Dynasty* actress Linda
15. River mouth formations
16. **Victorian-era showpiece: _____ Historic House**
17. Canadian figure skating "king" Stojko
18. Squeezed out resources
24. Task
25. Burrow for badgers
30. Plaza in ancient Athens
31. Mosque leader
32. Peaceful pace
33. Type of pork roast
34. Stow in the hold, old style
36. Daily allowance, say
40. First section of a play
41. Vegetarians' protein source
44. Topper for a Blue Jay
47. Write down the wrong day
49. Was not consistent
50. Silly folks, in 127-A
52. Jacques Cartier or Champlain, in Montreal
53. One type of discrimination
54. You might have one on your shoulder
57. Pinkish-purple
58. Long-running David Suzuki show: *The _____ of Things*

59. Part of Miss Muffet's munchies

60. Always, in old poetry

62. "Calm down!"

63. Indoor sports place with simulators

64. Bryan Adams classic: "Run to _____"

68. Whisper sweet nothings, say

69. *Frozen* reindeer character, et al.

70. UN currency stabilization org.

71. Wineglass part

72. Dawdling

74. Rather stinky

75. 1970 Quebec event: October _____

79. *Cheers* barmaid Perlman

80. Port city near the Red Sea

81. Attempt

83. Flavour

87. Three dots, in punctuation

88. This bird appears on a Canadian coin

89. _____ of Man

90. Irish Breakfast, et al.

93. Green mineral

94. Melchior or Balthasar

95. Woody plant tissue

97. Speak sharply to

99. Seoul citizen

100. Awestruck

101. Fabric for a Scottish clan

103. Having more wisdom than others

104. Foe

107. Pantyhose colour

108. Ricky Martin hit: "Livin' la _____ Loca"

109. Cans

111. Canadian polling firm: Angus _____ Global

115. Canadian Penny Oleksiak won four Olympic medals here

116. National Reconnaissance Office (abbr.)

117. Rank for a sailor (abbr.)

118. Colorado mountain

119. Canadian aviator Ward who founded Wardair

SOLUTION ON PAGE 173

64

By the Numbers

Famous films

ACROSS

1. Charlottetown _____ Club
6. Great white ocean predator
11. Depletes of energy
15. ETs' crafts
19. Hate
20. Lifted, in Laval
21. Luau dance
22. Near, poetically
23. Florida coastal city
24. Banish
25. Lily variety
26. Kitchener-based band Courage My Love, for example
27. Fugue components
29. It blows stuff up real good
31. Invitation answer, for short
32. Pines for
34. Texas city
35. Skin layers
36. **1937 James Stewart romance drama**
42. Céline or Shania?
44. Black cuckoos
45. Large Oklahoma city
46. Pile of rubble in the Rockies
48. Ignited
51. Wichita state
54. Broken arm support
56. Musical scale interval
58. And more, in brief
59. Moccaccino flavours at Second Cup
61. Owls' sounds
63. Carry a satchel?
64. Vacillates, at the park?
66. Ontario-born 2003 Masters champion Mike
67. Sin city, in the Bible
68. **1997 Bruce Willis sci-fi film**
74. Some underground NWT workplaces
77. Murder
78. Rubber band

82. Canadian Opera Company diva's moment
83. Flower part
85. Two-dimensional
88. Gilbert and Sullivan offering: *Princess* _____
89. Sock that measures airport breeze velocity
91. Imbecile
93. Order of Canada tennis inductee Daniel
95. Supersonic flyer, for short
96. Famed violin maker
98. Crack open a Molson Canadian
100. Insect's feeler
101. Pertaining to blood
103. **1999 Bruce Willis psychological thriller**
107. Nickname of Victoria's son Alfred
109. She's as busy as a bee
111. 2004 Michael Bublé live album track: "_____ Never Know"
112. This Canadian immigrant made the first phone call
113. Scary
117. National Ballet of Canada practice attire
121. _____ vera
122. "_____ stupid question…"
123. Phileas Fogg's creator Jules
125. NBC morning show
126. Ice sheet in the Atlantic
127. Japanese parliament
128. Latin year
129. Old-style word of encouragement (var.)
130. Alberta's Maligne Lake, for example
131. Sound, mentally
132. Robust
133. Knight's equine

DOWN

1. Sweet potatoes
2. Not much
3. Sear
4. Lacking lodgings
5. Neptune moon
6. Magician's skill: _____ of hand
7. Curse
8. Passionate
9. Bank on support
10. See 8-D
11. Tribal spirit guides
12. Bond bad guy: _____ Goldfinger
13. Wealthy ruler
14. Identical
15. Not a fact
16. **1982 Sylvester Stallone action movie**
17. Gothic style arch
18. Goes to Canadian Tire
28. Syn. for 29-A
30. Astonish
33. "Quiet!"
35. Bass _____
36. "Goodness gracious _____ alive!"
37. Related through your mother's side
38. US C&W star Gill
39. Jazz icon Fitzgerald
40. Phrase on a damaged merch tag
41. Abbr. for a BC coastal place
43. Fish without fins
47. Farmhand's job
49. Burst _____ tears
50. Abound
52. Some Asian domestic servants
53. 2016 Garbage album track: "_____ Can Stay Alive"
55. Liquid butter for Indian recipes
57. Shakespeare's play about Kate (abbr.)
60. National non-profit: Spinal _____ Leak Foundation

62. Major junior hockey team: Edmonton _____ Kings

65. Stand in good _____

66. 1970 Neil Young song: "Tell Me _____"

67. Entrap

69. Bit of land in the St. Lawrence

70. Travel by WestJet

71. Joni Mitchell classic: "Big Yellow _____"

72. Canadian new wave group: _____ Without Hats

73. Spiritedness

74. Big-mouthed moms?

75. Canadian optometry chain

76. **2015 National Film Board of Canada documentary**

79. Icon of industry, say

80. Fans' favourites

81. _____ *diem*

83. Medically induced state of sleep

84. State of feeling no pain

85. CIBC ATM nos.

86. Scenes of action

87. Lack of muscle coordination condition (var.)

90. Sharon, Lois and Bram cover: "The Cat _____ Back"

92. Payable on demand

94. Made explicit, in Exeter

97. Restate

99. Noted Greek mathematician and astronomer

102. 1982 Dexys Midnight Runners hit: "Come on _____"

104. Info on a Chapters door

105. Subtle colour

106. Slow-moving arboreal mammals

107. Toward the back, on ship

108. Guy, colloquially

110. Samuel Woodworth poem: "The Old _____ Bucket"

113. Crazes

114. BC speed skating facility: Richmond Olympic _____

115. Milestones list of options

116. Shoreline birds (var.)

118. Wood shaping tool

119. Demolish a structure

120. Group of two

124. Oddball

SOLUTION ON PAGE 173

65

Games People Play

Popular sports in Canada

ACROSS

1. Sibling of Seth and Cain
5. River that runs through Calgary
10. Rock faces in the Rockies
15. Large cake type
19. Hip bone
20. Careen
21. He composed "Bolero"
22. Sumptuous
23. Canadian voters, en masse
25. In an unfriendly manner
27. Broken down
28. Like a rainbow shape
30. Trees associated with Canada
31. *Calgary Sun* commentary
32. BTO song: "_____ It Like a Man"
33. One-named "Thank You" songstress
34. Salon services
37. The Source or The Brick
39. Chinese restaurant beverage
43. Cropped up in the morning?
44. Beekeeper's hazard?
46. Soften flax
47. CST or MST: Time _____
48. Slavic folklore figure: _____ Yaga
49. Nanaimo is on this side of Vancouver Island
50. This Canadian cyclist won three Olympic medals: _____ Harnett
51. Terminus
52. Some Weather Network personnel
56. Bipolar disorder symptom
57. Cosmetics item
59. Twosomes
60. **Canada's first game of this took place in 1876**
61. Bargain events at 37-A
62. **Sailors brought this sport to Canada in the 1860s**
63. Phlegm
64. **Canada's official winter sport**
66. Evergreen shrub with edible berries
67. Brings back together
70. Tracts for crops
71. Sailboat's retractable keel
73. International Longshoremen's Association (var.)
74. Luau wear
75. Prude
76. Bacardi and Captain Morgan, for example
77. Rogers Centre no-no
78. Traveller's guide
79. Concern of Health Canada and the Canadian Food Inspection Agency
83. Henry, Peter or Jane of acting fame
84. Poker player's foyer?
86. Accepted practice
87. Not open
88. Thin and tall
89. Metric weight unit
90. Harbour horn sound
91. Erase
94. Devours (with "down")
95. US retailer in Canada: Banana _____
99. Fashionable folks
101. Flatter excessively
103. Already departed
104. Dangerous household gas
105. Dorothy, to Em and Henry
106. Loan
107. Transmit
108. Get into the _____ of things
109. Ceremonial Jewish dinner
110. Mandolin's cousin

DOWN

1. Scored on a serve, in tennis
2. Tree trunk
3. CEO or CFO
4. **Canada's official summer sport**
5. Runs away to wed
6. Sensationally gory
7. Incorrigible child
8. Thanksgiving Day mo. in Canada
9. *Star Trek: The Next Generation* actor Wil
10. **Around 1867, this was so popular it was declared Canada's national sport**
11. Hindu royal (var.)
12. Ardent
13. Precious stone
14. Like the most reprehensible person
15. Quickly apply cosmetics
16. Cessation in the action
17. Shaft under a car
18. Olden days titles in Turkey
24. Conical tent (var.)
26. West Point enrollee
29. Like hen's teeth
33. Former reality show: *Say Yes to the _____ Canada*
34. Historical warship
35. Scornful literary technique
36. Like a boring writer?
37. Opposite of soused
38. Former Ford pickup: Sport _____
39. Growls at
40. Cut-offs?
41. Giving goosebumps
42. Essential oil sourced from roses
44. Rabbits
45. Like a shabby garden?
48. "Rasputin" pop group: _____ M.
50. Saguaro, et al.
52. They might be kept in a cabinet?
53. Fully grown
54. Half of a Guess Who medley: "No _____ Tonight"
55. Furniture piece
56. Rogers Centre pitcher's place

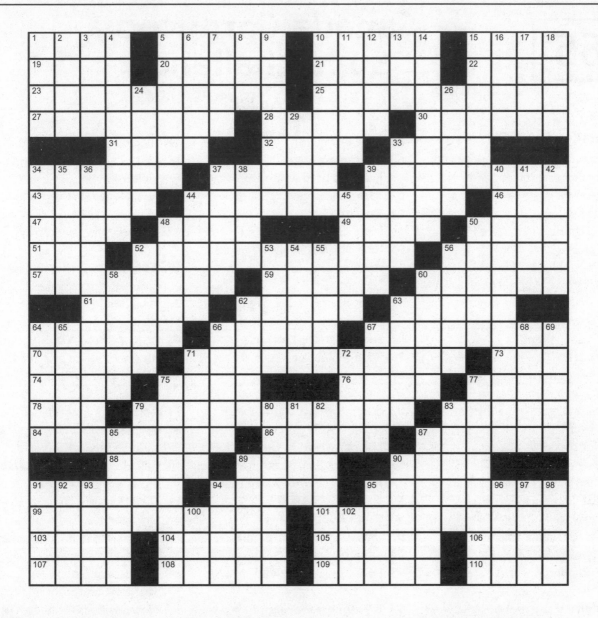

58. Nipigon and Nipissing, in Ontario
60. Cowboy boots adjuncts
62. Newfoundland chain: Long _____ Mountains
63. Tawdry, to the tailor?
64. Game with a board of 16x16 squares
65. Canada has one on three coasts
66. Earthquake
67. Defined way for a city bus
68. Avoid the fuzz, say
69. Pasta _____
71. Felon

72. Shipboard prisoners are confined here
75. Early Canadian settlers
77. **An early variation of this sport was first played in the 1860s**
79. Flowering leaf
80. **This sport arrived in Canada from Scotland**
81. American military air corps (abbr.)
82. Wild garlic plants
83. Bakers need this ingredient
85. Filled with joy
87. It's mined in British Columbia and Ontario

89. Amicably interacted
90. Canonical hour
91. They can be scrambled or poached
92. Ocean icefield
93. Helsinki resident
94. African gully
95. *It's a Wonderful Life* co-star Donna
96. "In _____ of flowers"
97. "Winning _____ everything"
98. Surrender control
100. Like uncooked vegetables
102. Canadian lingerie retailer: la _____ en Rose

SOLUTION ON PAGE 174

66 Canada Cornucopia Superchallenger

No FIBs

ACROSS

1. Jetés at a Royal Winnipeg Ballet practice
6. Flee from custody
12. Canadian accountants' designation: Chartered Tax Practitioner (abbr.)
15. One colour on Canada's flag
18. British boarding school leaves of absence
20. Festive gatherings, in Folkestone
21. Tool for tilling
22. Famed 1970s psychic Geller
23. Type of equinox
24. Toronto Raptors sport
26. "Sometimes When We Touch" singer Hill
27. Not friendly
29. Your lifeline is here
30. Official gemstone of Ontario
32. Flat-bottomed boat propeller
34. Provincial bird of Nova Scotia
35. Tire or tap troubles
37. Needlefish
38. Computer operating system abbr.
39. Makes sense to the accountant?
43. Johnson of *Rowan & Martin's Laugh-In*
44. Fibreglass unit
45. Fantastic
47. Priest's investiture, say
48. Canadian James who invented 24-A
50. Like one side of British Columbia
51. Weighty burden
52. Computer keyboard key, for short
53. Vow at the altar
54. Holler
55. Rushed
57. Moose Jaw-born TV host Linkletter
58. Type of bagel
60. African grassland
61. Pronoun used in Quebec City
62. African ungulate, for short
64. Coagulate
66. Have a premonition
68. Canada's Mike Holmes works on these on HGTV
71. "Disgusting!"
72. Goat-like mythology figure
73. Native American jewellery beads
77. Actor/director Lupino
78. Sixth Jewish month
80. Beethoven's birthplace
81. She often gets gifts in May
82. Health care assistant (abbr.)
83. Sudden bump
85. Use hyperbole, in the UK
87. First Canadian horse to win the Kentucky Derby (with 117-A)
89. Camry or Camaro
90. Tooth trouble
91. *Pretty Woman* star Richard
92. Egyptian fertility goddess
93. Canadian country and western star Paul
95. Psyche components
96. Ravens' cries
97. Kvetch
98. Use Listerine
100. Poisonous pigment
102. Like Hamilton's Dundurn Castle?
105. *The Da Vinci Code* priory
106. Stick shift option
109. Bible book (abbr.)
110. Free from all restraints
113. Lake Victoria country
114. Canada provides this to Ethiopia
115. Great Britain air force (abbr.)
116. Nova Scotia's second-oldest Anglican church is here
117. See 87-A
118. Tragically Hip drummer Johnny
119. Alexander Keith's product
120. Ukrainian city
121. Hockey legend Gretzky

DOWN

1. Bulgarian currency units
2. Donald and Ivana, e.g.
3. Canada's Snowbirds excel at this
4. Stampede Breakfast fare in Calgary
5. Elevator alternative
6. Subside, like the tide
7. Saint John or Halifax
8. Spanish cellist Pablo
9. Bodily joint
10. Canadian McCrae's "In Flanders Fields"
11. Direction on a compass in Quebec
12. Ali was one many times over
13. Not too bad
14. Bombarded
15. Two-time Governor General's Award winner for fiction (with 100-D)
16. Ears anagram
17. Mark left by a blow
19. Criticize, to a cockney
25. Hound owner's instrument?
28. Smoothly, on a musical score
31. Ontario's Darlington Nuclear Generating Station provides this
33. Hiking trail
34. Oaf's interjection
35. Highway 400 divisions
36. Rub out
38. Having two purposes
40. Northeastern Egypt peninsula
41. One-eighty, on the avenue
42. Savoury pasta sauce

44. US Joe elected in 2020
45. Good word on a Royal LePage sign
46. Hoist
49. Fruity cocktail
50. Type of Shaw service
54. 1998 hit from 93-A
56. Had a vision while you slept
59. First card in a deck
60. Alberta home of the world's second-largest pysanka
61. Person, place or thing word
63. Shorten a sleeve
65. Tropical fruit
66. Snake's tooth
67. Took an oath

68. Muslim woman's headscarf
69. Smell
70. Island in the Mediterranean
72. Stick-in-the-mud (var.)
74. Office held by 44-D
75. Tear out stitches
76. Clergyperson's home
79. Related to religious studies, say
80. Woodbine wagers
81. Smidgen
84. South Pacific place
86. Canada's Wonderland attraction
87. Salamander
88. Japanese writing system
91. Swimmers' acrobatic dives
94. Thornapple genus

96. Glee club, for example
97. Bauble, in Britain
99. Faux pas
100. See 15-D
101. Forte, to a pianist
102. French chanteuse Edith
103. Nepal's continent
104. Peerage female, in the UK
105. House framing board
107. Temporary capital of Yemen since 2015
108. Unusual
111. Confucian concept
112. Evidentiary crime scene substance

SOLUTION ON PAGE 174

By the Numbers 2

Songs that add up

ACROSS

1. Charitable donations, à la Dickens
5. 1940s PEI premier Campbell
10. 1983 Bryan Adams hit: "_____ Like a Knife"
14. Holy Hindu figure
19. Match for pugilists
20. Despises
21. Funeral home notice, for short
22. It follows Pisces
23. **1967 Marvin Gaye/Kim Weston chart-topper**
25. You might find soap on this
26. Islamic officiants
27. Quid pro quo
28. Excellent skier at Whistler?
30. Less restricted
31. 2004 Wayson Choy Giller Prize nominee: *All _____ Matters*
32. Got off a horse
33. Ceres anagram
36. Neil Young classic: "Cinnamon _____"
37. Fresh out of the box
41. Lacking in individuality
46. Assign a revised mark to an essay
47. Old Timmies slogan: Roll Up the _____ to Win
48. Change a backsplash
49. Iron _____ Company of Canada
51. Canadian artists: Group of _____
52. Like a free fiancé?
55. _____ rasa
58. Round at the Rogers Cup
59. Anaesthetize
60. Keep an Edmonton Elk off the field?
62. South Saskatchewan River structure: Gardiner _____
63. **Britney Spears 1998 smash single**

68. Sarah Palin's former AK job
71. Newborns
72. Obliged not to
76. Acid secreted by the bladder
78. Golden coins of old Europe
79. University recordkeeper
82. Stand for Canadian painter Pratt
84. Maple Leaf George Armstrong wore this jersey number
85. Plato's plazas
87. A Nigerian language
88. Tolerate bad grub?
90. Good time to contact Royal LePage
94. Canada's Karsh photographed this Mother
95. Sounds from 43-D
96. West Yorkshire city
97. California valley known for wineries
99. *Love It or List It Vancouver* realtor Talbot
100. Royal Canadian Navy warships, say
103. Former European Communist state
107. Make the grade, like a seamstress?
111. It separates the abdomen and thigh
112. Move a jet to the runway at YVR
113. **1971 Led Zeppelin track**
114. Past, to a poet
115. _____ gin
116. *The Red Green Show* setting: Possum _____
117. Mount Olympus was his mythological home
118. Doorbell chimes: Ding-_____
119. Cravings for Japanese food?
120. Spay or neuter
121. A deadly sin

DOWN

1. "This won't hurt _____!"
2. Lesotho currency unit
3. Mangy dog
4. Sheepherding employee?
5. At that place
6. Excessive rush
7. Tatar anagram
8. Petite amphibian
9. Edmonton Symphony Orchestra (abbr.)
10. Rounds up the horses?
11. WWII torpedo launcher
12. Cone-shaped dwelling (var.)
13. Stone pillar
14. Cruise ship departure schedules
15. Voltage coils
16. Hollywood actress Cameron
17. Red blood cell pigment
18. CDA's 1972 Summit Series rival
24. Asian country: South _____
28. **The Commodores 1978 number-one hit**
29. *Diamond Mine* band: _____ Rodeo
31. Cash register drawer
33. Vigourously clean
34. Beijing's country, to a Quebecer
35. Japanese noodle soup
36. Richardson HGTV show: *Sarah Off the _____*
38. Invested in a GIC, say
39. Tissue swelling
40. Fabric for Lee jeans
42. Found fault with the chowder?
43. Shearling
44. Warm season in Shawinigan
45. Like teetotalling Boers?
46. Fired up a boiler again
50. Golden _____
53. Little lump
54. Guy who works for the FBI
56. Tumults

57. Philosophy that all things have souls
60. Old-style road paver
61. Birds you might think about?
64. YCJA word
65. Fairy tale's first word
66. Flatbreads popular in India
67. Hamilton clock setting (abbr.)
68. Visitor
69. Speak like Erato?
70. Sun screen?
73. A kid pedals this
74. Canadian singer of 1998's "Spaceman": Bif _____

75. Slow paces in the paddock
77. Building a strong foundation?
79. Certain bucks?
80. "To _____ is human"
81. Esso sells this
83. Italian dishes (var.)
86. Elated
89. _____ Spear NL
91. They're next to ivories
92. Indigenous Alaskan
93. Convict's second shot in court
98. Dilettantish
99. Genus, for example
100. Family skirmishes

101. Pizza Hut pie size
102. County in England and town in Ontario
103. "Yikes!" of yore
104. Ti-Cat rival
105. Any time now
106. Boy or man
107. QB Warren who won five Grey Cups with the Eskimos (now Elks)
108. Light beige
109. Small guitars
110. Barely audible interjection
113. Achy illness

ACROSS

1. Emulated Canada's Penny Oleksiak
5. Spoken tests at U of T
10. Seven, in Saguenay
14. Hole for an anchor rope
19. American trumpet great Al
20. 13 species of this bird are found in Canada
21. 1942 Veronica Lake film: *This Gun for _____*
22. Flu symptoms
23. Loretta Lynn hit: "_____ on the Way"
24. Arranged a trip on VIA Rail?
26. Archaeologists' workplaces
27. Canadian restaurant chain: _____ Japan
28. Therefore, to Descartes
29. **One of two official provincial colours**
30. Move quietly through the tulips?
31. Vancouver _____
33. Jewish month
35. Apply your knowledge
37. Some hospital units, for short
38. Worthless, at TD Bank?
40. Yangtze river transport
42. Harper Valley grp. of song
43. Notable Spanish Renaissance painter: El _____
44. They tick past quickly (abbr.)
46. Guarantor, e.g.
48. Language spoken in Lahore
50. Emerge, in the chicken coop
53. "The darkest _____ just before the dawn"
55. Very attentive, like the otolaryngologist?
58. Bullring beasts
60. Prepare to drive a Tesla
62. Canadian prime minister Mackenzie, by birth
63. Ta-tas

65. Italia capital
66. *A Streetcar Named Desire* sister
67. Shot by a Toronto Raptor
69. **Tallest structure in the province**
71. 2012 Canadian film: _____ *Mine*
72. He fell into the Aegean after a failed flight
74. Kids' Saturday morning viewing, for short
75. Makes lacy doilies
78. Streets, in Saint-Sauver
79. Pontius _____
80. Prairie provinces river: _____ Saskatchewan
82. "Sweet!" to Rhett Butler?
84. _____ of a deal
86. Prelude
88. "No," in Novosibirsk
89. Skirt length
91. Red gemstone
93. Jungle vine
97. Banned substance for an athlete (abbr.)
98. Avoided a dragnet, say
101. Extremely small particle description
103. Doug McKenzie's *SCTV* sibling
104. Capone's rod
105. Sits for a photo shoot
107. Caviar on toast, for one
108. Water bugs (var.)
111. **Animal on Ontario's coat of arms**
113. Lakes, in Quebec
115. Pimple, colloquially
116. Sense or sensibility?
117. Proportional amount
119. Like some Swiss Chalet orders
120. Eaten anagram
121. 1951 Hugh MacLennan novel: _____ *Man's Son*
122. Has a meal at Earls
123. Before long, to a poet

124. Copenhagen residents
125. "_____, poor Yorick!"
126. Top Rogers Cup competitors
127. Feudal estate worker

DOWN

1. Farrier's task
2. **Southernmost city in Ontario**
3. These surround pupils
4. Manitoba Teachers' Society (abbr.)
5. Bake for too long
6. Boxer's favourite jewellery piece?
7. WWI battle site in France
8. Molokai necklace
9. "O Canada" and "Our Dominion"
10. 1980s pop star Easton
11. Ireland, old style
12. Fiancés' legal contracts, for short
13. Artist Harrison whose paintings highlight Yukon terrain
14. WWI spy Mata
15. Bra size
16. **Official provincial flower**
17. Lady of León
18. Letters that create plurals
25. Lengthy periods of time
28. Audience's call for more
30. Not substantial
32. Assimilated, in a nation new to you
34. *The Seven Year _____*
36. Window component
39. Shylock's lending practice
41. Voltaire play about religious fanaticism
42. Act of committing a crime
45. Calendar abbreviation
47. Littlest ones of litters
49. Light touch
51. **Provincial capital**
52. Black bird
54. In a broody mood
55. Thorny shrub

56. First half of Ontario's motto
57. Dissenting factions
59. Grammy-winning Canadian McLachlan
61. Lasses and ladies
62. Fall on ice
64. Pried
68. Robber's command: "_____ up!"
70. Go on the road, like Drake
73. Requirement for Canadian Coast Guard staff?
76. Steve Buscemi role on *The Sopranos*
77. Where pigs live

81. 2006 Canadian film: *Away from _____*
83. BC estuaries?
85. 1964 Oscar-winning actress Kedrova
87. Ponder
90. Gluten-free oats substitute
92. Specific route for a TTC vehicle
94. Mythical women warriors
95. Largest lake wholly within Ontario
96. Paint remover ingredient
97. California city
99. See 25-D

100. Rexall pharmacy vial info
102. A password or portal provide this
103. Made hay?
106. Remits
109. Chomp on
110. Speedy serves from Canada's Bianca Andreescu
112. Mammal seen in West Coast waters
114. Long in the tooth
117. Pod veggie: Snow _____
118. Tip Top purchase
119. Fitness workout: _____ Bo

69

Mechanics' Medley

Entertainment at the shop

ACROSS

1. Alberta Treasury Branches (abbr.)
4. Some provinces sell milk in these
8. Daisy type
14. Old-style seizure
19. Music star from BC: Carly _____ Jepsen
20. Autodrome Montmagny shape
21. Mexican liquor
22. Shania Twain hit in 1996: "_____ Needs to Know"
23. Groove
24. In attendance, at roll call
25. Breathe out
26. Oil sands deposit in Alberta
27. Become sluggish
29. **US composer who won two Pulitzer Prizes for Music**
31. TD TFSAs, say
33. MI's largest city
34. Ditty
35. Extremely punitive
38. Tenant's payment
40. Fort Nelson airport code
42. Slow down the pace
46. Multi-tasking musician: _____ band
48. Annual club membership payments
50. Dark colour, in Baie-Comeau
52. Greek letter
53. Attacks from the air
55. Word derived from an existing word
59. Governing board members
61. Nova Scotia Provincial Court proceedings
62. Heavy metric weight
63. Plummeted
64. Beat, resoundingly
66. Of the last month (abbr.)
67. Like a persistent pooch?
68. **1971 Guess Who hit single**
72. State of hypnosis
76. Doofus
77. Secular
78. Use a rotary phone
82. Like some ancient alphabets
83. Forcefully express your opinion
86. Like a raspy voice
88. One type of Church of England attendee
91. Preacher or teacher
92. Sue Grafton mystery: _____ *for Corpse*
93. Erato or Urania
94. High-pitched bark
96. Twist ties?
97. Bury a pharaoh
99. Early Canadian lawman Steele
102. U of M lodgings
104. They're swabbed on ships
105. Eastern Ontario apple type
107. High level of energy
109. Like Dorothy Livesay works
111. **"Wasted Days and Wasted Nights" singer**
116. Ancient Roman magistrates
120. Sayings attributed to Jesus
121. Like Marilyn's famous *The Seven Year Itch* dress
122. European mountains
123. *The Golden Girls* star McClanahan
124. Select group of VIPs
125. 2015 horror film
126. Slangy refusal
127. Glasgow School of Art (abbr.)
128. Israeli–Canadian architect Safdie who designed Habitat 67
129. Sunday supper servings
130. And others (abbr.)
131. Until now

DOWN

1. They taxi to the gates at YYZ
2. Rigid
3. See 52-A
4. **Richard Roundtree played this movies franchise character**
5. These contain irises
6. Leg band with a clip
7. Precipitated
8. Merganser
9. Group of six
10. Cape Breton fiddling star MacIsaac
11. Distracted while singing jazz?
12. Fairy's narrative?
13. Red warning?
14. This burns things up real good
15. Woman's lace-up garment
16. Blow your own horn
17. Word software menu option
18. Caught in the act, say
28. Canadian soldier's WWI protective gear
30. Jewish holy day
32. Rebuff
35. David Amber and Ron MacLean, on Canadian hockey broadcasts
36. Bone cavities
37. Show you've seen before on CBC
39. Udder
41. Ketone or ester
43. Copying a chimpanzee?
44. European river
45. Ate at Milestones
47. Stick for stitching
49. In a mangy manner?
51. Surgical suites, for short
54. Novi Sad native
56. James Bond franchise film: *A View to a _____*
57. 1987 thriller: _____ *Attraction*
58. Provide with clothing
60. Take to civil court
65. Beef stock, e.g.
67. Ten years
68. Make room for?
69. Edible tuber

70. Mattress dip
71. Put on the payroll
72. Vestige
73. Dispute between joggers?
74. Apprehension
75. Zero, at a Toronto FC game
78. Ricochet
79. Major artery name
80. Smart _____
81. Ancient Greek harps
83. _____ Cruces NM
84. Summers, in Sherbrooke
85. _____-à-terre

87. **Fast & Furious franchise star**
89. Small space for a little bear?
90. Clydesdale's hoofbeat sound
95. Barbecue fuel
98. Not so youthful anymore
100. Nighttime problem in Plymouth: Sleep _____
101. Canada won 24 of these at the Tokyo Olympics
103. Red wine serving
106. Bid on a property
108. Tiny, in Témiscaming

110. Cloth made from mulberry bark
111. 1967 movie: *The Flim-_____ Man*
112. Caramel-filled Nestlé confection
113. Cuirass part (var.)
114. Red *Sesame Street* puppet
115. Canadian Club sells these
117. Gluttonous spree
118. Crafty scheme
119. Chair for an MLA?

70

Speaking of...

Canada's plethora of languages

ACROSS

1. _____ Minor
5. RBC ATM output
9. Acacia's thorns
14. Hydro pioneer in Ontario: _____ Beck
18. Classify
19. Miscellaneous collections
21. Nail filing board
22. Paddy grain
23. Fissure
24. Comedy of errors, perhaps?
25. Month that follows Adar
26. Lams anagram
27. Experience all over again
29. Extremely unfortunate
31. Calgary Spruce Meadows buildings
33. Molson product
34. **Mandarin and Cantonese are part of this immigrants' language group**
35. Rani's wrap
36. Queen Elizabeth, vis-à-vis Canada
39. O.J.'s LA trial judge
40. Uber competitors
44. "Don't _____, don't tell"
45. Spicy Indian fritters
48. Approached
50. Tyke
51. Gather, at harvest time
53. Geological periods
55. Pitches in
56. Gaucho's weapon (var.)
57. Expanse of bamboo
59. Uses loam to fertilize
61. *Front Page Challenge* group
62. Air Canada magazine: *en_____*
63. Coyotes' calls
64. Sandy African expanse
65. **Some Indian immigrants speak this**
68. Gumby's sidekick

69. **It's spoken by Filipino immigrants**
70. Secret trysts in Trois-Rivières?
71. Long-time *Calgary Herald* columnist Don
72. *The Crucible* is set here
73. Cowboy boots add-ons
74. One type of terrier
75. Some chemical salts
79. "Tiptoe Through the Tulips" singer: _____ Tim
80. Petite lake
81. 1980 Richard Gere film: *American _____*
83. Big order of Canadian Grade A beef
84. End of an _____
85. Stretched your neck to see a bird?
87. Connections
89. _____-for-tat
90. Very altruistic
92. Opposite of nay
94. Rock concert souvenirs
96. Tirade at a tarn?
97. **An official language of Canada**
100. U of A advanced deg.
101. Weapons depot
104. One type of Marxist–Leninist
105. Unborn child, in Chelsea
108. Rival of an Argo
109. Victoria newspaper: _____ *Colonist*
111. Oahu greeting
113. "_____ Misbehavin'"
114. _____ Québécois
115. Regarding, in olden days
116. 2013 Avril Lavigne song: "Here's to _____ Growing Up"
117. Whit
118. Son of Eve
119. Gives a hand, say
120. Duration of a loan
121. Manitoba town: _____ Lake

DOWN

1. Brezhnev governed here (abbr.)
2. Job for Canada's Ryan Gosling
3. Resident of Colombo
4. Head Hun
5. Newfoundland town: _____ By Chance
6. He was dubbed "The Greatest"
7. Bruce Willis thriller: *The _____ Sense*
8. Muslim paradise nymph
9. Blessing, to a bard
10. Priest's shoulder cloth
11. Place to live at Queen's uni
12. Armour pieces that protect the upper arms
13. Sets of grammatical rules
14. **It's spoken by some Middle Eastern immigrants**
15. Canadian potato chip flavour: _____ pickle
16. Pinnacle
17. State of disorder
20. **Some South American immigrants speak this**
28. Rise or fall?
30. Understand
32. Description of 64-A
34. Indian man's griddle cake?
36. Quebecer Gagnon who won three gold medals in Olympic speed skating
37. Ontario Sustainable Energy Association (abbr.)
38. Infantile celestial beings
40. Animals' appendages
41. Discordant, in music
42. Famed Ravel composition
43. *Hogan's Heroes* milieu
46. It needs a punchline
47. Slippery surface
49. Gordon Lightfoot classic: "_____ Morning Rain"
52. Courtroom crime

54. By 1994, Air Canada banned this on all flights
56. Caribbean country
58. Wild swine
60. Amazed
61. It preceded the cellphone
63. Frosty coating
64. Wild West watering holes
65. Glues
66. Rogers Centre game official
67. Like person, place or thing words
68. _____ and Prejudice
69. Jewish prayer shawl (var.)
71. Pre-marriage announcement, in church

72. If this fits, wear it
74. BC's west side, say
75. Canadian multinational IT co. based in Montreal
76. Chemical analysis technique
77. Make changes to text
78. Djokovic's collections?
80. Before birth
82. **Language spoken by new Canadians from "The Boot"**
85. Hatfields or McCoys
86. Hereditary rulers
88. Dumb one (var.)
91. **See 97-A**

93. Psyche
95. Structure's steel components
97. See 77-D
98. Atoll kin
99. You might buy one at The Brick
101. Work attire for congregation leaders
102. Make irate
103. Filth in the flue
105. FCC word
106. "For _____ us a child is born"
107. Crock-Pot meal
110. Males
112. That female

SOLUTION ON PAGE 175

147

71

Blown Away...

By these breezy songs

ACROSS

1. Muscat is its capital
5. Cacophonies
9. _____ clock
14. US singer Khan
19. Ceremonial occasion
20. Black-purple drupe
21. For-profit thrift chain in Canada: _____ Village
22. More robust
23. **1963 Bob Dylan classic**
26. Fireplace nook
27. Hypothesize
28. Hit the _____ on the head
29. Reduces the temperature
30. First American League black baseballer Larry
31. Young boy
33. In a crafty manner
35. River in Bonn
37. Shakespearean-era wig
39. Toy dog's bark
40. Joint inflammation problem
41. Cookie container
42. Impudence
44. Kicks out of the CBA?
49. She shortens a written work
52. Pigs' enclosure
53. Deforest
55. Stunned a tile installer?
56. Eastern Canada prov.
57. McDavid or Crosby, e.g.
58. Have an instinctual feeling
59. Carrot family herb
60. 1-A shares a maritime border with this country
61. Yeats sonnet: "_____ and the Swan"
63. Pass judgment
64. **1998 Garth Brooks live album track**
68. HMCS *Chicoutimi*, et al.
72. Heat vent
73. Montreal's NHL team, colloquially
74. Haitian currency unit
79. Talons
81. Blue Jay's slugger
82. Canada's Sandra Oh won a 2019 Golden Globe for playing her: _____ Polastri
83. Former Canadian magazine: _____ *Standard*
84. Remove a cannon's support
86. Stun
87. Dramatis _____
88. Teats
89. Real Canadian Superstore section
91. Central
92. Settles a tab
93. Jogged
95. Little finger
97. Bonds out of the clink
99. Dazzlingly skilled musicians
103. Bears' lair
104. Vena _____
105. Virile fellows
106. Groove on an archer's bow
108. Southern end of a South America region
112. Desert plant
113. **1963 Ian and Sylvia ballad**
116. Employees' earnings
117. Lobbies encased in glass (var.)
118. River in Ireland
119. Cut and run, like a kitty?
120. Ties
121. Not those
122. Meniscus injury
123. Female parents

DOWN

1. Eye, to a bard
2. Thickness measurements, for short
3. At the peak
4. Boston R&B band formed in 1978
5. Budapest sits on the bank of this river
6. With a frosty attitude
7. Grandmother, colloquially
8. 12-year Toronto Maple Leaf Darryl
9. Street map abbr.
10. Ontario _____ Bowls Association
11. Pseudonyms
12. Quarrel at a track meet?
13. Canadian women won bronze in this type of relay at Tokyo 2020
14. Legumes for salads
15. Canada's embassy in Vietnam is here
16. Perseus star
17. Jay who fronted Crowbar
18. One of the Twelve Olympians
24. Coin anagram
25. Word repeated in an Anne Murray Christmas song cover
32. **1978 Kansas #1 hit in Canada**
34. _____-de-camp
35. California white oak
36. Sarnia abuts this Great Lake
37. Average score, for Canadian golfer Mike Weir
38. Cosmetics company: Mary _____
40. Fishing hook
41. *Beverly Hillbillies* Clampett
43. Metal fasteners
45. Raised Rhodesian Ridgebacks, say
46. Blackheads and whiteheads
47. Stratagem
48. Originate (from)
50. Jonathan Scott's TV property brother
51. Like much of Canada's North in winter

52. Arabian and Aegean
54. CCR got stuck here in song
56. Canadian artist Christopher
57. Military school freshman
60. NS driver's licence, for example
62. Rage
65. Canadian automotive shop: Mr. _____
66. Shania song: "Whose Bed _____ Your Boots Been Under?"
67. Crash in a flophouse
68. Bathtub grime: Soap _____
69. Forearm component
70. Salve that soothes
71. To win 13-D, the Canadian team had to do this

75. Ideal philosophy?
76. Pertaining to the kidney
77. Heavy carts
78. Some compass points (abbr.)
80. Intelligence
83. Marry
85. Beautiful boyfriend in Gaspé?
86. *Love Story* star McGraw
87. Dennis Lee poem: "Alligator _____"
90. Foodie
91. Mosque turret
94. Like some yogourt
96. Held onto
97. Blue Jay's triple: Three-_____

98. Swear
99. He eschews animal products
100. Pupa successor
101. Build stronger stone walls
102. Truth, in olden days
104. Showy flowering plant
105. Bird of prey
107. Long-time Montreal-born Penguin Letang
109. Ripped paper apart
110. Canadian mining co. purchased by Vale in 2006
111. Manitoba-born actor Beach
114. Common US lang.
115. Space Tourism Society (abbr.)

SOLUTION ON PAGE 175

72

Divine Desserts

Canadian creations

ACROSS

1. Accompany
7. Submarine's armament
14. Russian Blue's bite?
20. Less hirsute
21. Like negatively charged particles
22. Air Canada pilots do this
23. **Notable Nova Scotia cobbler**
25. 1960 Olympics pair skating Canadian champ Barbara
26. Short clerk?
27. Witch's spell
28. The yellow birch is Quebec's official this
29. Cooks mussels
30. Must pay up
32. Señor's snooze?
34. Get _____ out of
35. Zagreb country
39. Remain unsettled
40. Theatre stage backdrop
42. 2009 Giller Prize-winning author MacIntyre
43. 1973 Murray McLauchlan hit: "The Farmer's _____"
44. Beauty pageant contestant's ribbon
46. *Stars Wars* scoundrel: Han _____
49. Emulated Canada's Jim Carrey
50. Game defeat
51. Chatter
52. Tottenham trash can
54. Browse at The Bay
55. **Leavened dough Quebec treat**
58. Colorado NHLers, for short
59. Beatles smash: "_____ and Shout"
61. _____ Vegas
62. Piz Bernina, for one
63. Riddle-me-_____
64. Place to play darts
67. Northwest Germany river
68. Feathery

70. Auction house grouping
71. *Concorde*, for one
72. Oshawa-to-Kingston direction (abbr.)
73. Luau necklace
74. Feel fluish
75. Clergyperson
77. Ontario Cycling Association (abbr.)
78. **Indigenous bread**
82. River in England
86. American Indigenous group (var.)
88. Lily, in Lachine
89. Bolt or Volt
90. Saskatoon-born wrestler: Rowdy Roddy _____
91. Blueprint detail, for short
92. Italy city: San _____
94. Seasoned hors d'oeuvres spread
95. Use a Brita, say
96. River in France
98. Puts on loud suits, like Cherry?
99. Kidnappers' demands
100. Up and about
102. Submissions to Sun Life
105. Loudness unit
106. WWII Soviet leader Joseph
108. Allo, backwards
109. Pose for a painter
110. "No problem," at Pickering Nuclear Generating Station?
115. Ship's crew member
116. **Quebec-created dessert**
119. Genetic combination
120. Barge in
121. Straightened out a twisted pipe
122. Clean freaks can't abide these
123. Teeter-totters
124. Crystalline rocks

DOWN

1. Wanes
2. BC place: _____ Spring Island

3. Colonel Mustard's game
4. Japanese hotpot dish
5. Started a computer again
6. Three, in 92-A
7. Biblical weeds
8. Jet-black quartz
9. You might see one on an Alberta field
10. Carrying a bottle of dessert wine?
11. Accustomed to (var.)
12. Eats
13. Canada's women's eight, for example
14. Magpies' cries
15. 2009 movie from Canada's James Cameron
16. Like a fierce feline?
17. **Squares first made in BC**
18. Topical twosomes?
19. In itself, in Latin
24. Greek mythology goddess
31. Canada's Bianca Andreescu did this at the 2019 US Open
32. Touch or taste
33. Donkey
35. AB social support org: Community Living Alternative Services (abbr.)
36. Wealthy Canadian Little?
37. Cognizant of shenanigans
38. Very competent
39. Canada _____
41. Wild mustard plant
43. Categorize
44. Lippy
45. Middle Eastern capital: _____ Dhabi
47. 1971 Alice Munro offering: _____ *of Girls and Women*
48. Beginning
50. Timmy's TV dog
51. US island territory in the Pacific
53. Nasal membranes

55. Like an antique clock?
56. 1956 Gene Vincent hit: "Be-Bop-_____"
57. Tortoiseshell's colouring
60. Canadian actor Kenneth
64. Lowly labourers
65. Crack open a Kokanee
66. **Fried dough fare**
68. Kim Mitchell hit: "_____ Lanterns"
69. Some Parliament Hill pols
75. Elect your MLA
76. Stirs up seabed sediment
79. Dutch _____ disease
80. Bangladeshi breads
81. Pecans and filberts

83. Phrase that sets a limit
84. Come across as
85. Makes a moral mistake
87. Greek warrior with heel trouble?
90. Evergreen dropping
93. European economic org. created in 1957
94. Barbershop ointments
95. Vancouver Canucks supporter
97. Black-and-yellow bird
98. Water down
99. US campus military grp.
100. Black tea type
101. Not fresh
103. Strides, leisurely

104. 1990 Catherine O'Hara movie: *Home _____*
105. 1971 Five Man Electrical Band hit
107. UNBC prog.: Natural Resources and Environmental Studies (abbr.)
109. Frequent Weather Network word in winter
111. Pulpit
112. Require
113. _____ buggy
114. Dog bowl morsels
117. Irish grp. first formed in 1919
118. Embrace

73

The Best of Blondie

New Wave winners

ACROSS

1. Madagascar carnivore
6. Persona, in publicity
11. _____ of the D'Urbervilles
15. Rumple
19. Anticipate an arrival
20. Conspiracy plotters
21. Wings, to a zoologist
22. Tack _____
23. Excessive use of action words?
25. Scot's skirt
26. 1974 Guess Who hit: "_____ for the Wolfman"
27. Geographically focused disease
28. **Reggae-style 1980 hit**
31. Flax genus
33. Bills used in Colorado but not Canada
34. Huron and Ontario
35. Spicy meat jelly
38. Losing one's hair
42. One of the three green Rs
44. Clooney movie: *O Brother, Where Art _____*?
45. Soap opera, say
46. Cutlery set piece
48. Woodbine Racetrack loop
51. African nation: Guinea-_____
53. Tennyson poem, for example
55. **2017 single from *Pollinator***
57. Paul Rudd film franchise: _____-Man
58. Continuously persecute
60. Canadian music icon Bryan
62. Elizabeth Smart CanLit classic: *By Grand Central Station I Sat Down and _____*
63. Talmud study school
65. "No room to swing _____"
66. Brusque
67. **Hit from *Parallel Lines***
73. Limestone landscape formation
76. Flit
77. Castle's defensive embankment

81. The real thing, in Frankfurt
82. By _____ and bounds
84. Make neat
87. Paving substance
88. **First single from *Eat to the Beat***
90. Earthy pigment
92. Find a missing thing
94. Too frequent tippler
95. Olden days flus
97. Two of these don't make a right
99. Rose anagram
100. Language of old Italy
102. Porky Pig's paramour
104. Applies plaster, old style
105. Drug-busting cop
107. Potato or pasta, to a dieter
109. Defame
111. **Second single from *Eat to the Beat***
116. Burps
120. Half a Caribbean island name
121. Respiratory rasp
122. Most graceless
124. Hit
125. YYC postings
126. Famed Canadian figure skater Barbara Ann
127. _____ Carlo
128. Morays
129. Manitoba, directionally from Ontario
130. Bamboozles, like Bob and Doug McKenzie?
131. Banana family plant

DOWN

1. Preferred thing, for short
2. Ontario city: _____ Sound
3. Reddish-brown gemstone
4. Finnish classical composer Jean
5. **Fourth single from *Eat to the Beat***
6. Small block to keep your drink cold

7. 1968–84 Montreal exhibit: _____ and His World
8. Assist a robber
9. Open cut
10. If all _____ fails
11. Profits
12. Omit a vowel, in pronunciation
13. The Brick merchandise display area, for example
14. *The X-Files* org.
15. Tim Hortons flavoured coffees
16. Less probable
17. Shaw Festival performers' milieu
18. Second-year students, for short
24. ID issued by the GOC
29. Big weight
30. Threw over one's shoulder
32. **1999 UK chart-topper**
35. Cornered, near water?
36. Gleam
37. Mails
39. They top pots
40. Mardi and mercredi, in English
41. Not feeling well
43. Long historical periods
45. Charming
47. Greek philosopher
49. Nickelback tour equipment
50. Summit Series game two goal scorer Mahovlich
52. Suggest: Drop _____
54. _____-la-Croix QC
56. Jerk
59. Not refined
61. Ottawa-born NHLer Boyle who played for four teams
64. Hardy perennial
65. Regina museum: MacKenzie _____ Gallery
66. Musical timing
68. Maxim
69. Diminutive dog breed's bark
70. Roughly, in estimating

71. 1987 Dan Hill/Vonda Shepard duet: "Can't We _____"

72. Drags

73. Canvas shoes brand since 1916

74. Prefix with phobia

75. Like some questions

78. Early video game maker

79. Omnivorous African mammal

80. Lock of hair

82. Spanish pro soccer league: La _____

83. Clearly pronounce

84. Via, in Indiana

85. Club for Saskatchewan's Graham DeLaet

86. 1978 partially French single

89. Georgia city

91. 100 lbs., in the USA

93. Acquiescence through force

96. Most agile

98. Tactical manoeuvres

101. Dollops of ice cream

103. Flow back, like the tide

104. *American Gigolo* **soundtrack song**

105. Calgary Foothills Hospital caregiver

106. Doddering

108. You'll find a map of Manitoba in this

110. Ending for eight

112. Canada's men's eight, for example

113. Like BC's Butchart Gardens

114. Strange, to a Highlander

115. Psyche parts

117. They rule a roost

118. Compass point in Spain

119. Opposite of dele, to a proofreader

123. Ingested a meal

SOLUTION ON PAGE 176

ACROSS

1. Smarmy
5. Decorative wall panel
9. US singer Erykah who won four Grammy Awards
13. Alumni of 80-D
18. Ice crystals on windows, say
19. At any time
20. Karpluk who starred in CBC's *Being Erica*
21. Crew member for 71-A
22. Ad lib, in Liverpool
24. Electrically charged particles
25. Esoteric
26. Physicians provide these
27. Fibre for rope and sacks
28. Like a multi-layered cake
29. One who makes a choice
30. Fumble your words, in Florida?
32. She often wears a saree
33. Packing rope
35. Hiker's hostile mood?
40. Abruptly arose
42. Former Quebec premier (with 57-A)
44. "Instead of" word
45. Performs eye surgery
50. Spoke
51. Kisses from actor Gregory?
52. Seabird
53. Video game players, for example
55. Length measurement, in Canada
56. CBC show ensembles
57. See 42-A
58. Old-style adverb
61. Church service songbook
62. Chemical element B
63. Skin inflammation condition
68. Listening to a case again in court
71. Canada's "Raise A Little Hell" band
72. Chairs
76. German Surrealism artist Max
77. Study of visual imagery
79. Ethereal (var.)
80. Ex-Ottawa Senator Neil who scored the franchise's first modern-era goal
81. Lose control, when irate
82. Twangy, in tone
83. Former BC premier Clark
84. *As For Me and My House* scribe from Saskatchewan Sinclair
85. Pertaining to elementary substances in medieval times
87. Javelin-like weapon in Africa
89. "March King" John Philip
90. *Gone with the Wind* protagonist Scarlett
95. Occurrence
98. City slicker's opposite
101. Within reach
105. They might be picked
106. Extreme attentiveness
107. Australian songbird
108. Couple's evening out
109. Diseases
110. *Pride and Prejudice* author Jane
111. Privy to
112. Stepped down onto the ground
113. This duke was Queen Victoria's dad
114. Canadian Indigenous group
115. Campbell River is on this side of Vancouver Island
116. Batten down a sail
117. Uses an abacus

DOWN

1. In total, *O Canada Crosswords 23* has 150 of these
2. More citrusy, in taste
3. African antelope
4. Candice who starred in *Murphy Brown*
5. Allocates resources for a specific purpose
6. French military boat
7. Richard Burton played one in a 1953 movie
8. Lode finds
9. Canada's Eric Lamaze won equestrian gold at these Olympics
10. Enkindle suspicion
11. Swats, old style
12. Like loose gemstones
13. More bloody, in the movies
14. Event for Canadian sprinter Andre De Grasse
15. Month following Shevat
16. Enjoy a repast
17. An aril encloses this
21. East Indian climbing palms
23. Just a single time
30. You might change this?
31. Get up for the day
34. Skirt strengtheners
36. Humble request
37. Broadcasts on Global
38. Shelter for a pup?
39. Undertones
41. Barely audible summons
42. Many Air Canada aircraft have these
43. Lightish panty hose colour
45. Polish statesman Wałęsa
46. Light grey in complexion
47. Fraudulent scheme
48. Bring home the bacon
49. Lances
51. First Lady of Argentina Eva (1946–52)
54. Skye, near Scotland
55. Deserve
56. Canadian Hume Cronyn starred in this 1985 sci-fi favourite
59. Toddler's toy that rocks (var.)
60. Gull's kin
64. 19th-C. French writer Émile
65. Pose anagram
66. Supersized prefix?
67. Chemical radical

69. Like Terry Fox, to many
70. Stats for Blue Jays hurlers
71. Safari participant's helmet
72. This Canadian band has sold more than eight million albums
73. Snakelike fish
74. Warmongering Greek god
75. *Cagney & Lacey* co-star Daly
78. Courtiers' clique, in Córdoba?
80. Manitoba university
81. Close

85. Give permission
86. City, gulf and isthmus name in Greece
88. Redheads, colloquially
89. Wimbledon brawls?
91. In fine fettle
92. Yukon's western neighbour
93. Washed off soap
94. Climb Alberta's Mount Temple
96. Musical genre of Canada's Arcade Fire

97. Juno-winning singer/pianist Krall
99. Citrus fruit hybrids
100. Exams at 80-D
101. Olympian van Koeverden who carried Canada's flag at 9-D
102. Factual
103. Cheryl Hickey's role on *ET Canada*
104. Not in favour of
106. London Drugs pharmacy bottle

SOLUTION ON PAGE 176

Jailbird in a Pear Tree

Some holiday humour

ACROSS

1. Persistent pain
5. Piece of pond scum
9. Vigour
13. Served up a scandal?
19. Hamilton landmark: Mountain _____
20. Roll of fabric or wallpaper
21. Tear apart
22. "Is there an echo _____?"
23. Electricity or gas company customer, for example
25. Not at all certain
26. Amulet for Akhenaten
27. Diluted espresso beverage in Boston?
28. Hair-smoothing products
29. Outdoor bowling surfaces
30. Historical Russian coin
31. Old-style lighthouse
33. Element #76
35. Lets up
39. Yukon tourism slogan: Larger _____ Life
40. Meander through
42. Juno-winning sister: Tegan and _____
43. More mocking (var.)
44. Blouses and polos
46. Safecracker, in Sussex
48. _____ appeal
49. **Ten holiday voyeurs?**
52. Molson makes this
54. Dance music from Jamaica
55. Refuses to admit
57. Get boiling mad?
61. Facing away from the sea
66. Copies, for short
68. Shallow stretch on the beach
69. Some arthropods
70. Speech hesitation sounds
72. Front hall rug
73. Snare anagram
74. Open a seam, in sewing
75. Oracle's city in ancient Greece
79. Edible root
81. Subterfuge
83. It borders Brazil and Suriname: French _____
85. Some York uni degs.
86. Snotty person
88. **Eight Xmas embezzlers?**
94. Ontario Cattlemen's Association (abbr.)
97. Baby talk syllables
99. "_____ the Snowman"
100. Birds' cliffside roost
101. Keister or caboose?
103. In a precise manner
105. Canadian Lee's "Alligator Pie"
106. How you're addressed?
107. City in Saudi Arabia
109. Belonging to other people
111. 1995 Travis Tritt hit: "Tell _____ Was Dreaming"
112. Swings around (var.)
113. Seafood serving
114. Some iconic pianos
120. Total shambles
121. _____ acid
122. Sumatran simian
123. Measurement at Tip Top tailor
124. Pal, in Perthshire
125. Ladder crosspiece
126. On one's own
127. Tease a seamstress?
128. Firefighters' tools
129. Hardens
130. Spit out

DOWN

1. First two syllables of a magician's catchphase
2. Study all night
3. Fixed-price meal: Table d'_____
4. Jug for a sheep farmer?
5. Old-style adding machine
6. Part of Ontario's motto: "..._____ she remains"
7. Ontario resort: _____ Eden
8. Shrivelled muscles description
9. Two-masted ship with a cell?
10. Mention (with "to")
11. Stream of revenue
12. Homer epic poem
13. Pushes out of place
14. Ancient Peruvians
15. Renaissance woodwind instruments
16. Abdominal ruptures
17. Word that's been rubbed out, say
18. Cotillion belle
24. **Eleven yuletide robbers?**
32. Former prime minister Stephen
34. Canada's Lord Beaverbrook: _____ Aitken
35. Tool for punching holes
36. Henrik Sedin, to Daniel, for short
37. _____ Transat
38. *The Mary Tyler Moore Show* newsman Baxter
39. Old CBC show: _____ *Kids in the Hall*
41. Canadian energy regulation agy.
44. Gave clemency
45. Trim a bit
47. **Six merry murderers?**
50. Alias initials
51. Micro-organism
53. Post-injury recovery regime
56. Rise into the sky
58. Afghanistan place: _____ Bora
59. Guess Who song: "_____ on to Your Life"
60. English actress Lanchester
61. Praise
62. Stridex might resolve this
63. Drug pusher's pursuer

64. Wipes wet dishes
65. Tea leaf flake
67. Old-style bottle for 52-A
71. Ghetto
76. "La Vie en Rose" singer Edith
77. Extensions and toupées
78. Like some swimming pools
80. _____ chi
82. Delectable, to the dentist?
84. Tax department employees
87. Spectator's contemptuous interjection
89. Scotiabank foyer machine
90. Notable Canadiens goalie Dryden
91. Canada's Seth Rogen's character in *Funny People*

92. Math-based strategy game
93. "Oh my gosh," to an astronaut?
94. Hockey icon Bobby
95. Nestlé Canada brand: Lean _____
96. Starch-converting enzyme
98. Mandarin orange variety
102. Took a hiatus
104. The heart is here
106. People
108. Licence renewal sticker
110. Cream of the social crop
111. Had in mind
115. Canada's James Cameron wrote/directed this 1994 film: _____ *Lies*
116. Wimpy one

117. On the peak of Mount Robson
118. BC First Nation
119. St. John's receives the most this annually in Canada
120. Vancouver Canucks mascot

Author's note: Many moons ago, I used this theme in a smaller crossword, but two clues were incorrect. I always wanted a second chance to make things right and now I have!

SOLUTION ON PAGE 176

157

1 ▪ The Sporting Life

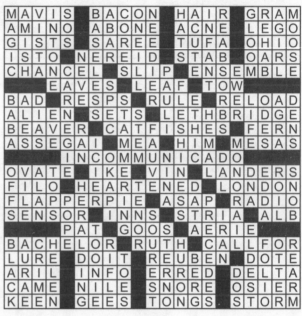

2 ▪ Canada Cornucopia 1

3 ▪ A Dozen Theme Clues

4 ▪ Come On Over

5 ▪ Drive Time

6 ▪ Across the Aisle

7 ▪ Famous Fauna?

8 ▪ Home Sweet Canada

9 ▪ Toys in the Attic

10 ▪ Canada Cornucopia 2 Challenger

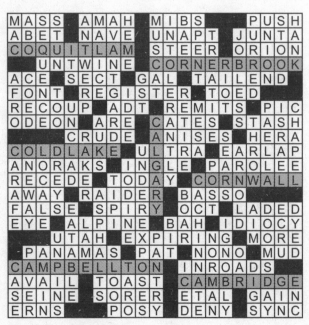

11 ▪ Give Me a C…

12 ▪ Take Off, Eh?

13 ▪ Ooh, a Trip to BC

14 ▪ Spice Up Your Life…

15 ▪ From Commencement to Conclusion

16 ▪ Rock On…

17 ▪ Rock On 2…

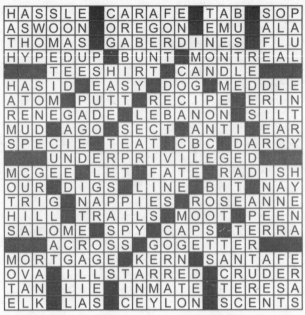

18 ▪ Canadian Cornucopia 3 Superchallenger

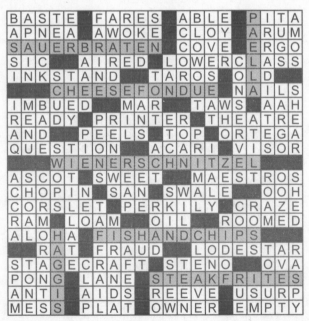

19 ▪ International Flavours

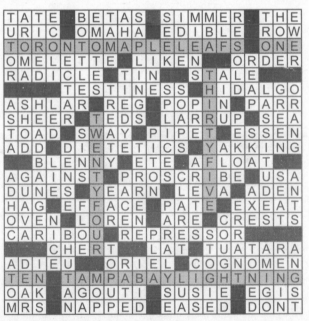

20 ▪ Here's to the Habs

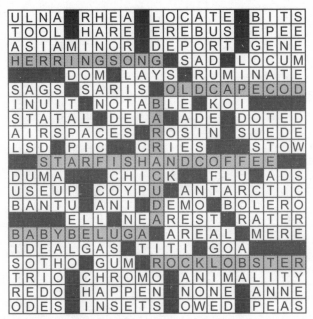

21 ▪ Something Fishy

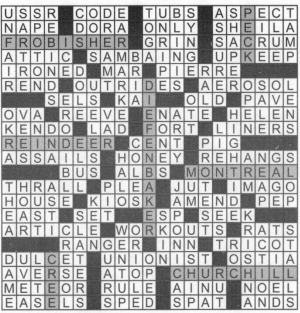

22 ▪ Land O'Lakes

23 ▪ Catch(phrase) Me If You Can

24 ▪ They're in the Army Now

25 ▪ Colourful Comestibles

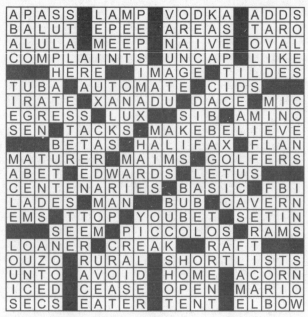

26 ▪ Canada Cornucopia 4

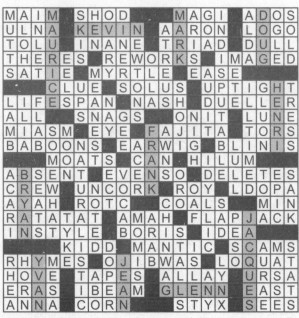

27 ▪ Their Cups Runneth Over

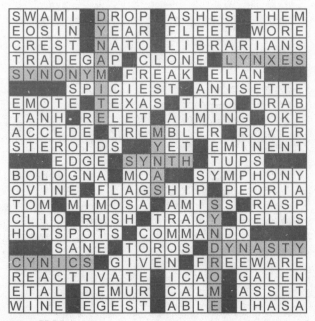

28 ▪ Y Not…

SOLUTIONS

29 ▪ Who Am I? 1

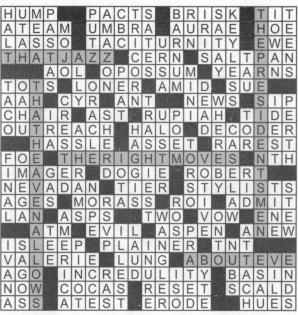

30 ▪ *All* In…

31 ▪ They All Fall Down

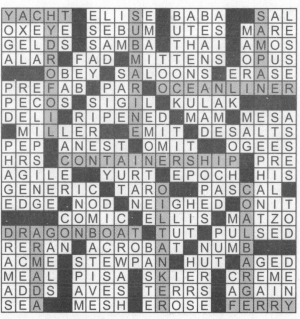

32 ▪ Come Sail Away…

33 ▪ Murder, She Wrote

34 ▪ Canada Cornucopia 5 Challenger

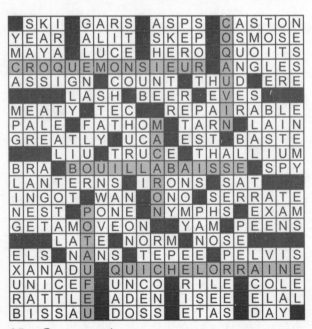

35 ▪ *Gastronomie*

36 ▪ C-A-N-A-D-A Sixpack

37 ▪ Rhyme Scheme

38 ▪ Beijing Bonanza

39 ▪ On the Move

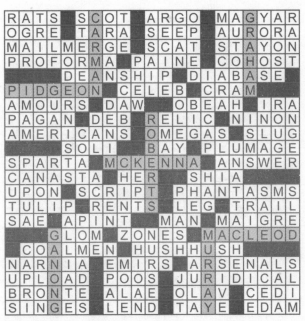

40 ▪ Illustrious Alumni

SOLUTIONS

41 ▪ What's the Tea?

42 ▪ Canada Cornucopia 6 Superchallenger

43 ▪ A Star Was Born Here

44 ▪ X Marks the Spot…

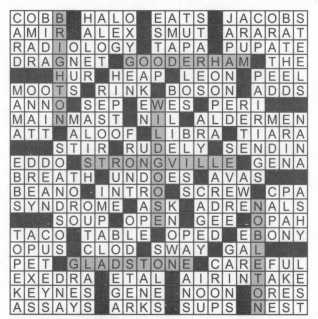

45 ▪ Optimistic in Ontario

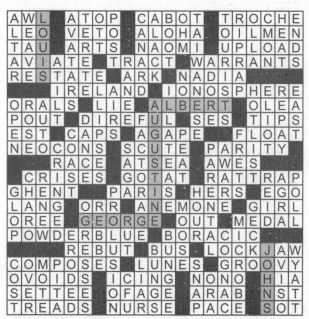

46 ▪ Wanna *Stay* Here

47 ▪ Eat Drink and Be Musical…

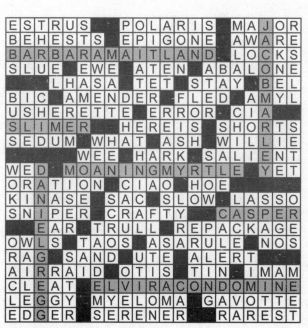

48 ▪ Cinematic Spectres

49 ▪ Eminent Universities

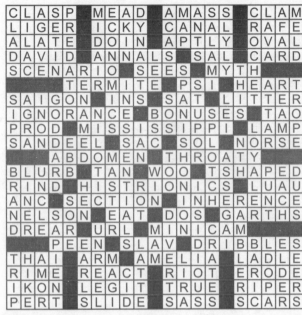

50 ▪ Canada Cornucopia 7

51 ▪ Ready for the Runway

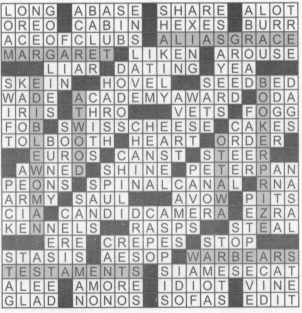

52 ▪ Who Am I? 2

SOLUTIONS

53 ▪ Ships Ahoy!

54 ▪ Whoo Are They?

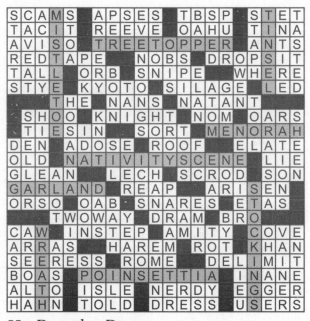

55 ▪ December Decor

56 ▪ The Greatest of All…

O CANADA CROSSWORDS ▪ BOOK 23

57 ▪ Les *Liz*

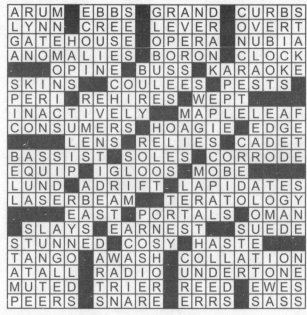

58 ▪ Canada Cornucopia 8 Challenger

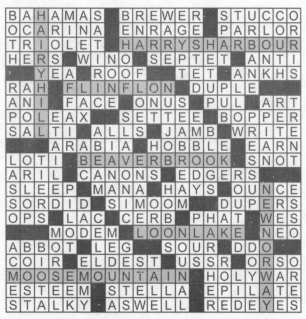

59 ▪ Echo Location

60 ▪ Big Tech

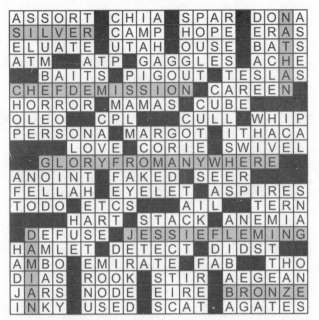

61 ▪ Olympics Flashback

62 ▪ Keep On Truckin'

63 ▪ Destination: Charlottetown

64 ▪ By the Numbers

65 ▪ Games People Play

66 ▪ Canada Cornucopia 9 Superchallenger

67 ▪ By the Numbers 2

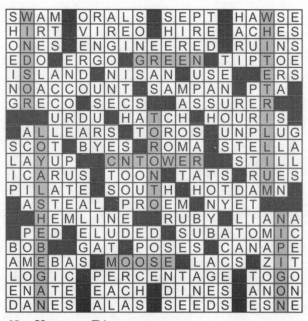

68 ▪ Yours to Discover...

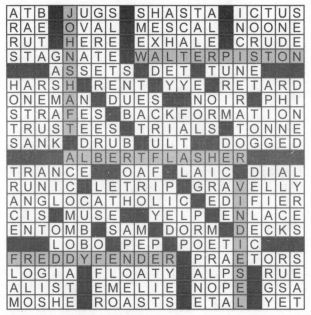

69 ▪ Mechanics' Medley

70 ▪ Speaking of…

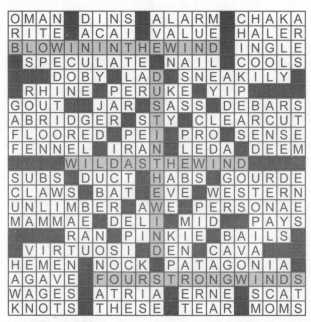

71 ▪ Blown Away

72 ▪ Divine Desserts…

73 ▪ The Best of Blondie

74 ▪ Canada Cornucopia 10 Super-duper
Challenger

75 ▪ Jailbird in a Pear Tree